D1609789

PROSPERO AND ARIEL

PROSPERO AND ARIEL

THE RISE AND FALL OF RADIO

A Personal Recollection

by

D. G. BRIDSON

LONDON
VICTOR GOLLANCZ LTD
1971

ISBN 0 575 00610 2

PRINTED IN GREAT BRITAIN
BY EBENEZER BAYLIS AND SON, LTD.
THE TRINITY PRESS, WORCESTER, AND LONDON

TO JOYCE
who was so much a part of the great days

CONTENTS

ILLUSTRATIONS

A*

ACKNOWLEDGEMENTS

A few paragraphs of this book first appeared in *The Listener*, to the Editor of which, Karl Miller, I am grateful for permission to use them again. I am also indebted to him for the title of my book, *Prospero and Ariel*, which he himself gave to the article in which they were first printed. I trust that I shall not be confused with the master that, like Ariel and all the others, I have merely tried to serve.

A few paragraphs on my relations with Wyndham Lewis appeared in a longer article published in *Agenda*, and to the Editor of that review also I am grateful for permission to use them in a shorter context.

I am grateful to the BBC for permission to reproduce the following photographs which are their copyright: plates 2, 3, 4, 7 and 12. Plate 9 is the copyright of RKO Radio Pictures, Inc.

The Editors of the *New Statesman*, *The Observer*, and *Musical Opinion* have kindly allowed me to quote from reviews which appeared in their columns.

FOREWORD

THIS IS IN no sense a history of broadcasting in Britain; such a work having already been undertaken by Professor Asa Briggs. Nor is it intended in any sense as a history of the Feature Programme, that form of writing peculiar to radio, which has been studied by Douglas Cleverdon in a book still unpublished. This is a purely personal story of my own career as a staff writer and producer for the BBC from 1935 to 1969.

In the course of that career, I have worked with many valued friends and colleagues to whose excellent work for radio I have been able to give far less notice than it deserved. This is something I regret, but to have noticed it more than I have done would have been to swell the account beyond all measure. Everyone who has worked for the BBC knows how much his own work is beholden to that of others, and mine has been no exception. The evolution of the Feature Programme, with which I have been largely concerned, has been a matter of group activity, and I claim no more for myself than an early place in the group.

But one man's view of a shared experience is sometimes interesting, particularly when it has taken him so far afield and enabled him to work with so many people in so many different ways. The BBC is a large and fascinating institution, of which an individual view may still be valuable when tracing its influence and achievement. No individual can hope to contribute more than a very little to either.

I have subtitled my book *The Rise and Fall of Radio*, and perhaps that needs a word of explanation. Radio had been thriving for some dozen years before I became involved in it. No doubt it will continue to thrive for many years in the future. But there are

13

many kinds of radio, far more than the four channels on which it is broadcast currently would suggest. The kind of specially written radio in which I am interested only began to emerge in the thirties. During and immediately after the Second World War, it was paramount in broadcasting; and it was only during the fifties that the rise of television deprived it of its largest following. But though it ceased to be a medium for entertainment and information for the many, radio still continued to exercise a powerful influence as a cultural medium for the few. It was only with the approach to the seventies that it first began to abrogate that role. But once the programmes had been parcelled out into the four channels that we know today, there could be less and less future for the kind of radio writing in which I am primarily interested. With the end of the Third Programme, the call for it was reduced still further, and that is the kind of radio to which my subtitle refers.

It is no more than a coincidence that I should have joined the staff of the BBC when the Feature Programme was coming to birth, and should have retired from the staff as the Third Programme was being abolished. But so far as I am concerned, the coincidence was a lucky one. New forms will be developed to replace it, but the radio that I knew and the radio I respected the most may soon have been forgotten. For whatever happens to it in the future, radio will clearly be different. It is my own part in some of the radio which went before that this book tries to recall.

D. G. B.

CAFÉ ROYAL

AFTER AN HOUR, the caryatids were growing more familiar, the crimson plush more cosy and the gilding mellower. Two half-moons on the marble were all that remained of my lager, and the time was five to seven. The appointment had been made for six o'clock, but unpunctuality in Londoners was what every Northerner had come to expect. And in any case, back in the early thirties, the brasserie of the old Café Royal was a place in which to see and be seen. I ordered another lager.

My appointment was with that one-time apologist for Communism, Claud Cockburn, with whom I had been put in touch by that one-time apologist for Fascism, Ezra Pound. The conjunction may seem unlikely, but my friendship with Pound had begun in a far more unlikely manner. A couple of years earlier, in 1931, he had published his microseismic *How to Read*, a book which I had ordered and eagerly read. For Pound was a figure whose cosmopolitan aura was very well calculated to dazzle any young would-be writer of the time. As leader of the *avant garde* in the twenties, as Eliot's own *miglior fabbro* and godfather of *Ulysses*, even as a friend of *The Enemy*, this self-styled 'specialist in genius' had everything to recommend him to one of my reading tastes. Even so—at the time—*How to Read* had not particularly impressed me as How to Write. Myself a bait for factious rather than factitious bait, I had risen in wrath at such an infuriating attack upon my insularity. In the heat of the moment, I had even fired off a counterblast—which served at least as a sop for my out-raged sense of the usual. After all, why Chinese? Why Provençal? Why Propertius rather than Tibullus? And so on. As for his thesis that language could be 'charged'—how did he hope to prove it by writing so sloppily himself? A week later, I had been startled (and highly gratified) to find my quibbling answered in a letter from Rapallo that had been charged with almost nuclear energy. Everyone should know, even in the transpontine murk at *my* end of my great fahrt of a country . . . And so on again; and who the hell was I anyway? Which, as it proved, was to be the start of a stimulating correspondence extending, off and on, over the next thirty odd years. During which time, we continued to differ on points of opinion, as I need hardly add.

That summer of 1933, however, I was in London on holiday from office work in Manchester. In the last couple of years, I had groped my way through the murk at least to the point where I could see more lively prospects ahead. All my spare time from office work, by then, was going into writing. My poetry was beginning to appear in the right places, and I was making a modest pittance out of criticism and book-reviewing. A. R. Orage had gone out of his way to be helpful, and gave me regular space in the *New English Weekly*. In short, I was well in process of writing myself out of a boring job and unhanging my hat from a pension. Depression or no Depression, I was all for taking a chance with life. As a desk-tied Mancunian, on the other hand. I was still rather short on London literary contacts. My two weeks annual leave were accordingly devoted to trying to widen the circle.

Among other people who might prove helpful, Pound had suggested Claud Cockburn, one of whose stories had taken his fancy in *The Dial*. I had promptly dropped Cockburn a note, and he had offered to meet me that evening in the Café Royal. I have to admit that at the time his name was still unknown to me: he had not yet begun to twist the world by the nose in *The Week*. I certainly didn't know him as the only correspondent on *The Times* ever to turn down a job with their Washington bureau out of an honest preference for life on the *Daily Worker*. And if I had not stayed on for an extra lager, I might never have learned the fact until he published his autobiography *I, Claud*.

As it was, I had finished my lager and was paying my bill at the desk when a tall and rather improbable figure hurried through the doorway. American horn-rimmed spectacles rode high on a predatory nose, which hovered in turn above an extended upper lip; and he wore a dark fedora. He suggested more of the federal agent than the private eye as he loudly made enquiries after a Mr. Briddson. But the Oxford voice was distinctively *un*-American as it jerked out in explosive stammers. I introduced myself, and explained that my name was pronounced Brideson—which only a Manxman might be expected to know. Cockburn uttered apologies for his being late, and added more apologies for his mispronunciation. This I much appreciated: all too many people are prepared to start an argument on the lines that Bridson *must* be pronounced Briddson. I have even had to explain before now that the 'i' is long—as in Christ.* No such explanation was called for with Cockburn, however: in his case, the 'o' was long as in Al Capone.

Further drinks were ordered and the conversation grew animated. I never knew anyone whose talk could be wittier or more disruptive; but on this occasion, Cockburn's only concern was to be helpful. I explained my problem to him, and asked whether he knew any editors who might be interested in my literary work. He shopped around the back of his mind in a friendly way, but finally had to admit that he didn't. His one good story in *The Dial* notwithstanding, his contacts were journalistic rather than literary. But then an idea suddenly occurred to him: I said that I lived in Manchester . . . I also happened to be a friend of Ezra Pound's . . . Had I ever thought about writing for radio?

I had to admit, in turn, that I hadn't. *The Listener* had taken a poem of mine, but radio was a different matter: indeed, I mentally bracketed the BBC with Parliament, the Monarchy, the Church and the Holy Ghost. Cockburn could understand that well enough, but explained himself more fully. An Oxford friend of his was a BBC producer: he was shortly being sent up to Manchester,

* If people still remain unconvinced, or perhaps have never heard of Christ, I am always prepared to refer them to the Bibble, where they'll find him written up as the Holy Chilld. By then, they have generally got the message—Brideson.

where he had just been appointed Programme Director to the North Region. More to the point, he also was an admirer of Pound's, and had lately produced Pound's opera on the life of François Villon for the National Programme. Most to the point of all, the BBC were looking out for new writers: they even *paid* for the plays and talks and other things that they broadcast. It might be a good idea to get in touch with his friend: perhaps I could meet him when he came up to the North. His name was Archie Harding.

I made a note of the name and agreed to do so, though not convinced that the idea was all that promising. Having nothing better to suggest, however, Cockburn went on to matters more in his own field. His inside knowledge of politics was highly illuminating, and his attitude to them no less refreshing. He gave me a quick run-down on the international situation from China to Prussia, if not to Peru, finished his drink and glanced at the time: he was, of course, late for his next appointment. Glinting sardonically through his lenses, he shook me by the hand: perhaps I might find in the BBC—what he had found in America—that there really was 'more room for scope'. We parted on that happy suggestion.

What Cockburn had tactfully kept to himself was the reason for Harding's impending transfer to the North. The story only emerged after he had joined me there and we had become close friends, later that year. But the story proved him a man very much after my own way of thinking at the time.

It seemed that the previous year (1932) he had produced for the BBC the first of their celebrated Christmas Day programmes—an event which had certainly made radio history. For the first time ever, he had linked all parts of the Commonwealth in a vast radio hook-up which circled the earth in sixty minutes and ended with a message to the peoples of the Commonwealth, broadcast from Sandringham by King George V. The programme had been a spectacular success throughout the world, and Broadcasting House (opened earlier the same year) had assumed a sudden new dignity as a centre of world communications. "Nation shall speak Peace unto Nation," the motto of the BBC proclaimed in those days, and surely such a message should not be confined to the Commonwealth alone.* Accordingly, Harding had been given the task of uniting Europe on New Year's Eve in an equally inspiring way. Radio circuits were promptly booked to a dozen European capitals, and evocative sound-sequences bespoke in a dozen languages and manners. New Year carols were offered by one, New Year parties laid on by others, with watch-night services, crowds and ceremonies on tap from hither to yon. As on Christmas Day, the whole panorama was to be linked in London by a colourful commentary (written by Harding) to point up dramatic effects as the spotlight flashed from country to country.

No doubt Cockburn himself—among others—had helped Harding with background information, for Europe was Cockburn's oyster. But from one source or another data had been gathered together: significant facts about life in France, vital statistics about the Italians, inside stories from Germany and Austria. Harding had even established what proportion of her national income Pilsudski's Poland was spending on armaments. And though the figure sounded rather high, not much notice might have been taken of the disclosure, if Warsaw had not then followed it up on the air with a rather truculent military march. On this occasion, even the Germans had come up with nothing but sweetness and light, for Hitler and the Nazis were still not quite in power. As for the Soviet Union, they, of course, had not been represented at all. Poland's contribution had therefore sounded the only militant note in an otherwise peaceful evening, as Harding had rather expected that it might. But if the inference was somewhat unfortunate for the *ancien régime* in Poland, the repercussions might have been even more so for lively-minded radio. The Polish Ambassador had called at Broadcasting House the following morning, claimed that his country had been

* When their foreign language services began countering the Axis propaganda shortly before the war, the BBC changed its motto to "Quaecunque", which has been variously translated. "Where the Hell" is my own favourite. In 1948 peace was restored—in plain English.

affronted, and demanded an almost national apology. Heads, he insisted, must roll—assistant heads at the very least—and Harding was duly carpeted by the Director-General.

As Harding recalled it later, Sir John Reith had been magisterial. "You're a very dangerous man, Harding," he was reported as having decided. "I think you'd be better up in the North, where you can't do so much damage." In which opinion we see clearly enough how little was known about the North in Portland Place during the Depression years.

But every country has its own Siberia, and like Dostoevsky before him, Harding had been marked down for the House of the Dead. That the North should prove to be a very lively house, where even the dead refused to lie down quietly, was one of the lucky accidents of radio history. For nobody could have been more bent upon making the inmates articulate than Archie Harding himself. I was only too happy, in my own way, to try and help him in the attempt.

PART ONE

RADIO FOR THE MANY

I

Floreat Mancunia

ALTHOUGH I HAD been born in Manchester in 1910, I spent my childhood and schooldays at Lytham St. Annes, a quietly pleasant oasis on the Lancashire coast, almost entirely surrounded by golf-links. I was seventeen when I left school and returned to my birth-place to earn a living. The Manchester in which I then grew up was a grimy and despondent city wallowing in the backwash of the Cotton Slump. For in most parts of Lancashire, this had long been giving an ominous foretaste of the so-called Financial Crisis and the general Depression of the thirties. Throughout the Cotton Towns, people were already trying to inure themselves to the ills of unemployment, under-payment and under-nourishment.

It was a year after the General Strike that I came back to the city with my mother: it was a year after the Manchester blitz that I finally said goodbye to it. I could hardly have chosen fourteen more significant years in which to know it. I was there at a time to see how degrading industrial poverty can become, and how ordinary people can accustom themselves to live with it. I was there to watch the May Day parades, when the red banners were publicly blessed by a pillar of the local Church and when Dr. Hewlett Johnson was Dean at Manchester Cathedral. I was there for the national ignominy of 1931, when the crowd seemed likely to storm the local branch of the Bank of England, next door to which I worked. I watched the rough-house at the Free Trade Hall, when Mosley's Fascists began to beat up hecklers, and them-selves took the worst of the beating. I also watched the annual gathering of the Hunger Marchers, limping away to the Hyde Park rallies in London, which many of them were too hungry to reach. Not all of us, in the early thirties, found Manchester a haven of affluence and opportunity; whichever corner prosperity was just around, it needed re-armament and a Second World War before the corner could be turned.

At the best of times, Manchester has never had much in common with London; it has always had its own peculiar way of life, no less than its own particular problems. But during the slow strangulation of the Cotton Trade, with unemployment growing from year to year, Manchester had an almost embattled air—that of the waning capital of a grimly autonomous Northern republic. To draw a ridiculous comparison with the Spanish Civil War, Manchester was almost like some unfortunate travesty of Barcelona; the enemy was at her gates. But Manchester's final stand was being made as much against what the world was becoming, as in defence of what the city had once invented and imposed upon the world. For whatever was happening in the South, the North still held on stubbornly to what it remembered of earlier habits. All of which gave it, in the eyes of the South, a dourly alien, somewhat alarming apartness. For leaving aside the Hunger Marches, only occasional Cup Finals at Wembley then brought Northerners down to London in force, cloth-capped hordes of rude barbarians, talking incomprehensible dialects, and gawping round the West End like so many Goths in the Roman forum. Such incursions were hardly calculated to waken feelings of brotherly love and affection. Little affection, in return, was felt by the Northerners for the South; the place was much too smug and well fed and comfortably well off for that. The South was a green and pleasant garden suburb, far more green than anything that the Cotton Belt remembered since Crompton got astride his mule. But I for one preferred my vistas to show the darker shades of the Pennine country. They seemed more appropriate to life in a dying economy.

Not that Manchester itself had suffered from the Depression so much as some of the smaller Pennine towns. Spinning centres like Oldham and Ashton, Rochdale, Bolton and the rest were generally far harder hit. To them, Manchester was indeed a capital city—with many of the advantages that capital cities have to offer. They saw their future, often enough, decided on the floor of the Manchester Royal Exchange, and their viability solemnly debated in leaders in the *Manchester Guardian*. But whatever they thought of her, Manchester was still a part of the North. Whatever they thought of London—that was a part of something else.

Obviously enough, poverty and hard times are comparative. In the worst days of the Depression, life in the North could be just as gracious, as comfortable and plain luxurious as life any-where else. It could, that is, for those who happened to have the money. This a few Northerners undoubtedly had: many of them had far more than they actually deserved, remembering how some of them had acquired it. But leaving the wealthy out of it, even in the lower income brackets life could be comfortable enough. I myself was never really badly off; I worked at a regular job which paid me a small but regular salary. My father and uncle were both managers of something or other, and bourgeois standards reigned supreme in the family. All that I personally missed out on was a chance to go to the University: call-ups from a score of cotton mills in the twenties had taken care of that. But I made very little of the lost opportunity: a degree would only have grounded me in one of the so-called professions. And to-wards them I had no leanings whatever.

After a short flirtation with physics, my interest had been firmly given to the arts—particularly writing and painting, music, the theatre and the cinema—all of which I could enjoy in Man-chester probably better than anywhere outside London. I had a stimulating circle of friends, and they were mostly people who shared my interests. Many of us belonged to the Manchester Salon Club, the Unnamed Society and the Manchester Film Society. Most of us went regularly to the Hallé Concerts at the Free Trade Hall, and the pre-West End openings at Manchester's three theatres. Most important of all, there were plenty of opportunities for lively discussion and conversation: not many people, after all, can learn to write until they have taught themselves to talk.

And teaching ourselves to write was what quite a few of us

27

were doing. The *Manchester Guardian* was there for an outlet, to start with, and three or four other local papers. Then there were the London weeklies, the monthlies and the quarterlies—from which rejection slips came fluttering back like snowflakes.

First of us all to achieve a breakthrough was the novelist Frank Tilsley, whose *Champion Road* was later to prove one of the better evocations of the North. As secretary of the Salon Club, he wrote his first book, *The Plebeian's Progress*, on the club typewriter and a salary of fifty pounds a year. The novel was accepted by Victor Gollancz, and earned them both considerably more than that.

Walter Greenwood's success with *Love on the Dole* was even more spectacular; but when Jonathan Cape brought the novel out, Walter was still earning twenty-eight shillings a week as a door-to-door salesman in Salford. Among the painters, Laurence Lowry, Eric Newton and Emmanuel Levy were still prepared to sell their friends a canvas for a fiver: the pity was that not all of us had a fiver to spare at the time. Francis Dillon (later to join me as one of the liveliest writers at the BBC) was rather more comfortably off than most of us: he had a job with the Inland Revenue, to which the rest of us turned over most of our meagre profits. Also, of course, there were the lucky ones who actually worked for the *Manchester Guardian*—people like Neville Cardus, Paddy Monkhouse and Donald Boyd. Until he took himself off to Moscow, there was even Malcolm Muggeridge . . .

Those were the times, indeed, when Pound described me in a letter to a friend as "the somewhat savage and wholly impecunious Bridson raging in the backstreets of Manchuster". If a little romanticised, the general picture was a fair one. I was still comparatively impecunious, and certainly savage about social conditions as I found them in Manchester at the time—backstreets and everywhere else. But it was actually in the more respectable purlieus of Manchester's King Street that Archie Harding found me in October, 1933.

I must admit, he proved to be something new in my experience. For apart from my first brief meeting with Cockburn, Harding was the only Oxford intellectual Marxist that I had so far met.

And nobody could possibly have been more Oxford than Archie Harding always remained. A slight peccadillo at Cheltenham College had landed him at Keble rather than Christ Church or Balliol, but the true stamp of the place was upon him. His accent was so distinctively Oxford, that he had only to open his mouth and Deansgate turned round in astonishment. German, Egyptian, Armenian or Japanese accents passed in Manchester without remark, but an Oxford accent in the thirties was a true exotic—as Harding was himself. He was not so remarkable in appearance, though certainly good looking enough—tallish and slimly built. A lock of hair fell jauntily down to his eyebrow, and he was faintly grey at the temples; he wore well-tailored clothes, a little frayed at the shirt-cuffs out of eccentricity. His face, when he was not smiling, was faintly petulant, podgy but full of authority: he rather reminded me of the Child Jesus in the Leonardo Madonna of the Rocks in the National Gallery, London. He had an engaging sense of humour, a wittily mannered turn of speech, and an incisive burst of laughter. His father was a Colonel (retired) in the Royal Marines, and his background was impeccably Upper Class. It was just this background which Oxford and intellectual restiveness had taught him first to challenge, then finally to reject.

Manchester, he told me, reminded him in a curious way of Leningrad. As he had been there and I had not, I accepted the fact with interest. As for the Manchester people, they had been no surprise to him: they were all that Engels had led him to expect, from the suffering and exploited masses to their comically nineteenth-century masters. His interest in both was that of a sociologist—I had almost said an anthropologist. He delighted in relating stories about them as he gradually came to know them, which were often highly amusing to one of them like myself.*

* Harding found the Northern version of the London clubman the most comical of all. On his first appearance as a guest at the Manchester Reform Club, he was asked by an elder citizen what he thought of the Manchester girls. He admitted—by and large and for all their no doubt sterling qualities—that he found them rather plain. Lowering his *Guardian*, the oldest member remarked—with splendid alliteration—that we didn't do that to faces in Manchester. With its obvious analogy to grinding the faces of the poor, Harding happily insisted that the phrase had great social significance. He felt that the qualification "Not now, anyway," was virtually implied.

He was much intrigued, for instance, as he first emerged from the station by the bold enquiry which straddled every Manchester lamp-post—WHY WEAR A TRUSS? Natives, of course, were aware that this was an oblique advertisement for another patented appliance marketed by a local manufacturer. Harding preferred to see in it one more affirmation of Northern freedom from restraint. How many of us, he wondered on the other hand, still wore an *intellectual* truss?

His passionate interest in radio was something that he brought to the North along with him. Starting in London as an announcer, he had soon moved on into radio production, in which he quickly distinguished himself. The first of the Christmas Day programmes had merely been one of many successes. Along with Lance Sieveking, E. J. King-Bull and Mary Hope Allen, he had created the Feature Programme, for which the BBC was soon to become renowned. He had worked along with Val Gielgud in pioneering radio drama, and with Eric Maschwitz and John Watt before the Variety Department had even been formed. His whole attitude to the medium was stimulating and somehow exciting. To him, the microphone had been an invention no less revolutionary than the printing-press, and the spoken word was far more immediate in its impact than printed words could ever be. Marshall McLuhan might have learnt a great deal from Harding's theories, back in the early thirties.

As for the use to which radio had been put, that was a matter on which he held strong views. All broadcasting he insisted, was propaganda; because it did not attack the anomalies of the capitalist system, it became propaganda in tacit support of them. Average people everywhere were painfully inarticulate; but how much less articulate than most were the average people here in the North? As he saw it, that was hardly an accident. For where economic collapse had brought the people so much hardship, continuance of the system required that the people should remain unheard. As part of the system itself, he maintained, the BBC had been careful to see that they did.

In Harding's view *all* people should be encouraged to air their views, not merely their professional spokesmen. And that went for the Working Class no less than the Middle and Upper Classes. The air at least should be open to all, as the Press quite obviously was not. As it was, both Press and the BBC were equally tools of what we should now be calling 'The Establishment'. They stood for order and orthodoxy, the *status quo* and all that the *status quo* implied when the whole economy was dying on its feet. One didn't have to be committed to Marxism to agree very largely with what he said.

In some ways, of course, Harding could be quite unintentionally amusing—particularly to Northerners. He was always a convinced theorist. In argument, he affected the exploratory pause, rather than Cockburn's explosive stammer; and this, along with his Oxford drawl, was easy enough to parody.* But the fact that he always retained the power to laugh at himself was one of the most engaging things about him. His belief in the vital importance of radio's role in the modern world was perhaps the only belief that he took quite seriously. As to the use to which radio should be put, that was a matter he was prepared to debate —provided that standards were not debased, and attitudes were never allowed to be anti-social. That once assured, many things could be tolerated, much could be excused, and much laughed out of court. With Harding, radio came first; politics were a slightly cynical runner-up, with doctrine largely a talking point.

Through Archie Harding, I was to make many new friends in Manchester. Edgar Lustgarten I had known slightly, but soon came to know much better. Apart from his gifts as a mimic, he had a mind like a needle for any matter involving the law: in a more unlikely way, he also had a very good ear for jazz. His weekly jazz programme, which he introduced for the North Region under the name of Brent Wood, made him one of the earliest disc-jockeys on the air.

* Edgar Lustgarten, who had known Harding at Oxford and was then a Manchester barrister, could hit his manner off to perfection: "I was quite mmmmmm AT A LOSS to understand the political mmmmmm INDECISIVENESS of the Northern proletariat, until I finally mmmmmm realised that the Lancashire working class mmmmmm TO A MAN still insists that Lunacharsky mmmmmm was a BLANQUIST!"

Kenneth and Ruth Adam had moved into the North from Nottingham. Adam was then on the staff of the *Guardian*, and had achieved the distinction of talking himself out of the job of leader-writer by protesting that he really didn't know what he was writing about. His plea to be reduced to the ranks as a run-of-the-mill reporter, so that he could really learn his trade, must have shaken his editor more than somewhat. At least the gambit seems to have paid off handsomely. In later days, he was surely the only BBC Director of Television ever to make more money by writing about the job than the BBC had paid him for actually doing it.

Among the Londoners who arrived in Manchester about that time, two stood out as unassimilable, though none the less congenial to me for that. Robin Whitworth, a pleasantly young Old Etonian, came to the North Region as Drama Producer, with an inescapable aura of fashionable affluence to mark him out in a crowd. The impact of Northern poverty and unemployment was something of a traumatic experience for him. Indeed, he could scarcely understand how revolution had been avoided, where life had so little to offer to people he soon learnt to admire.

Giles Playfair, on the other hand, was bothered less by the poverty than he was by the wealth and ostentation of life among his richer industrial friends—the vast mansions discreetly tucked away in Cheshire, and the extravagant banquets that were tucked away inside them. His own background, needless to say, was theatrical, and the parties that he gave along with Grace Lovat Fraser pulled in a regular galaxy of visiting actresses and ballerinas.

Closest of my earlier friends was Francis Dillon, whom I introduced to Harding, and who subsequently joined the BBC as feature writer in the West Region. Jack, as his friends knew him, was ten years older than me and had fought in the First World War. He had landed at Archangel with Ironside's expeditionary force, and then at Constantinople with the occupying forces. He had moved on to India, and finally come to rest collecting Income Tax in Manchester. He was a man of infinite and strident wit,

whose croaky voice had been raised to its unusual pitch by a dose
of mustard gas in Flanders. The parties that he threw with his wife
Tanya were focal points for the brighter part of local Bohemia.
Jack himself was one of the liveliest minds I knew at the time—
indeed, he still is.

Almost immediately after Harding's arrival in the North, I
resigned from my office job to devote myself whole time to
writing. For the first few months, I was busy about my own
affairs, but by the spring of 1934, he had got me to read through
some of the radio scripts that he had been writing in London. He
had liked the poetry I was publishing, particularly the social
protest poems like *Song for the Three Million*, and my *Second Hymn
for the People of England* which Pound had included in his *Active
Anthology*. Harding felt that these would speak well, and could be
broadcast effectively, given the right context. He pointed out that
radio offered a new field for poetry. Not only could it be given
the occasional straight reading, but it could also be a lively
ingredient in the sort of documentary programmes he was interested in promoting. Auden was writing poetry for documentary films: why shouldn't I write poems for documentary radio?
The idea sounded a good one and rather appealed to me.

Perhaps a contributory factor to my interest was the news that
back in 1930, Harding had tried to interest T. S. Eliot in radio as a
medium for serious writing. Unfortunately for radio, he failed to
do so. But after I had read some of Harding's experimental scripts,
I could see what he meant when he wondered whether the form
of *Triumphal March* had possibly been suggested by one or two
of them. Eliot's roll-call of the armaments at least seemed rather
reminiscent. It also seemed to hold out promise for similar roll-
calls on the air. How many tons of crude ore, how many thousand
tons of steel . . . I was to try out the method myself, over the next
few years.

The first of my programmes to be broadcast went out on St.
George's Day, 1934. It told of the oak tree planted on Parliament Hill by a party of working men to honour Shakespeare's

tercentenary in 1864. The leader of this literary-minded battalion was one George Moore, a Cumbrian philanthropist, not the Irish novelist. I forget why Harding required such a quaint piece of Victorian gothic: perhaps, like the young man of Newcastle in one of his favourite rhymes, it was just to oblige a relation. At least the programme gave me my first insight into radio production methods, then in its multiple-studio phase, and far more complicated than today. I attended all the rehearsals and was made privy to the mysteries of the dramatic control panel. Fired by the experience, I came on the air a week later with something rather more promising.

Harding had invited me to try my hand at a programme about May Day. Briefly, the idea was to contrast the old bucolic three-times-round-the-maypole tradition with the new conception of May Day as the day for social protest. Here at least was a theme which offered me possibilities. I built up a pleasantly varied mosaic in which Robin Hood plays and the May Day games gave way to the May Day rioting against imported Flemish labour under Henry VIII. May Day had soon become a cause of contention between the Puritans and the people: the Strand lost its maypole. Herrick and others restored the May Day jollity. But dancing Jennies gave way to the spinning Jenny: the Industrial Revolution began to pave the way for another. As for the nineteenth century, that gave me the chance really to try for a little fun! Tennyson, in the role of an increasingly hysterical Queen of the May, found himself cross-cut against a rising tide of industrial militancy, petering out in a final despairing squeak before the advance of organised labour. From there, of course, was a short step to the Hunger Marches, machine-guns in the Berlin streets, and the Internationale blared out over the loud-hailers in the Red Square. The programme ended on a quiet but equally ominous note in a poem of mine read by Robin Whitworth:

> Cause enough, then, for their spending
> One day in the old fashion—
> All under way and the land mending . . .

Winter over with its winter ration—
    Salt meat, dried fruit and the rest:
May gave them milk again and churns to freshen.

Yes . . . And the Spring, then, and the men out.
    Spring again—and the men 'out' still . . .
May Day, then, and a new order of things . . .
May Day, yes . . . And a new order of things . . .

This was sounding rather a new note in British Broadcasting—
or so Archie Harding decided. But the newest note of all came in
the reading of a couple of stanzas from my *Song for the Three
Million*, the number of the Unemployed in Britain at the time.
The stanzas were snarled out in seething anger by a vigorously
proletarian voice that must have rattled the coffee-cups in sitting-
rooms all over the country:

Cut the cost somehow, keep the balance whole;
Men are in the making, marching for the Dole.
Payday and May Day drawing to the poll,—
There's a time to truckle—*and* to take toll.
    Time to take toll—so watch where you tread:
    The lesson in the bleeding is *not* to be the bled.

Bats are from the baking, cooling on the slab:
The duster at the knuckle, waiting for a dab.
Shout for your chauffeur or call for your cab:
Our kind of scathing is difficult to scab!
    And stooping to the tramline, you can hear the tread
    Of the done-brown damnfools—the living and the dead.

The voice was a new one on the air, the voice of Ewan MacColl,
but there was no mistaking the message of the tramping feet
behind it.

Ewan MacColl was himself a victim of the Depression. The
son of an unemployed Glasgow steelworker, who had moved to

Salford in search of work during the twenties, he had suffered every privation and humiliation that poverty could contrive for him from the age of ten. His memories of his early years are still bitter—like his recollection of how to kill aimless time in a world where there was nothing else to do: "You go in the Public Library. And the old men are there standing against the pipes to get warm, all the newspaper parts are occupied, and you pick a book up. I can remember then that you got the smell of the unemployed, a kind of sour or bitter-sweet smell, mixed in with the smell of old books, dust, leather and the rest of it. So now if I pick up, say, a Dostoievsky—immediately with the first page, there's that smell of poverty in 1931."

MacColl had been out busking for pennies by the Manchester theatres and cinemas. The songs he sang were unusual, Scots songs, Gaelic songs he had learnt from his mother, border ballads and folk-songs. One night while queueing up for the three-and-sixpennies, Kenneth Adam had heard him singing outside the Manchester Paramount. He was suitably impressed. Not only did he give MacColl a handout; he also advised him to go and audition for Archie Harding at the BBC studios in Manchester's Piccadilly. This MacColl duly did. *May Day in England* was being cast at the time, and though it had no part for a singer, it certainly had for a good, tough, angry Voice of the People. Ewan MacColl became the Voice, a role which he has continued to fill on stage, on the air, and on a couple of hundred L.P. discs ever since.

Shortly after *May Day in England* went out, a letter appeared in the correspondence column of the *Radio Times* over the signature of one George Potter. It gave high praise to the programme and ended: "Broadcasting produces, or displays, a creative writer of real force, and the critics continue to retail nothing but the latest band-room and bar-room gossip. It is high time this particular temple is cleansed." I was surprised, when I met him a year later, to find that 'George Potter' had been a discreet pseudonym for Laurence Gilliam, who had just moved over from the *Radio Times* to become a London feature producer himself. We were to see a great deal more of each other.

From then on, it seemed that so far as radio was concerned, I was hooked. I was to devote myself to writing for it more and more—and in due course was to end up doing virtually nothing else. Not only did radio give me a wide outlet for what I wanted to say; it had its own absorbing interest as a medium still to be opened up and developed. For as Harding had said, it soon seemed to me that radio was being used in the wrong way. It stood apart from a vast audience which it still merely condescended to address. The sort of radio both of us wanted was something very different.

Because of my sudden interest in the medium, I offered to write a column of serious radio criticism for the *New English Weekly*, along with the other reviewing that I was still doing for them. This Orage agreed to carry, and the column started up in July, 1934. Previous to that, as Gilliam had complained, no such column had existed, though Collie Knox, Jonah Barrington and others had long been running their gossip columns. A couple of years later, Grace Wyndham Goldie started a critical column in *The Listener*. I was amused when she subsequently told me that the editor had handed her some of my back-files by way of showing her what was wanted. Finally, even Eliot himself began to carry a Broadcasting Commentary in *The Criterion*. Radio criticism had at last arrived.

That same summer of 1934, Northern radio made one truly unique recruit. While in London, Harding had acted as an adjudicator at R.A.D.A., where he had been asked to award the first gold medal for microphone technique. The girl who won it had a warmly engaging voice, excellent diction, and absolutely no fashionable affectation of accent whatever. She was not remarkable at R.A.D.A. for that alone: she also happened to be a girl from a working-class home in the East End. As it transpired, she heartily detested R.A.D.A., for which she had won a scholarship, and equally detested the genteel mediocrity of the West End theatre of the time. Harding had been impressed with her, and had asked her to come and see him at Broadcasting House. She preferred to hock her medal, and go over to Paris for the Stavisky riots. By the time her money had run out, and she was back in London needing work, Harding had been transferred to Manchester. As he had promised to find her whatever radio work he could, she decided to follow him North. But where most girls would have borrowed the train fare, Joan Littlewood preferred to cover the hundred and eighty miles on foot. This she did with a small rucksack.

Sleeping under hedges, living on raw potatoes and turnips dug up out of the fields, hitching lifts and all that went to the usual picaresque tradition brought her finally to the Potteries. There she rested up in communal quarters with a group of families fighting a running battle against eviction from their homes. Perhaps it was the loss of the battle which eventually brought her on to Manchester. True to his word, Harding at once put her on the air; her story was also taken up by the Manchester papers. Beds were laid on for her in flats around the city, and Joan became a part of the Northern way of life. As she chose to put it herself: "I was a bum, but I was adopted for the first time in my life, as part of the whole humming scene. I was adopted by the autonomous republic."

I sometimes wonder whether I ever met in anyone quite the same warmth and charm and utter sincerity with which Joan made the North her own. Over the next few years, I was to watch her captivate hundreds of people in every sector of Northern life. Her sense of fun was highly infectious; but only her power to deflate the pretentious was really dangerous. For her, the people who mattered were those who knew they had something they must create; the people she despised were those who had never found it necessary. She had no real ambition to act herself: her burning urge was to gather together a body of people equally devoted, who could be taught to act and react instinctively as a group. There was something of Stanislavsky about it, but very much more of Joan Littlewood. In a way, it was almost exasperating that being such a natural actress herself, she preferred to try and coax good acting out of material far less talented. So far as the stage was concerned, perhaps she felt that appearances were against her: she looked too full of fun, and her gap-toothed grin was too engaging to carry conviction in very much more than comedy. As for her acting for the BBC, this she could never take seriously as more than a comic interlude. The BBC as a whole she found as absurd as it mostly was, and her parody of the BBC manner could embarrass even a BBC announcer. Harding and I and the rest had to endure her mockery, which was salutary for all of us. But despite her derision of the BBC, Joan was to play a very important part in making the sort of radio that I wanted. We worked at it happily together over the next few years.

Among the beliefs that I shared with Orage and Ezra Pound, was a firm assurance of the need for some sort of monetary reform. Various economic panaceas have been suggested. Once there was technocracy and today there is fluidity, but in 1934 there was Social Credit. And whatever one thought of that, the world-wide recession of trade at the time was more than enough to prove the need of an urgent shot in the economic arm. By way of publicising the need, I had just written a verse play called *Prometheus the Engineer*. It was written in the form of classical tragedy, and set in what I described as the Workshop of the World. Its hero, the Engineer, was vainly attempting to hold a balance between the factory floor and management. As was to be expected, he ended up as a victim of neo-luddite violence: the workers threw him to the machines.

Despite its anti-Marxist economics, Harding liked the play and accepted it; in due course it was cast and billed and went into rehearsal. Once again, Ewan MacColl was given a major part to play; there couldn't have been a better choice for the militant leader of the workers. Robin Whitworth and I were billed as co-producers, he looking after the technical aspects at the control panel and I the speaking of the verse dialogue and the various choruses.

It happened that Harding had recently had his knuckles rapped again by Sir John Reith. He had put some hunger-marchers onto the air in an interview, and what they had said was not very complimentary to the National Government. At the last moment, therefore, he felt the need to take out insurance, and sent the script of *Prometheus* to London for what was known as 'policy scrutiny'. Needless to say, no one in Broadcasting House had ever heard of Social Credit. To a policy scrutineer, an argumentative play written around a revolt of the workers was manifestly inspired by the Comintern. *Prometheus* was banned by the BBC Controller of Programmes, Colonel Dawnay, as being dangerously seditious. Rehearsals immediately had to be stopped, and a substitute found to take its place. A few enquiries were made by the press, as the *Radio Times* had billed the play quite prominently; but no official explanations were offered.

In view of his current interest in the writing of dramatic verse, someone in London had sent a script of the play to T. S. Eliot, and had even invited him to Broadcasting House to hear the transmission. As no transmission occurred, profuse apologies had to be offered, and he went away somewhat mystified. When I met him shortly afterwards, he asked me the reason for the sudden cancellation—and was highly delighted when I told him. Dangerously seditious as it was, he printed the play in *The Criterion*, that organ of rigid conservatism for which I had recently begun to do reviewing.* The BBC continued to abide by its own ideas of the conservative.

But trouble over *Prometheus* notwithstanding, a few weeks later I was invited by the BBC North Region to apply for the post of their Drama Producer, shortly to fall vacant when Robin Whitworth returned to London. The idea had been Harding's; but it had the blessing and full support of Ted Liveing, the North Regional Director. The application was made, and duly endorsed by Liveing, it was forwarded on to London. But before I could be accepted into the fold, I had to go down to London in person and offer myself for inspection in Portland Place. A series of interviews were laid on for me, and in a couple of days I had caught a train and found myself in front of Broadcasting House.

* *Prometheus* was written in a stylised amalgam of North Country and Americanese— an idiom as artificial as that used by Pound twenty years later for *The Women of Trachis*. On the printed page (for which it was never intended) this looked distinctly odd. But belted out by MacColl and the others above the steady roar of the machines, it made exciting listening.

I had seen the building before, of course, but since I had come to know what broadcasting meant, the place had assumed a new interest for me. Many people had likened it to a stranded concrete battleship, and such it appeared to me then—with a double figurehead at its prow. Over the door stood Prospero and Ariel, elegant and elongated—the one young and eager, the other bearded and sedate. I remembered the story I had heard about the sculpture shortly before, which deserves to be better known. It seems that when Broadcasting House was opened, a couple of years earlier, the BBC Governors had been invited to climb up to the platform where Eric Gill was putting the finishing touches to the statues behind a tarpaulin screen. They were startled by what seemed to them a palpable exaggeration in the size of Ariel's pudenda. A meeting was called to discuss the matter. As one of the Governors happened to be the ex-headmaster of a famous public school, he was held to be better qualified than the rest to express an opinion as to whether the figure was in any way abnormal. After careful thought, he is reported to have given his verdict thus: "I can only say, from personal observation, that the lad is uncommonly well hung." Like Michelangelo before him, Gill was tactfully asked to remount his ladder and cut things down to size.

I thought at the time, there was something highly significant in the story. Indeed, there was something highly significant in the BBC's whole approach to life, as Harding had maintained. When he had asked for a drawing in the *Radio Times*, for example, to illustrate Pound's Villon opera, the artist had drawn Grosse Margot leaning out of the brothel window, her breasts bare to the breeze. Like Ariel's before her, it was felt by the editor that the lady's nudity would have to be 'scrutinised' upstairs, and this was duly done. The directive that came down to him from the think-tank on the third floor was worthy of Solomon: "*One* of the lady's breasts might be bare—but certainly not both." In all such matters, it was implied, the BBC employee should know exactly where to draw the line. The *Radio Times'* artist accordingly drew it down the cleavage.

With that ruling in mind, I had given some thought to my own dress—and carefully adjusted it before entering Broadcasting House for the first time. I was told at the desk that four people expected me in their offices. The first was the Appointments Officer and the second a Programme Planner: both proved amiable and encouraging. The third was Val Gielgud, BBC's Director of Drama, known to me by repute and from his photograph in the papers. He matched the latter admirably: his neatly pointed black imperial also matched the sword-stick that stood in the corner of his office. (As it was still only the afternoon, his crimson-lined opera cloak was not yet in evidence.) But Polish nobleman as he nearly was, and rude Bolshevik as I must have appeared to him, we hit it off surprisingly well, as we have done ever since. We talked of this and that, and in due course he passed me on to the last of the four people I had to meet, the BBC Director of Internal Administration.

Later to be Sir Basil, at the time he was plain Mr. B. E. Nicolls, known to the staff as Benjie, but only addressed as such by those who enjoyed his favour. He was certainly an impressive figure, built on somewhat the same lines as Sir John Reith, though not so tall. He was even more imposingly bald, and equally elegant in his pin-stripe trousers. He had a strongly handsome face, and his eyes glinted from under jutting silvery brows and a loftily domed forehead. He greeted me affably, but I was careful to show him all due deference; he did not look to me like a man to tolerate over-familiarity.* To do him justice, however, he couldn't have been more friendly, or done more to put me at my ease. He told me that my programmes had been much appreciated and those he had heard himself he had found original and lively. He had

---

* Moray McLaren, later the Assistant Head of Drama, once told me a cautionary tale. At one of Nicolls's weekly meetings, discussion had been droning along until his attention began to wander. "What would *you* do, Moray?" Nicolls had suddenly fired at him out of the blue. As Moray hadn't the faintest idea what was the point at issue, he decided to play it firmly. "If I was you, sir," he declared, "I should go at it bald-headed." Hearing the stifled laughter, and catching the look in Nicolls's eye, he desperately tried to cover the gaffe. "That is," he added unwisely, "if you'll pardon the expression." Though everyone else appeared to be, the Director of Internal Administration was clearly not amused.

seen my name in the reviews and knew that I wrote for Orage, an editor whom he respected. He talked easily about literature and the theatre, even enquiring what music I liked. I told him that I would settle for Bach, Mozart and Beethoven: he advised me not to neglect Brahms. This I cheerfully promised, and after the tea was finished, he rose benevolently to his feet: as the last of my four scrutineers, I felt he was definitely well disposed. "I think," he said as an afterthought, "that the *Admiral* might like to see you . . ."

Who 'the Admiral' was, I hadn't a very clear idea; he certainly wasn't on my list, and so far no one had mentioned him. As we strolled along the corridor, Nicolls filled in the picture for me: Royal Navy, of course, Sir John Reith had brought him in to run the business side of things. Admiral Sir Charles Carpendale was in fact the BBC Controller of Administration, and shortly to become the Deputy Director-General. "I don't say that he knows his *Waste Land*," Nicolls conceded, "but I think you'll find him quite a decent sort of a chap." We threaded our way past a secretary, and I followed him into the presence.

The Admiral proved to be something of a surprise. He was a small, lean man with thin grey hair and a somewhat desiccated look. Hardly an Admiral in the bluff Elizabethan tradition, he rather reminded me (when I saw it later) of Charles Laughton's Captain Bligh in *Mutiny on the Bounty*. Perhaps I reminded him of Fletcher Christian, for his face was about as bleak as the North Cape in February. He motioned me to a chair and began his examination. What school had I been to? *Which?* Then which University? *I hadn't???* What was my occupation? Writing? Writing what—and for whom? Why did I think I was a producer? Had I ever produced plays in the theatre? Then had I ever produced plays on the radio? What did I mean—*helped* to produce? Helped to produce what? Helped to produce my own programmes? What was that supposed to prove? Why did I think I'd be able to produce anyone else's? What? Then why had I said that I could?

By this time, I was beginning to get a bit more Northern in

my responses. I *hadn't* said that I could—I'd said I was pretty sure I could. The Admiral observed that he wasn't trying to put words into my mouth. I pointed out, on the other hand, that the BBC appeared to share my opinion—those, at least, who knew my work. The Admiral pursed his lips: he was clearly one of those who *didn't* share my opinion.

To the ebb and flow of this little interchange, Nicolls had been listening with tactfully hidden amusement. No doubt he was interested to see how I reacted under pressure, though he admitted some years later that the look on the Admiral's face was what he remembered with most pleasure, confronted as he had been by "a rather gingery young man in gay, bohemian clothes . . ." Gingery I admittedly was; but as for the clothes I was wearing, they seemed to me quite impeccably formal. Whatever the truth of that, throughout the spirited cut and thrust, Nicolls himself had remained impeccably neutral. He rather conveyed the impression that his sole purpose in being there was to try and prevent us actually coming to blows.

The Admiral fidgeted in his chair, carefully primed himself, then fired off a truly decisive broadside: "Do you speak French?" he reverberated.

"I've not yet found it necessary," I answered with equal annoyance. "It takes me all my time to write English."

That one rather took him aback, and he chewed it over once or twice. Before he had quite decided whether it was impertinent, Nicolls had tactfully led me off his quarter-deck. No doubt it was fortunate that he did.

Out in the corridor, he grinned at me rather quizzically and made a few noncommittal noises; a pity the interview had run into rather a blind alley . . . Far more closely in touch with production matters himself, of course . . .

We shook hands in front of the lift, and he told me I should be hearing from him. "The Admiral," he mused, "appears to have a bit of a *bee* in his bonnet . . ."

I didn't enquire whether it wasn't rather a matter of bats in the Admiral's belfry.

Needless to say, I was not given the job. I console myself with the thought that there really was some distinction in being turned down flat by Sir John Reith's elected deputy.

The letter which followed me back to the North regretted my unsuitability for the post on the grounds of under-experience.* The letter went on to express the hope that I should still continue to write for radio, for in that way experience might be increased. The letter was signed by B. E. Nicolls.

Not only did I continue to write for radio: I continued to write provocatively. Harding's inherent fondness for the North had not interfered with his power to find occasional fault with it, and many aspects of Manchester life exasperated us equally. In the Autumn of 1934, we thought it might be amusing to vent our exasperation over the air. The result was a show called *Jannock*, a declaredly Malicious Medley, written by me and produced by Robin Whitworth. Knowing my Manchester businessman, by virtue of having worked with him, I set out to portray some of his more tiresome sides with all my natural candour. My poem *The Northern Dance of the Seven Deadly Sins* provided one section of the programme, others were written around the boorishness of public servants, and the gloomy acceptance on all sides of the fact that 'business was terrible'.

The response to *Jannock* was vigorous. The Manchester *Daily Dispatch* came out with a roaring attack on the programme, ably abetted by the Manchester *Evening Chronicle*. To them (and to their readers, apparently) it constituted a "Libel on the People of Lancashire", and their posters proclaimed to the world that the BBC had insulted the North! To most people, of course, the BBC implied the South, and the fact that I was myself a Northerner rather confused the issue for them. People began to take sides in the quarrel: it *was* a disgusting travesty, or Manchester busmen *were* like that . . . (When busmen actually proved the point,

---

* I was intrigued to learn eventually that the official reason for my rejection, as noted in my BBC staff-file, was that I had "an unpolished personality". It was also darkly hinted that I was "politically minded". As Michael Standing established, however, the latter charge was later amended: I was then credited with "a strong sociological sense". We both much enjoyed the reassessment.

"Jannock" was promptly hurled at them by the passengers as a new term of abuse.) Certain listeners had been thrown into a downright frenzy of indignation, however; among them a one-time business colleague of mine. A friend in the cotton trade, known to appear regularly on the BBC as a spare-time hobby, was almost ostracised when he next appeared on the floor of the Royal Exchange. He meekly pointed out that he hadn't played any part in *Jannock*. "A good thing for you that you didn't," growled one of the most respected members. "If you had, I should never have done business with you again!"

For the next few days, Ted Liveing, the harassed Regional Director, went round clutching the press-clippings with a hunted look in his eye. Harding, on the other hand, was jubilant: "The cap fits!" he shouted, slapping himself on the thigh. As for myself, I was glad to think that my boring years in an office had not perhaps been entirely wasted.

I followed up *Jannock* with a few shows that were not so controversial, and for New Year's Eve wrote *Frost at Midnight*, the first of some hundred literary features. This nostalgic study of Coleridge in his declining years was superbly acted by Robert Farquharson, one of the most remarkable actors I ever heard on the air. It was much liked by the critics, and also in influential circles at Broadcasting House. As the *Manchester Guardian* put it, "Mr. Bridson's work has not hitherto always been free from some particular angle or prejudice, which has lessened its artistic value." On this occasion, Mary Crozier declared, all was exactly as it should be.

Alas, I was not so fortunate with *The Scourge*, the play which I wrote next. I had intended it mainly as an essay in the imaginative use of sound effects. The story concerned a man whose car was wrecked by a train at a level-crossing: the sound of the train continued to thunder in his head. The motivating theme of the play was adultery, which seemed to me usual enough. But since the adultery happened to be committed between a youth and his uncle's young and attractive wife, I found myself taken off the air again—this time, curiously enough, on the grounds of condoning incest! I protested that incest was no more involved than it would be if someone were to have an affair with his step-mother. "Who on earth would ever do that?" was the scanda-lised response. I agreed that Phaedra had found the buskin on the other leg, but still held out for the possibility. Nevertheless, the train was cancelled—much to the irritation of Jan Bussel, the new North Regional Drama Producer whose first production it should have enlivened. Once again, there were press enquiries: I was even credited with being the only writer to get himself twice into the *Radio Times* without being able to get himself onto the air.

Perhaps it was just as well that I suddenly came up with the first of my *Harry Hopeful* shows, a series which was to set a new trend in actuality broadcasting. To prove my respectability further, I even helped to celebrate the twelfth centenary of the death of Bede. So venerable was that death-bed, that London promptly com-missioned me to help them celebrate the fourth centenary of the death of Sir Thomas More. And though I did as much for the first centenary of the death of Cobbett in a rather more inflammatory way, word seemed to be getting around that I had acquired a new orthodoxy.

Earlier that summer, Scottish Region had taken John Gough onto their staff. He was a rugged Australian writer-composer, a friend of Jack Lindsay in the old Fanfrolico Press days. His job was the writing of radio feature programmes, and he was in fact the first creative writer ever to be taken onto the staff of the BBC as such. His sponsor was Moray McLaren, then Scottish Pro-gramme Director, and the appointment was certainly a wise one; for radio's need of creative writing was growing as fast as the radio audience. Harding promptly asked for a similar post to be sanctioned in North Region, and shortly afterwards it was.

In the summer of 1935, therefore, I found myself invited by the BBC for the second time to apply for a staff position—this time the post of Feature Programmes Assistant. My feelings were a trifle mixed, but the humour of the situation rather appealed to me. What appealed to me far more was the chance of working in more closely with Archie Harding. So much of my time was already being taken up by radio that it seemed quite reasonable to start in working for it exclusively—at least, for a year or two.

I filled in my application form and was once more summoned to London. Making obeisance before Prospero and Ariel, I carefully groomed myself, and entered Broadcasting House for the second time. Four people were waiting to see me, the same four people that I had seen exactly nine months earlier. Whatever had been in process of gestation, the period seemed to be somehow apt, and much play was made of the fact. Val Gielgud was particularly sardonic; such delays, he declared, were typical of everything in the building. He only hoped that my time would not be wasted on this occasion.

My second interview with Nicolls was no less friendly than the first. He observed that history has a habit of repeating itself, but this time we left Brahms out of it. We talked about what the new job involved, and I even took upon myself to haggle a little over the salary. I had been much saddened by the death of Orage the previous winter, but the *New English Weekly* was still in being —now edited by Philip Mairet, for whom I was still writing a regular column of radio criticism. I pointed out that this would have to be given up if I joined the staff of the BBC; I hoped they could take this loss of my earnings into consideration. Nicolls cheerfully argued that as Orage had never paid anyone, loss of earnings could hardly be involved. I answered, with some warmth, that Orage had certainly paid *me*—and that Mairet still continued to do so. Nicolls said that no doubt a suitable salary could be agreed upon, and I let the matter rest at that. Only the one impediment now remained to the marriage of true minds. "I think," he said reflectively, "that this time we'll *not* go and see the Admiral . . ."

The contract reached me in Manchester a couple of days later. The salary was what I had hoped, being rather more than had been mentioned the previous year. I signed the contract on 17 June 1935, and reported for duty a week later.

No doubt I had been smuggled in by a back window—but even so, I had joined the Club. The Welsh Regiment had its goat: the BBC now had its Bolshevik.

2

Seed-time in the North

I ONLY MET up with the Admiral one more time—about six months after I had been infiltrated onto his staff. He sat down opposite me one evening in the BBC canteen, when I happened to be in London on one of my routine visits. He obviously recognised me, and eyed me with some suspicion: Wasn't I that young fella . . . ? Hadn't he given express instructions . . . ? I eyed him blandly back over our fish and chips, but didn't wish him good evening. Hesitating to question me, he retired baffled into his evening paper. Luckily, I never even saw him again: a bosun's whistle piped him (literally) into retirement and left me to more congenial colleagues.

Up in the North, I found them all remarkably congenial. Apart from Harding, Ted Liveing proved himself a staunch supporter of mine. He remembered readings by Vachel Lindsay at Oxford back in the twenties, and poetry was accordingly on his list. He was the only man I ever knew with marmalade coloured hair, his nickname of Red Ted having reference to that rather than to his politics. Victor Smythe, the long-time impresario of Northern Outside Broadcasts, was known in every hotel bar throughout the North: in his cigar digesting way, he was probably the nearest thing to Lew Grade that the BBC ever managed to acquire. The Manchester Control Room was cheerfully run by Bruce Purslow, an ex-radio operator from the Merchant Marine, who took me under his wing and taught me what little I ever knew about radio engineering. Jan Bussell, who held the job of Drama Producer from which I had been debarred by naval action, was another good friend and neighbour. His true ambition was to find fame as a puppeteer, and this he finally did along with his wife Ann

Hogarth, when television brought us Muffin the Mule.* Donald
Boyd, who shortly joined me as a Talks Producer, I had known
while he was still on the *Manchester Guardian*; we were to do
many things together before joining forces finally on the BBC
War Report. David Porter, a non-sectarian Ulsterman, also joined
us as Variety Producer: along with Edgar Lustgarten, Giles Playfair and Henry Reed the composer, he carved out a new line for
the Region in light music and entertainment.

I might remark that the local Director of Administration was
a certain Captain Henry Fitch, also of the Royal Navy. Despite
my refusal to play bridge, he appeared to find me acceptable, and
we mostly managed to keep off all political issues. On one occasion, however, we failed. During the Spanish War, he declared
himself to be firmly behind Franco, and needless to say I didn't
share his enthusiasm. One afternoon, over tea and toast in the
boardroom, he managed to draw me into an argument. "If you
were a Republican commander, Bridson," he asked me suddenly,
"and I fell into your hands as an Insurgent officer—what would
you do with me?" I always felt that a straight question called for
a straight answer: "I should stand you against a wall, sir," I
declared with some vehemence, "and have you shot by a firing-
squad." The news delighted him: he commended me for my
honesty and shortly after backed me for a rise in salary. No doubt
the Royal Navy was far less bigoted than I had been led to suppose.

I have said that Harding's belief that radio should reflect the
life of the people was one with which I fully concurred. I also
believed that radio was there to put people in touch with each
other, not merely to instruct or inform or even to entertain
them. It seemed to me that since its inception, broadcasting by
the BBC had been the exclusive concern of 'us', and listening the
lucky privilege of 'them'. That the man in the street should have
anything vital to contribute to broadcasting was an idea slow to

* He also derived some lustre from showing the then Queen Elizabeth how to work his
puppets at a local Garden Party. "The Queen," he solemnly reported to the local press,
"is a born manipulator."

gain acceptance. That he should actually use broadcasting to express his own opinions in his own unvarnished words, was regarded as almost the end of all good social order. Never once in history had the man in the street been even consulted. As a member of the electorate, he had been invited to express a preference for either side of somebody else's question—but that was as far as social order had so far been prepared to go.

This is another way of saying that very few 'actuality speakers' —as the BBC chose to call the vast bulk of their licence payers— had yet been heard on the air. Eric Maschwitz had begun to put a few of them into *In Town Tonight*, but there they had hardly been heard to advantage. Stumbling awkwardly through their scripts, they had suggested anything but the actual, and had mostly proved a painful embarrassment. The reason for this was simple enough: they were none of them trained readers, the scripted dialogue in which they were asked to take part with professional announcers was in no way natural to them, and the awesome surroundings of the studio—in many ways reminiscent of a dental surgery—were not the best setting in which to meet up with a microphone for the first time.

One has to remember that during the thirties—indeed, until after the war—nearly all speech on radio was live, and had to be pre-scripted. The microphone was regarded as such a potentially dangerous weapon that nobody was allowed to approach it until it was fully known what he intended to do with it. Perhaps an exception might have been made for the monarch, but to him a script was probably a convenience. (There was nothing at all spontaneous about the abdication speech of Edward VIII, for example.) As for the rest of us, almost nobody was exempt.*
Even Bernard Shaw had been firmly refused a chance to come to the microphone and *talk*. By him, as by everyone else, a script had first to be written and submitted, carefully vetted by a producer, referred to a higher authority if necessary, and then read

---

* Somewhat later, odd spontaneous answers were elicited in the London streets by Michael Standing in *Standing on the Corner*. I believe that carefully chosen speakers were also heard *extempore* in *Midland Parliament*.

at the microphone exactly as it had been sanctioned. Failure to
keep to the written text would merely have meant being taken
off the air by a vigilant programme engineer. So far as my recollection goes, no completely spontaneous broadcast was heard on
the air live before the wartime experiment of an unscripted debate
between Quintin Hogg and Aneurin Bevan. In that, the stam-
mering Welshman ran such rings round his Tory opponent that
Churchill himself is said to have insisted that no such politically
dangerous exercise should ever be indulged in by a member of
his party again!

A case can be made out for checked and censored scripts in
wartime on the grounds of national security. But that spontaneous speech should have been banned by the BBC for the first
odd twenty years of broadcasting is almost unbelievable. The fact
remains that it was. The result, needless to say, is that few beside
professional actors, professional speakers, and what one might
call professional personalities ever got near the microphone at all.
First of the last category, perhaps, was John Hilton in 1933;
Mr. Middleton-the-garden joined him in 1936. But apart from
these and one or two others, the voice of the BBC remained the
voice of the upper-middle class, and almost the only accent heard
on the air was Standard Southern English. Out on the perimeter,
in Scotland and Wales and Northern Ireland, occasional purlings
of the genteeler local Doric were permitted. But not until 1941
was Wilfred Pickles allowed to read the news in a voice identi-
fiably non-standard. Some surprise had once been felt that King
George V himself had not appeared to speak what the BBC regarded as King's English. Sir John Reith—once—had announced
a few English election results in tones reminiscent of the auld
manse. Listeners had rung up to complain, and from then on the
English ear had been left reassuringly unsullied. The radio audience had been taught to expect the BBC to speak BBC—just as
the simple traveller had long grown used to the fact that in France
even the children spoke French. The *Harry Hopeful* programmes
undoubtedly helped to change all that.

I have already mentioned the first of them, which I wrote in the spring of 1935. It was called *Cam Houses to Tan Hill*, and was the outcome of a trip which Harding and I made round the Yorkshire Dales in search of radio material. The material was there for all who had eyes and ears—the splendid look of the country and the splendid sound of the dalesmen. Not only was their dialect a wonderful speech to hear, their character was implicit in every word they uttered—dialect or straight North Country. Although myself a townsman, I had always had a great fondness for the Northern countryside, and admired the Northern countryfolk no less. I knew them on the Cumberland fells, on the Yorkshire moors and in the Derbyshire dales—and I wanted the world to know them too. But I wanted the world to know them as they really were in their own setting. And how was that to be brought about—the rules of the game being what they were?

I was quite convinced that it *could* be brought about. But first of all, it seemed, I had to think up someone whom they could accept as one of themselves and talk to purely in their own terms. As it finally emerged, the answer was a comic invention of my own: an out-of-work glass-blower's assistant, a natural picaresque who tramped the roads of the North in search of a different kind of job. I thought of him as a foil for the countryman's innate sense of humour, one whose leg could be pulled as they talked about country matters. Looking for work as he was, all the jobs they did could be made to sound utterly beyond him— far too skilled or complicated or plain exhausting. Playing back at them in his turn, he could at least pretend that they were— being far too happy in his travels ever to want to settle down. The tradition was almost that of the Music Hall; and as a spokesman for the BBC, such an unlikely character could soon become a figure of fun.

Inventing Harry Hopeful was easy: bringing him to life might not have been easy at all. Luckily for me, the man to do it was there at hand in the person of Frank Nicholls. By trade, Nicholls was a clock repairer who lived in the little Lancashire town of Irlam. He was fond of amateur acting and had passed an audition with the North Region: he appeared regularly in their Children's

Hour with Eric Fogg, Muriel Levy, Doris Gamble and the rest, and had played parts in most of my own features to date. In point of fact, he was really too old for the present part, being grey-haired and in his fifties: I had thought of Harry Hopeful as rather more of a jaunty lad, and as such he was always drawn in the *Radio Times*. But nobody else had half the charm and humour and dialect acting ability of Nicholls. He soon proved himself, beyond all doubt, to be one of the world's great broadcasters.

As for the dalesmen, they took to him at sight. He cracked with them in their pubs, took tea with them and their wives at home, and was followed about by hordes of delighted children everywhere that he visited. Nobody I ever knew had a greater gift for putting people completely at their ease. They showed him around their farms, their quarries or wherever they worked, and talked about everything under the sun. Copy was hardly in short supply but boiling it down into speakable dialogue involved a certain amount of trouble. Nicholls was easy enough: he could play any character I gave him. But those he was up against must be written in character just as they were. I jotted down their stories, noted their favourite tricks of speech, their dialect usage and turn of phrase, while Nicholls continued to draw them out. From a couple of hours' listening, I then had to distil the essence of what they really were—told entirely in their own words and cast into a cross-talk act which gave them the edge on every topic. The dialogue might look well on paper, but that was merely the start of it: they still weren't ready for the studio.

I finished the script back home in Manchester. Posting on their separate parts to the dozen or so speakers concerned, I went back to the dales a couple of days later with Nicholls and a radio engineer. We took portable gear with us, for I wanted everyone in the show to have seen the microphone first rigged up in his own front sitting-room: after that, it could hold no fears for him. In one home after another we tried the acts out over it, changing the words here and there, and listening to the result on head-phones in our car at the front gate. If a speaker sounded unnatural, his family was invited to listen over the phones as well—

and no critics could be more exacting. After pillow sessions in bed with his wife for the next few days, few men were below production pitch when the whole group came down by bus for the final studio rehearsal and transmission.

In the event, the *Harry Hopeful* shows proved immensely popular, no less in the South than in the North. The rich variety of the Northern dialects and accents, the toughness and humour inherent in the Northern character, struck a new note in broadcasting at the time. So did the waggish character of Harry Hopeful himself. The broadcasts, furthermore, were all of them country shows—whereas radio normally tended to reflect only life in the towns. The Yorkshire and the Derbyshire Dales, the Lake District and the Scottish Border, the Trough of Bowland, the East Riding, Cleveland and Upper Teesdale—each brought its breath of fresh air into the listening suburbs, and each had its own attraction as landscape and splendid walking country. The crowd of tourists which followed them into the various districts covered was proof in itself of the interest that the shows aroused. As for Harry Hopeful, he became something of a national figure: one heard his theme-song whistled in the streets. It was a sad day for many people when Frank Nicholls died, in February 1938.

Perhaps the most important thing about the series was the new conception of the North which it helped me to project. To me, as I have said, Manchester was far more than a grimy, industrial city in the provinces. To me, the North was not provincial at all; it was an entity standing upon its own. So far as industry went, the rest of the country revolved around it. So far as the people went— and they were far older than the Industrial Revolution—the Northerners were a people apart. My first desire in radio had been to *project* the North. Frank Nicholls was the first of three people who helped to make it possible.

The shows that we did together had taken me into every corner of the North Region, from Berwick down to the Wash and from Chester up to the Solway Firth. I had always loved the fell country, and walking tours in the Pennines, the High Peak or the Lake District accounted for most of my holidays. In 1932 I had walked my way through much of the Scottish Highlands, ending up on Skye with my first sight of the Western Isles. From that particular holiday, I got the idea for another of my earlier programmes. For over much of the way I had followed—though in reverse—the route taken by Charles Edward Stewart in the Jacobite rising of 1745.

The March of the '45 was written during my first year with the BBC. It was probably the most successful of all my single programmes, and certainly the most widely heard. It was to be broadcast nine times over the next thirty-three years, and played back over closed circuit more times than I care to remember. During most of that time it was available as a BBC Transcription recording, and thus broadcast repeatedly in the United States and all parts of the Commonwealth. Judging from BBC statistics, it must have been heard by anything up to a hundred million listeners—no small audience for a programme mostly written in verse.

For those who heard it first in the sixties—and found it, perhaps, a strange survival—it might be as well to recall the circumstances in which it was written. In February 1936, when it was heard for the first time, there was still no television service: that was to open up, in a small way, later the same year. The only other dramatic medium known to the vast majority of listeners was the cinema. As for poetry—or verse, as I still prefer to call it in this context—that was something acceptable to only about one listener in every thousand. There was no tradition at all of spoken verse as we know it today.

The radio audience of the thirties was a vast, popular one: it was not by any means the audience I had been writing for in the *New English Weekly* or *The Criterion*. My idea in writing *The March of the '45*, therefore, had been to do for radio something comparable in its way to what had been done for the cinema by D. W. Griffith or Cecil B. de Mille. I wanted to tell a dramatic story, panoramic in scope, and to make it more immediately exciting than anything that had been heard before. I wanted to make the listener become emotionally involved; I wanted to make him grip his chair and get caught up in the action. I chose verse for the narrative part of the programme—two thirds of the whole—because I knew that verse could be *made* exciting and 'charged' in a way that prose can never be. The only question remaining was—what kind of verse to use?

The poetry I had been publishing was far too 'literary' for mass appeal: something far more rousing and declamatory was wanted. Walter Scott, as I soon realised, had solved the problem for me a hundred and thirty years before. He had proved that the fast-moving narrative verse of the Metrical Romances could still muster for the poet a wider audience than any since the fifteenth century—without forgetting Pope's *Iliad*. And thanks to Scott, that style of verse was admirably suited for any tale with a Scottish setting. *Marmion* and *The Lady of the Lake* may not be poetry of the highest order, but they can make superb radio—as anyone who has heard them knows. Rhyming narrative verse has a strongly hypnotic beat to it, comparable in its way to the pounding beat of earlier jazz: it can hold attention riveted and it can heighten emotional response.

Those who supposed that the verse of *The March of the '45* was the sort of verse I normally wrote had obviously not seen anything of mine in print. Indeed, the only verse in the programme which bore any relation to my normal style were the bleak lines of the middle section, which traced the dispirited march of the clansmen through the freezing cold of a North of England winter. For all who remember the rising crescendo of *The Clans are Coming*, I wonder how many may remember my own comment upon the march?

> Those days knew little enterprise.
>   All was undeveloped—pastures—cottages . . .
> Now, of course, it is otherwise.
>
> Headstocks line the lanes they followed. The fields
>   Are smouldering slag-heaps. We have not been idle,
> And staple industries have their yields—

Wigan her coal and iron. Also the mills—
  In combine, mostly—and the rubber proofers:
Power and light by pylon from the hills.

Bye-passes have straightened out that route—
  Housing schemes, ribbon building—both new features:
Money talks where men are astute.

As for Salford, it is a different place—
  Manchester also. We can hardly remember
Where or when he came among us.

Not many joined him, as it was;
  And traces vanish as the years lapse.
Very few would join him now—
  Apart from the unemployed, perhaps:

Monotony tries everything once . . .

Monotony certainly does—even Dostoievsky . . . As for the unemployed, they were becoming so monotonous—as a continuing
national reproach—that the thirties were doing their best to forget
all about them. It was felt that they posed a far greater threat to
government than the Jacobites had ever done; and the very mention of them was getting to be tendentious. Accordingly, I was
ordered by the policy scrutineers to remove the reference. This I
reluctantly did; and until re-armament had improved the national
situation, 'corner-boys' had to be substituted for the offending
word! I rather wonder which constitutes the greater menace
today . . .

  Much of a gamble as I had taken in writing *The March of the '45*
in the form I did—too popular for the few, and too poetical for
many—the success of the programme was remarkable. For the
next twenty years there could be no mention of radio drama or
the feature programme without dragging it into the act; and
Audience Research Reports have continued to show it a very firm

favourite even in times as anti-romantic as ours. Its wide popularity within the BBC, no doubt, was due to the fact that it was played back and its technique discussed for years by all producers attending the BBC Staff Training School. When Harding became the Chief Instructor there, it was his favourite demonstration piece, and as his students included radio producers from all over the world, news of the programme naturally got around. Archibald MacLeish referred to it as a prototype (unheard by him) in his preface to *The Fall of the City*. Milton Allen Kaplan quoted from it copiously in his *Radio and Poetry*. Louis MacNeice paid handsome tribute to it in his foreword to *Christopher Columbus*.

But undoubtedly the impact of the programme on listeners was mainly due to the inspired production of the Scottish cast by Gordon Gildard. Only when the story moved south of the border did Harding and I take up the thread with the march from Carlisle down to Derby. The final third of the show, from Falkirk on to Culloden, was Gildard's responsibility again. I have had many exciting moments in radio, but few so strangely exciting as my first hearing of what he had done with the verse. As declaimed by the Scottish narrators, Douglas Allen and Rex de la Haye, it came down the line from Glasgow like a Highland river in spate. This was radio with all the stops out—crowds, pipes, orchestra, choir and gunfire adding their quota to the whole effect.

It was gratifying to all of us to receive our personal accolades from London two days later: "I should like Bridson, Gildard and all the Effects people concerned to know that I consider this to have been one of the best conceived and handled radio-dramatic programmes that I have heard in the course of my experience." The note was signed by Val Gielgud, and it made me begin to think that radio might keep me busy for longer than I had intended.

Various other programmes followed, in which I continued to experiment with popular verse forms. *Steel*, described as an Industrial Symphony, was an attempt to extract as much excitement from an industrial process as I had done from armed rebellion. The recordings I made in a Sheffield steelworks were dramatic enough, but the programme was only partly successful. Even so, it still continued to be played back regularly to the Training School, where it was heard by the Irish playwright Denis Johnston, then limbering up to join the London Features Department as a producer. *Multiple Studio Blues*, the parody which he wrote on *Steel* and my other programmes, was funny enough to find its way onto the air. It must have baffled many listeners, for it was a very 'in' joke, but it was hugely enjoyed by most of my fellow producers—and most of all by me.* As for my next historical show, *King Arthur*, apart from its remarkable cast it was notable chiefly for its incidental music—the first work commissioned by the BBC from a promising young composer called Benjamin Britten.

In *Coronation Scot*, I returned to the formula of the romantic journey, this time tracing the course of the beautiful stream-lined blue and silver express from London via the North-West route to Glasgow. Voices greeted its passage along the way from field and factory, the whole journey being reflected in a spectro-scopic change of accent from Cockney up to the final Gorbals. The show was again an interesting one to do by reason of the early use it made of mobile recording gear, this time carried on the train itself with a microphone installed in the driver's cabin. Every bridge, junction, tunnel, station and gradient had its own distinctive note to add to the constantly changing sound pattern. The straining climb up Shap Fell made the high-spot of the action, the train finally breasting the rise and racing away again for Carlisle like a filly coming into the straight.

Coronation Scot marked a further step in my plan of linking the various Regions into a composite national broadcast hook-up.

---

* *Steel* had used the statistical roll-call of *Triumphal March*, which I had first tried out in *Tunnel* in 1934. In *Multiple Studio Blues*, D'Artagnan has left for England to recover the Queen's necklace. He is stopped at Dover by the Customs, and asked whether he has any-thing to declare. "Yes," he replies in the voice of Ewan MacColl. "Fifty thousand tons of white-hot steel, five and a half miles of chromium-plated steel railing, eight hundred and fifty thousand adjustable two-way sprockets . . . Etc."

On this occasion London, Midland and North Regions and Scotland were all tied in to the control point in Manchester, where the running narration, music and recorded sound were blended into a single entity. Nothing quite so elaborate technically has been heard on the air for some time. The London section of the programme was handled for me by Laurence Gilliam.

Gilliam had taken Harding's place in Drama Department when Harding had moved North in 1933. Along with the job, he inherited the annual Christmas Day broadcasts, which he continued to mount each year until the sixties.* He was put in personal charge of all London feature programmes, under Val Gielgud, in 1936. He was quite certainly one of the outstanding personalities of radio. During the war and after, he was to show a gift for leadership which inspired devoted loyalty in a group of the most talented writers and producers in radio history. But back in the thirties, he was merely one more talented documentary producer himself, and a friendly rivalry grew up between us in our respective bailiwicks. We collaborated on many occasions and I much enjoyed the frequent visits which he paid me up in the North.

There was a flamboyance about Gilliam which impressed everyone who came in contact with him and quickly earned him the nickname Lorenzo the Magnificent. He was lively, generous and witty—a man with a gift for making friends, and among the most amusing company I ever kept. To the physique of one of Michelangelo's Sistine athletes, he joined the grin and features of a genial white Negro. That, in fact, was how he described himself; and his broad nose and crinkly hair well fitted the description. It only remains to add that nobody could be more thoroughly and

---

* Apart from 1949, when I relieved him of the chore. On that occasion I nearly achieved the unique distinction of taking King George VI off the air. I was following the text of his Christmas message at the control panel in Broadcasting House. When he had reached the end of his speech, I signalled the programme engineer to cue the London Symphony Orchestra for the national anthem. As he was fading Sandringham out, we heard a faint breath intake. Whipping the orchestral channel out just in time, Ladbrook went back to the King for further words. It seemed that he had suddenly decided to add an unscripted—and unexpected—Christmas greeting. The world would have been surprised to know how lucky they were to hear it.

delightfully English. He was a keen cricketer, and to watch him in action on the field revived one's memories of A. P. F. Chapman and other giants of earlier, more expansive days.

Gilliam was a voracious eater and a dedicated drinker—provided the food and drink were all that he demanded they should be. He was also an impulsive cook, whose *bouillabaisse* was a meal to remember—in the dish or halfway up the wall. I once had the pleasure of taking him on a gastronomic tour of Blackpool—a town that could match exacting standards, provided one knew which doors to enter. In a crowded fishmonger's shop at lunchtime, he noticed some crayfish on the slab, and shouldering his way to the front, selected ten of the largest and most succulent. As the shopman reached for the *Lancashire Daily Post*, preparatory to wrapping them up, Gilliam waved it firmly aside. "Put them on a plate," he ordered, "we'll eat them here at the counter." Encouraging me to join in, this he proceeded to do—to the stunned surprise of the management. Watching him with no less awe, the customers edged away to a respectful distance. After we had demolished half of the pile, Gilliam handed the plate back to the shopman again, explaining that he needed some Black Velvet. "Keep them on one side," he said, "we'll be back to finish them later." This again the fishmonger accepted: the plate was carefully placed on a shelf behind him. I led the way round the corner to a nearby Yates's Wine Lodge, where Black Velvet was still to be had for a mere one and sixpence the half-pint tankard. Only at closing time did Gilliam deign to return to the shop, where the rest of the crayfish were again made available to us on the counter. Near Old Blackpudlian though I was, I should never have dared to try that particular gambit out myself—or got away with it if I had.

For a couple of years or more, Gilliam had been trying to inveigle me down to London to join him, but this I had always refused to do. Being far too free in the North to get on with anything that I wanted, I pleaded that I preferred life where I was. At the end of 1936, Harding had been recalled to London to become the first Chief Instructor at the BBC Training School, as

I have already mentioned. His place in the North was taken by John Salt, a London talks producer with whom I got on almost equally well. Salt came from a Yorkshire family, and could boast in Saltaire, not far from Bradford, a town called after his great-grandfather. Sir Titus Salt, an apostle of self-help who endeared himself to Samuel Smiles, had amassed a considerable fortune by learning to weave alpaca. Unfortunately, his family had promptly lost it again down a non-existent silver mine in Arizona. At least I could thank the mischance for John Salt's presence in the North where he made an admirable Programme Director. But apart from my growing friendship with him, I now had support in the North from two new feature writers. Cecil McGivern had been appointed producer in Newcastle, and was destined to write some of the finest documentaries of the war. Olive Shapley, who had been in charge of Northern Children's Hour was then appointed second Features Assistant in Manchester. Between the three of us, I liked to think that we could take on London at any time—and teach it what feature writing was all about.

Even so, and on renewed application, North Region agreed in 1937 to release me for three months, so that I could study London production techniques. Exchanging my Manchester house with John Pudney for his flat in Hammersmith, I accordingly moved down to Broadcasting House for a spell with Gielgud and Gilliam.

The only production that I had time to mount in London was a radio dramatisation of *The Waste Land*, for which I had Eliot's blessing. So far as I was concerned, this made quite remarkable radio, but I have to confess that Eliot did not share my own enthusiasm for the result. It will be remembered that the substance of the poem, on Eliot's own showing, is 'what Tiresias sees'. As dramatised, the substance of the poem becomes 'what Tiresias had heard'. Apart from his linking narration, therefore, the poem resolved itself into a medley of remembered sounds and voices—the Lithuanian woman, Madame Sosostris, the girl in the pub, and the rest of them. As it transpired, the girl in the pub

1. D. G. Bridson, a drawing by Michael Ayrton,
March 1969

2. E. A. Harding

3. Frank Nicholls as
Harry Hopeful

4. Joan Littlewood and D. G. Bridson, 1939

faced me with my only serious problem; for unlike poor Lil, the BBC flatly refused to swallow any abortion pills. I suddenly found myself under strict orders to omit all mention of them— vital as they were to the argument of the poem! Eliot was so incensed by this ridiculous censorship, that he only allowed the mangled text to go on the air at all out of a friendly feeling for me as the producer. But what principally dismayed him about the production was Robert Farquharson's performance in the key role of Tiresias.

Farquharson took to his role of the old man-woman with natural relish; his interpretation gave to it new shades of implication which Eliot little supposed were there. Never was sexual ambivalence heard more convincingly on the air—at least before *Round the Horne*. But to get the full flavour of the performance, one has to have known Robin as he really was.

To begin with, his real name was not Farquharson but de la Condamine. One of the most intelligent and distinguished actors on the air, he liked to encourage the belief that he was anything up to a hundred years of age. He had been educated at Rugby— "a frightful place," he once confided, "where Marshall would never speak to Snelgrove, and Derry was far too fond of Toms." That was not the only cause he gave me for wondering whether he had been there in Dr. Arnold's day. But whether or not, he was an almost unique survival from the days of Oscar Wilde—for whose delectation, report had it, he had danced wreathed in vine- leaves on Hampstead Heath. His reputation had been made in an early production of *The Importance of Being Earnest*, which had won him a highly appreciative notice from Max Beerbohm. At some period in his life, he claimed to have inherited a couple of castles in Italy from old gentlemen whom he liked to imply— purely by inference—that he had poisoned. (The Medici poison ring, with its hollow emerald, was still there for all to see on his finger.) He also affected diabolism, being unusually well read in the literature of demonology and witchcraft. His guests were frequently startled by bursts of blue flame that roared up the chimney whenever he poked the library fire. (The poker had been carefully treated with chemicals: the flames he pretended not to notice.) His house in Chelsea was handsomely furnished with renaissance marbles, canvases and silverware: his personal goblet was reputed to be the work of Benvenuto Cellini. And although it proved to be something of a disappointment, he was the only man who ever opened for me a bottle of Imperial Tokay which came from the cellar of Prince Bismarck, he in turn having acquired it from the Czar Alexander III.

But of his many accomplishments, it was his wickedly witty conversation which chiefly endeared Robin to his friends. His carefully stuttered *bons mots* were collected by a whole army of Boswells, and though I could personally add a number of anecdotes to the canon, one will do to establish his manner. Carleton Hobbs, the best of all his mimics, was telling Robin one evening how he had just been enjoying a rugby match at Twickenham. He had been amused by the derision of one disgusted fan who had constantly barracked a player. "Call yourself a footballer?" he had yelled, "Marleen Dietrich could play better!" "Indeed!" said Robin acidly, "and c-c-c-could he?" Hobbo went on to enquire whether he wasn't fond of rugby, having gone to the school which invented it. "No!" said Robin with some venom, "I always think it's such a pity that b-b-b-both sides can't *lose.*"

But to get back to *The Waste Land*, Robin found in Tiresias a role that was custom-built to his talents. Unlike the rest of the cast, he knew exactly what the poem was all about. The rest were frankly awed by its ambiguity, so that before rehearsal began, I had to give them an hour-long line-by-line exegesis. The cast grew more and more respectful as one mystery after another was carefully explained. In the almost religious silence which followed the final *shantih*, Robin loudly blew his nose; there was only one detail, he said, which rather puzzled him. I courteously gave him his cue. "Why," he asked, "did M-m-m-madame Sosostris have a bad cold?" I must admit I was quite unable to give him the answer to that one . . .

I was sorry, however, that Eliot failed to appreciate Robin's quality, for it spoiled his enjoyment of the entire production.

After all, to get *The Waste Land* onto the air at all, before the days of the Third Programme, was quite an achievement in itself. Odd as it may seem, the poem was still known only to a small circle of devoted readers: I doubt whether a hundred people in the BBC had even heard of it. If the National Programme audience knew him at all, Eliot was known as a playwright, the author of *Murder in the Cathedral*.* Even so, an audience of millions accepted *The Waste Land* on the air with surprising enthusiasm. For one thing, resolution into its different parts made it a great deal easier to follow. The mail which reached me after the broadcast was something of a surprise even to Eliot himself. One enthusiastic listener, I remember, introduced himself as "only a bricklayer . . ."

On my return to the North in 1938, John Salt suggested that I accompany him on a programme reconnaissance to Norway. In Oslo we were well received by the Norwegian radio staff, with whom we arranged a large-scale hook-up between Norway and Manchester. This was merely by way of underlining North Regional hegemony: Newcastle, after all, was Norway's traditional maritime link with Britain.

I had long been interested in the tie between Norway and the North of England, which dated back to the Viking Age. The links were still there to find, in the Northern place-names, dialect words, farming methods and local customs. All such survivals were easy enough to illustrate in radio terms, and this our broadcast *Norway* was designed to do. Sigrid Undset and others followed our story up from Norway itself, and there were many colourful illustrations of modern Norwegian life. So far as the

---

* Gilliam and I had been to watch Robert Speaight in the play when it first opened in the Chapter House of Canterbury Cathedral. Indeed, we might be said to have taken part in it. Arriving late for the performance, after a splendid lunch at Whitstable, we were stopped on the steps by one of the actors who, finger on lips, peeked quietly round the door to see how the action was going. We waited respectfully for a few minutes, till the actor flung open the door and briskly went inside. Thinking he was leading us to our seats, Gilliam and I followed him somewhat unsteadily down the aisle. Only when halfway to the front, faced by the startled gaze of the backward craning audience, did we realise that this had actually been the dramatic entry of the First Tempter. On that occasion, there happened to be three of him.

North went, I had only to alert a roster of trawlermen, farmers, dialect speakers and folk-singers, who promptly came flocking in to the summons from every fell and village in the Region, eager to have it known that they too had Norse blood in their veins.* They were very well received in Norway, where the hour-long programme was carried entirely in English.

I followed up on Norway with a programme devoted to the Isle of Man. For that, my name alone was an adequate qualification: my father had left the Island as a child, when his parents moved over to the Mainland (as Manchester is called by the Manx) and I was anxious to know his countrymen better. There again the Norse influence was paramount, as many Icelandic sagas had been at pains to remind me.

Since the death of Frank Nicholls, I had been looking around for someone who could take his place in a new series of Northern actuality shows. My choice fell on Joan Littlewood, whose charm and sincerity would have won the confidence of an anchorite. No *persona* was needed for her: she was everything in herself and became almost as popular in the North as Harry Hopeful had been before her. After covering the Isle of Man, further country shows took us to Furness Fells and the Cheviots.

But it was in the trio of major industrial features that we did together that Joan achieved her greatest success in actuality radio. By 1938, the worst of the Depression was over, but unemployment was still at a desperately high level in many of the Northern towns. For our production *Cotton People* we went to Oldham to

---

* As an example of the loyalty on which I could count in the North, the following incident is fairly typical. One of the speakers I suddenly needed for *Norway* was a young dry-stone waller from Wensleydale whom I had met with Harry Hopeful. I sent him a telegram the night before the broadcast, asking him if at all possible to attend a rehearsal in Manchester the following afternoon at three o'clock. He arrived an hour late (for which he humbly apologised) bringing along with him a girl who seemed to be rather nervous. Only after the broadcast did he introduce her to me as his bride. The wedding had been that morning, but when he received my telegram, he at once postponed his honeymoon and set out for the studio immediately after the wedding breakfast. By way of seeing them off, his best man had driven part of the way with them. At Scotch Corner there had been a terrible accident, in which his best man and another friend had been killed. Police enquiries after the accident had delayed him: he hoped I had not been inconvenienced. I only hope that his marriage proved luckier to him than my broadcast.

find the group of spinners and weavers that we needed. In the Oldham area there were more than three hundred mills: the week in which the programme was broadcast, only four of them were working full time.

Yet it was far from a depressing occasion when fifty Oldham operatives took to the air. Lancashire was my home county: I knew exactly the stuff that went to make up the Lancashire character. Once again, we relied upon careful scripting and home rehearsal to set the people on their mettle. Once again the method paid off handsomely, for the lively humour and sheer vitality of the mill folk whipped up over the air like an autumn gale on Blackpool promenade. This was Lancashire telling the world, and telling it inimitably. It was all I had hoped to do on radio with ordinary people telling about their ordinary lives—but facing up to living with quite extraordinary self-possession.

After Lancashire it was the turn of Yorkshire, but the broadcast that hit the air with most impact of all was the one we did with the Durham miners. Ever since the General Strike twelve years before, the plight of the miners had been deplorable. The towns that most of them lived in were little short of a national disgrace: their work was backbreaking and dangerous, the conditions in which they worked were primitive and intolerable. Seams only eighteen inches deep were not uncommon in Durham; the workings were generally damp, and pithead baths were still to come.

A month's work went to making the programme, during which time Joan and I familiarised ourselves with every aspect of the miner's life. We went on shift with the men by night and morning; we helped with the hewing, loading and putting; we got the dirt engrained into our scalps and every pore of our bodies. Joan lived with a miner's family—the son had been killed in the pit—while I put up in no greater comfort at the local miners' pub. By the time that *Coal* came on the air, there wasn't a miner at the pit who didn't know us and treat us as one of themselves.

In Durham again, of course, there was a high rate of unemployment: many men had been out of a job for the main part of their

working lives. One of the most moving stories in the broadcast
was that of the hewer who had been out of work for so long, that
when a job was found for him at last, his body had gone too soft
for him to be able to hold it down. The sob in his voice as he told
the story was hard to get out of one's mind.

On this occasion, response to the broadcast was more than a
matter of critical bouquets: money poured in from all sides, with
requests that it should be passed on to the miner in question. He
was the lucky one: I wished there had been enough to have
helped the ones who had not been mentioned. But one of the
letters gave me particular pleasure. Enclosing his own contribution, the writer told me that the broadcast had given him a new
pride in his office. It was signed by the Lord Lieutenant of County
Durham.

Broadcasts such as *Coal* gave millions of listeners a new realisation of the true dignity and importance of men and women like
themselves. Such broadcasts proved that everyone had something
to tell his fellow-men, and a point of view that deserved a hearing.
They also proved that everyone was capable of putting his point
of view across, often far more pungently than those who were
paid to do it for him. And that, let me emphasise again, was
something new in the land.

Frank Nicholls and Joan Littlewood were soon to be joined by
Wilfred Pickles, for whom I created the character of *Billy Welcome*
shortly after the start of the war. Between them, that remarkable
trio probably did more to help the country to find its voice than
anybody had done before. Within a matter of ten years they had
won an appreciative audience for the man in the street. Since
nothing succeeds so well as a good example, hearing one's neighbour sounding off is the shortest way of becoming vocal oneself.

By the time that the war was over, and *Have a Go* was able at
last to bring unscripted spontaneity to the air, people were no
longer afraid of standing up to a microphone. The boiled-shirt
image of the BBC as 'us' had been swept away for good; and the
free-for-all which followed had left 'them' with important parts
to play in radio and television. The age of the Common Man had

actually arrived; and that he could often be so superbly *un*-common, Frank Nicholls, Joan Littlewood and Wilfred Pickles must all be thanked for helping to prove.

Perhaps it was no coincidence that a vital new theatre movement was born in Manchester at the time when *Cotton People* and *Coal* were giving new vitality to radio. For it was there that Joan Littlewood first gathered together the group that was later to form the nucleus of Theatre Workshop. Known at the time as Theatre Union, that body of young enthusiasts had something they wanted to express in movement no less than in voice. Ewan MacColl was one of them, for in those days Joan and he were married: they had first met up in my broadcast *Tunnel*. Others were recruited by Joan from among the hundreds we got to know in all parts of the North.

I asked her in a broadcast recently what the North had meant to the movement she had founded there in pre-war days. She admitted it had meant everything—that what she had been able to start in Manchester could not have been started then in London. As the seed was later to bear such splendid fruit, I like to remember where the seed was first nurtured. So does Joan Littlewood.

3

Radio at War

WHEN WAR BROKE out in September 1939, I had just returned from Iceland, where I had once again been following up on the Norsemen. As the Russo-German Pact was signed while I was still in Reykjavik, and my only way back to London involved a six-day voyage to Copenhagen, I was a trifle apprehensive. War was obviously imminent, and since the Danes gloomily assured me that the Nazis would take them over in the first twenty-four hours of hostilities, I rather expected to spend my war in a German internment camp—if I lived to spend it at all. With the BBC label in my passport, I hardly expected Hitler to give me a very friendly reception. As his only English passenger, the Danish captain even offered to put me ashore in Norway, rather than bottle me up in the Kattegat.

This course didn't prove necessary, as I was safely back in England before the shooting began—my baggage plastered with swastikas, which also happened to be the emblem of the Danish-Icelandic shipping line. Technically, I was due to start my annual leave; but immediately after Chamberlain's broadcast speech, I reported to the BBC for duty. I was told to go away again, since apart from the news and gramophone recitals, broadcasting appeared to have come to an end. Rather baffled, I sat down in my office to write a verse play which had been on my mind for the last six months or more. It was a modern morality play called *Aaron's Field*.

The masterly inactivity of the BBC during the early days of the war now seems almost unbelievable. I have always respected the old North Country adage, "When in doubt do nowt", but never can it have been taken so literally as it was by the BBC during those first few weeks. No doubt the lack of any positive approach to their responsibilities reflected the change in the BBC's direction. Sir John Reith had resigned in 1939,* to be succeeded by F. W. Ogilvie, a charming man in himself, but hardly the sort of dynamic leader called for by events. Fearing immediate bombing, Broadcasting House had been almost emptied in the first couple of days: only a skeleton staff remained on duty— rather like the three hundred at Thermopylae. As it happened, the bombing did not occur—reportedly, because no BBC administrator had remembered to send Hitler a memo explaining that it should have done. Various evacuation centres had meanwhile been commandeered all over the countryside. Features and Drama Department had been banished to a mansion outside Evesham, known by the code name of Hogsnorton, where they found it almost impossible to produce anything at all. Radio, in fact, had gone almost as dead as it had the night of King George V's death. The moribund state of British communications, however, was fairly general. Sir John Reith had made a brief reappearance on the scene as Minister of Information. But despite the fact that BBC administrative types had hastily been enrolled to help him— or perhaps because of that—virtually no war information appeared to be available. In due course, Reith was succeeded at the Ministry by Lord Beaverbrook, and the rumour soon ran that his lordship was about to annex Broadcasting House as a

* I only met Reith once while he was still with us. Hearing I was in Broadcasting House, he summoned me to his office. Most improperly dressed in the country's first green corduroy jacket, I hesitantly appeared. Rearing up in his morning-suit, Sir John extended a massive hand and enquired knowledgeably about my family. As I was not aware that he knew anything about me—much less, my private life—this rather jolted me. As he obviously intended, I began to wonder what else he knew about.

He told me that when I was writing the '45, he had had to act as referee, as the Scots had formally objected to any Sassenach trying to purloin their national epic. He had bluntly refused to forbid the banns, which was very civil of him. But then, of course, he was not a Jacobite.

He proceeded to grill me as to whether I ever rehearsed my shows on Sunday. I humbly confessed that I often did—not because Mancunians were pagans (apart from myself, I should have added) but because the local actors were amateurs who had to work at their jobs during the week. He nodded his head in understanding, while mentally shaking it in dismay. He even conceded that in broadcasting such enormities had occasionally to be condoned.

more convenient centre of operations. Luckily for the rest of us, he was dissuaded from doing so.

I had written *Aaron's Field* in the first days of September; but despite the enthusiastic backing of Val Gielgud, it was mid-November before a space could be found for it on the air. Not that much was happening by way of competition, but everything in the BBC took a long time to happen. When it finally got itself heard, it was greeted by Grace Wyndham Goldie in *The Listener* as "the first new radio play since the war". Being "both 'radiogenic' and in verse," she added, "it breaks into the week's programmes like an explosion. So, slightly deafened but delighted, we sit back to consider its thunderous reverberations." The explosion might have been less noticeable if anything else had been going on at the time. But the Phoney War was never so phoney as it sounded by courtesy of the BBC in 1939.

The plot of *Aaron's Field* was simple enough. Aaron is a little man who has retired after a hard life in the city. He has bought himself a cottage and a field which he hopes to enjoy as a corner of peace and quiet. But this proves far too much to expect in the modern world. The lawyer wants to manage his field, the squire wants to hunt across it, the local council wants to build a road across it, the tourist wants to come and camp in it, the industrialist to develop it, and so on. With the outbreak of war, the field is commandeered for the digging of air-raid trenches, for which purpose Aaron cheerfully surrenders it. His private vision of salvation has been to enjoy his field in peace and on his own. As the first bombers come roaring over, he dies of fright and achieves his simple ambition.

As I have said, *Aaron's Field* was a modern morality play, and I fancied the moral was clear enough. Spelt out later with the printed text, the message was simply this: "Individual decency is not enough; the tragedy of Aaron and his kind lies in their inability to realise as much." A similar thought had been implicit in almost everything I had broadcast up to then. On this occasion, however, the message appeared to have been obscured by what the

Americans would call the play's 'inspyrational ending'. For all her appreciation of it, even Mrs. Wyndham Goldie complained that it preached the philosophy of despair. I still beg leave to differ—unless one is unable to draw a simple inference.

But whatever the listener made of it, *Aaron's Field* again proved highly popular. It was broadcast seven times in this country, and many times round the Commonwealth. I later was asked to mount my own productions of it in South Africa and New Zealand. Much of its first success was due to Ivor Barnard's very moving performance in the title-role of Aaron—the nice little man who is always being pushed around. That nice little men should refuse to be pushed around—and can't be if they hold together—was what the play was trying to infer.

And before the end of 1939, a number of people in the BBC were refusing to be pushed around any longer. Thanks to a brisk campaign by Val Gielgud and Laurence Gilliam, whatever gods might be in Portland Place had reluctantly changed their minds: Features and Drama Department ended its country exile and moved up to Manchester, where at least production facilities were available. Greeting them all on my own doorstep, and mindful of past persuasion, I rather felt like Mahomet: the mountain had actually come to me. We quickly pooled all Northern and National resources, and began to plan a documentary and drama schedule that could play a rather more creditable part in the gathering war effort.

They were a genial crowd of writers, producers and actors who flocked into our Northern sanctuary. Eminent in the van was Val Gielgud himself, almost overrun by Siamese cats, but only too anxious to mount the sort of spare-time listening for which the land was pining. Until he and Gilliam could set up house on their own account, Laurence came to stay with my wife and me. Later, with Maurice Brown and others, they set up a sort of open house in Rusholme, much to the neighbourhood's delight. Stephen Potter I had scarcely met, but his talent for lifemanship—no less than his flair for one-upmanship—made him a crony after my own heart. Equally so was Moray McLaren (by now the Assistant

Head of Drama) whose Scottish geniality was much warmed by the local wine-bars.* Another Scot, Robert Kemp, had recently joined us from the *Guardian*, his pawky humour soon proving to be exactly what the times required. Most amusing of all, perhaps, was the bitterly sardonic John Cheatle, whose copious flow of limericks, written around the landed gentry, threw many illuminating sidelights on Debrett. As for the Drama Repertory Company, also moved in from Evesham, they brought a splendid accession of acting strength to the North. Gladys Young and Laidman Browne, Philip Wade, Ronald Simpson, Ivan Samson and Bryan Powley, Mary O'Farrell and Vivienne Chatterton, Valentine Dyall, Robert Eddison and Edana Romney—these names and a score of others lent new lustre to all our joint productions. The North had never enjoyed such a sudden galaxy of talent before.

I had been told by the BBC as soon as war broke out that they had asked for indefinite deferment of my military call-up. It had occurred to them that a trained writer-producer of documentary radio could easily be turned into a trained writer of propaganda.† I had no objection to that, provided that such work had to be done; after all, there were plenty of people doing it for the other side. And happening to believe sincerely in all we were fighting for, I had only to write what I felt—and propaganda it duly became. As it transpired, I was the only member of the BBC staff, under thirty when the war broke out and medically fit, who was never released by them for military service. Coming in for my full share of the bombing and other wartime hazards, I had no undue qualms in the matter. Indeed, the only time that the Services took a look at me, after I had broken the IQ test record at

---

* He was particularly fascinated by my favourite Yates's Wine Lodge. Ordering our midday madeira one week, we were told that the barrel was empty. The same went for the malaga, the marsala and even the tokay. A be-shawled and toothless ancient nodded at us sagely: "Them was *foreign* wines you was asskin' for," she observed. We agreed that they probably were. The old lady shook her head in disgust; "There you are," she said. "It teks a war to show 'em up. I used to think they brewed all their *own* stuff here."

† Those who dislike the word I would refer to its etymology. Agnostic as I am, I have no objection to being bracketed with the Old Testament prophets and the writers of the canonical gospels.

the centre, they could offer me nothing better than mixing concrete for building airstrips. In the circumstances, I rather preferred to write about such processes.

The main thing, of course, was to get radio linked up purposefully behind the national war effort. This was easy enough to do, once the brakes had been taken off. As the writer best informed in industrial matters and most experienced in the handling of actuality speakers, I soon found myself editor of one actuality series after another. First of them all was *Go to it!*, the slogan popularised by Herbert Morrison, then Minister of Supply, who spoke in the first programme. For this series we gathered a cross-section of workers from the munitions factories all over the country. At that time, a Dunkirk spirit at the work bench was desperately needed, if we were going to survive. The spirit was there all right, but everyone wanted to hear it at work: thanks to those I brought to the microphone, they did. The programmes were invigorating not because they were saying the right things, but because they were real and genuine. To quote Grace Wyndham Goldie again: "These working men and women had been allowed to put their emotion into the words they habitually use." After all the time I put into mastering their speech-patterns, I can only say that they had indeed.

To encourage them in the habit, I then mounted *We speak for ourselves*, in which for the first time Wilfred Pickles became the catalyst. We again went after the armaments workers—by now with active servicemen on loan from the Forces and ready to tell the men and women at the benches just what reliance was being placed in the work they were all doing. The men and women not only spoke for themselves: the shows were staged in the factory canteens, and playing to lively audiences they spoke for the country as a whole.

Wilfred Pickles had acted in most of my pre-war programmes. He shared all the qualities which had made Frank Nicholls so popular, including the same earthy sense of humour. He was a Yorkshireman (his family came from Halifax) and he had devoted himself over the last few years almost exclusively to radio. In due course he joined the North Region as an announcer, along with Frederick Allen and Humphrey Donner. His Northern vowels were soon to impinge upon the South, when he became the first of the BBC News readers to inject them into the nine o'clock bulletins. (One gathers that Tunbridge Wells never recovered from the shock.) Before *We speak for ourselves*, he had done no actuality shows, but soon established himself as one to the manner born. The cross-talk acts became shrewder, the byplay faster and more instinctive; as the manner became established, I found that less and less rehearsal was necessary. After a year or two, the scripts could probably have been written by half of those who were taking part.

There comes a point, of course, where morale building is no longer necessary, and where incitement to extra effort becomes a downright insult. So far as I was concerned, that point was reached comparatively soon. It seemed to me that people who spent their days in a factory were entitled to forget the place when they came home for the evening. It was for this reason that I suggested getting away from work in 1941, and taking listeners back to the sort of scenes they had known before the war, and could hope one day to visit again. Whatever war had brought to the towns and cities, the countryside remained unchanged. You don't have to black out the fells and moors: night has done it effectively ever since they were first there. As for talk in the country pubs and cottages, that requires no impetus: country life has a continuity to it that only actual invasion can upset. When life in the towns gets drab or difficult or just plain boring, it sometimes helps to remember that country life can still be pleasant. Just to remind themselves of the fact, most people continue to cultivate their gardens in the murk.

The *Billy Welcome* programmes were intentionally reminiscent of the *Harry Hopeful* series: they took the listener out of doors. The name of his new *persona* was thought up by Pickles himself, and it was quickly apparent that he thoroughly lived up to it. As a character, Billy was rather more spry than his forebear, and more inclined to give as good as he got. But even so, comparisons can sometimes be embarrassing, and unless the ghost of Harry was to go on haunting us forever, the ghost had to be firmly laid. For his first broadcast appearance, therefore, I took Billy Welcome back to the same Yorkshire Dales where Harry had made his own début. And if any proof were needed of his ability to win people over, Pickles triumphantly gave it there. At first, he was much depressed by the general opinion, freely expressed on all sides: this Billy fellow was all very well—but *nobody* could be like Harry Hopeful! Needless to say, we never intended that anybody should be: as we saw him, Billy Welcome was a character very much in his own right. Of this Pickles finally convinced even his fellow-Yorkshiremen, and they ended up by liking Billy precisely for what he was. The new radio character caught on, and Pickles played him all over the British Isles, bringing back to the air a vast new fund of wartime country humour. Unfortunately, I was soon too busy with other matters to script all the shows myself.

Just before Christmas 1940, Manchester had been badly blitzed for two consecutive nights. Ted Liveing had resigned before the war, but I stood on the roof of the BBC building in Manchester's Piccadilly with my new Regional Director, John Coatman, and watched my city burn. It was a sad sight for both of us, and a frightening one as I remembered it in a broadcast more than a quarter of a century later: "On the opposite side of Piccadilly Gardens, a line of cotton warehouses had turned into so many blast furnaces. Their central hoists or lift shafts—now become roaring flues—were sucking the blazing bales of cotton from all six floors of the buildings, and firing them into a blood-red sky like rocks from a line of erupting volcanoes. Drifting down again over the city, the burning cotton started a further chain of fires. The Manchester I had known in the thirties was going up in flames."

Six months later, I had left the city with Gilliam for London, which from then on was to be my working headquarters and my home. Apart from occasional visits, I had said goodbye to the North Country.

In May 1941, the BBC direction had finally given way a second time: it had reluctantly agreed to the return of Features and Drama Department to London—which it should never have been forced to leave in the first place. By then the war had been waged for over eighteen months, and much as the North had played its vital part in them, London, after all, was the centre of all war operations. The Service and all other Ministries were there, all government departments, and the governments of all the Allied Powers. The difficulty of mounting a steady flow of wartime documentaries from a centre remote from all its first-hand material had become increasingly obvious.

Furthermore, apart from the needs of the domestic services, there was now a world-wide audience for war stories from Britain. The North American, African, Eastern and Pacific Services—wartime successors to the old Empire Service—were desperately in need of feature material. Britain was still standing alone—the whole of the allied war effort was being directed and waged from her shores—and the world was avid to hear about it. The feature programme as such was purely a BBC invention: no other radio service in America or anywhere else had developed it so effectively. It was admirably adapted for telling the story of Britain at war, and never had there been such a clamorous demand—in America and throughout the Commonwealth—for feature treatment of wartime news.

It was to organise Overseas Features, and to act as Gilliam's deputy, that I finally came to London with him. Oddly enough, I had just been offered another job, which carried far higher status. In the early days of the war, John Salt had been charged with stepping up foreign language broadcasting, and soon some thirty-six services were in operation. Early in 1941, he had offered to put me in charge of all foreign language productions—a job I should have been very happy to accept. Hearing the rumour, Basil Nicolls promptly stepped in and refused to release me, no doubt at Gilliam's instance. I was quite happy either way, though sorry to miss promotion. My transfer to Features and Drama Department from North Region was merely a step sideways—but overseas feature editor I became.

My new office was in Bedford College, peacefully tucked away in Regent's Park—with a suddenly trebled roster of feature writers and producers to draw upon. There was plenty of work for them to do.

Most distinguished of the new arrivals was Louis MacNeice. Like others of his particular age group, he had been in America when war broke out. But unlike many of them, he was far too interested in experience to be able to keep away for long from such an exciting phase of it: he returned to take his place in the front line. His interest was less in the impact of the war upon individual lives than in the wider patterns of life which war imposed on the community. The nightly rush of people cascading into the shelter of the tube stations; the nightly huddle of tin-hatted wardens in blacked-out Civil Defence posts; gin-rummy among the ambulance crews till the first calls brought them racing out for their vehicles; the sweltering work of the firemen picked out in silhouette against the flames of the blazing buildings; the morning sweeping-up of the broken glass, tinkling like Japanese gongs in a high wind—these were things which he could report dispassionately. Steeped in the classics no less than in modern literature, he had a keen feeling for all the damage that was being inflicted on London's historical homes and monuments, and his notable programmes in the series *The Stones Cry Out* reminded the world of our vanishing heritage. But it was not so much as a writer of documentaries that MacNeice became outstanding. His creative work was infinitely more important, and his *Christopher Columbus* was probably the most memorable programme written during the war.

Cecil McGivern, who joined us from Newcastle, was at his best in describing the new techniques of war and the ways in which ordinary men and women adapted their lives to cope with them. He shared my interest in people, and had an unusually good ear for everyday dialogue. His tremendous capacity for hard work was to prove itself once more in the formative days of postwar television. Meanwhile, his output of wartime radio was remarkably effective, and in the later days of the war he was to write some of the most impressive documentaries ever broadcast. *Bomb doors open* gave an exciting picture of the R.A.F. raids on Germany; *Junction X* told the story of railway operation during the blitz; *A Harbour called Mulberry* told of the building of the two floating harbours which made the D-Day landings possible; and *Radar* told the story of its invention and increasingly effective use in bomber interception.

Francis Dillon, my pre-war friend from Manchester, came in to join us from the West Region. He was a witty and thoroughly competent radio craftsman whose fantasies, like *The Nightingale* and *Rumpelstiltskin*, were heard far too rarely on the air. He had a peculiar knack for the handling of actuality programmes, and a true devotion to the chronicling of country life. His *Country Magazine* was the most popular series that Features Department ever mounted, and ran for many years. Also from the West Region came Douglas Cleverdon, whom I was able to recruit for us from routine duties with the BBC Home Guard in Bristol. He was probably the most meticulous and imaginative producer that we had, his virtuosity being reflected subsequently in the number of Italia Prizes that he won for the BBC. During the darker days of the war, like the rest of us he had far more mundane tasks to employ him.

As for the many other gifted writers and producers who joined our London nucleus during the war, their names included some of the best remembered in feature writing. Robert Barr, Alan Melville, John Gough, James Hanley and Leonard Cottrell, Robert Speaight, John Glyn Jones, Michael Barsley and Walter Rilla, Nesta Pain, Marjorie Banks, Jenifer Wayne and Brigid Maas—each had an individual style which gave a new distinction and variety to the wartime feature output. Their scripts and productions continued to roll off the assembly line—and still failed to glut the voracious demand of a couple of hundred million listeners from London to Sydney and Wellington, from North Africa to Cape Town, from Delhi to Singapore and from Boston to Vancouver.

My own concern was partly with helping Gilliam to maintain

the flow, and still more with my own writing and production. Of my forty-eight programmes in 1941, forty were broadcast over-seas—many of them exclusively. For the rest, I was able to keep my work regularly before the audience at home and to write occasional programmes which gave me rather more personal pleasure. *We love this land* told the story of the invasion of Nor-way, in which many of my Norwegian friends had been killed or interned. *Hail Freedom!* dealt with the subjugation of Greece, another country for which I had a particular fondness. *East by North* dealt with the northern route of the Atlantic crossing, and contained some of the Iceland poems that I had written before the war.

In June 1941, war came to the Soviet Union: in December it also embroiled the United States. Reflecting the war effort and the fighting quality of both quickly became a major concern of mine. But the Soviet Union, at least, posed something of a prob-lem for the BBC in terms of programme policy.

Nobody could claim that the Russians were Britain's favourite allies in the first heat of the German attack. In some quarters, it was bluntly suggested that they fully deserved to suffer all that was happening to them. Their occupation of Eastern Poland after the German invasion of 1939 had seemed disgracefully treacherous to most people. So had their 1939 invasion of Fin-land. As for their many reverses in the latter adventure, ably reported by Edward Ward, they had been greeted on most sides with elation. And the rapid advance of the German armies up to the gates of Moscow and Leningrad had given small cause, at first, to suppose that as fighting allies they were likely to hold the onslaught for very long.

I cannot claim to have been remarkably pro-Soviet during the darker times of the Stalinist régime: the various purges and the more ruthless aspects of Russian Communism depressed me. At the same time, I was certainly far from being *anti*-Soviet. I had been much impressed by the comparative success of the first Five Year Plans, and when war came I could at least understand the thinking behind the Russian military moves. After all, there *had* been a total disregard by the Poles under Pilsudski for the ethnic frontier of the Curzon Line, and the pushing of their eastern border so far into Soviet territory could hardly be defended. The Mannerheim Line *had* posed a direct threat to Leningrad, as the German-sponsored invasion from Finnish territory amply demonstrated. The Russo-German pact *must* have been suggested to Stalin by our own unwillingness to negotiate any pact with him ourselves—as Lloyd George, among others, had warned us that it inevitably would be.

But apart from all such arguments—true or false as they might be—I had far more sympathy for Russian achievements under Communism than had most of my colleagues at the BBC. Indeed, such sympathy was confidently expected of me: in the eyes of Nicolls and the hierarchy, it would have been quite out of character if I had failed to show it! After all, I had been taken on as the BBC's original left-winger—and here was a new twist to events where left-wing loyalties had suddenly assumed outward respectability. Accordingly, I found myself saddled—cheerfully enough—with various Russian programme commitments.

First of them was a gesture of solidarity with the besieged people of Leningrad. As narrator for this programme I brought in Frank Owen, then editor of the *Evening Standard*, whose strongly pro-Russian leaders were well known at the time. I gathered together a representative body of like-minded Civil Defence and factory workers—easy enough to find, now that the Russians had begun to show such courage and skill in fighting back. Wardens, firemen, policemen, ambulance workers and armament workers—each had a special message to send to their Russian comrades in the beleaguered city. London had beaten back the German attackers: Leningrad would do so too. It was only when the programme had been recorded that I learnt that the BBC did not propose to broadcast it.*

* Even in wartime, the vast majority of broadcasts continued to go out live, but when any of the European or Overseas Services were involved, pre-recording was allowed in view of the time differences. Each Overseas Service, of course, went out at its own appropriate time.

Somewhere around this time, it ought to be explained, the BBC had agreed to accept a certain amount of editorial advice from the Foreign Office. Sir Ivone Kirkpatrick had been appointed Controller of the European Services, with a watching brief in domestic programmes so far as foreign policy was concerned. Perhaps it did not seem to him that any such statement of solidarity with the people of Leningrad was called for at the time. Or maybe the Foreign Office believed that Leningrad was about to fall—and that all such gestures were therefore unnecessary. For whatever reason, he decided that the broadcast should be cancelled. I must admit that my own opinion was not based upon any information from the Kremlin, but I still had a strong belief that Leningrad would survive. Apart from that, I had a rooted objection to having my work interfered with on what seemed to me insufficient grounds. With Frank Owen to back me up, I fought to get the programme put on the air; and whatever the Foreign Office thought about it, I am glad to say that I won the battle. I won it, that is, all but for a word and a date.

Owen had ended his peroration with a truly clarion call: he relied on the people of Leningrad, he said, to beat the Germans back and "make this the most memorable October—since 1917". If the BBC allowed the recording to go out, I was told, "since 1917" would definitely have to be clipped from the recording. On the old BBC principle that one breast is better than none, I advised Frank Own to agree to the excision. This he did only with the greatest reluctance, darkly threatening to expose our censorship in the *Evening Standard*. When his political opinions inverted some years later, he may have felt rather relieved that I finally dissuaded him from doing so.

In 1942, I was asked to write an hour-long feature to mark the first anniversary of the launching of the German attack. For this I dramatised the lives of three Red Army soldiers and their families, tracing their adventures through the various phases of the fighting on Russian soil. For the anniversary of the October Revolution, I mounted an actuality programme, *Arms for Russia*, from the canteen of a Midlands armaments factory. By now, of course, the counter-offensives of the Red Army were providing almost the only heartening news from the many war fronts. But although they were rapidly becoming the heroes of the time, the Red Army were still being driven inexorably back in Hitler's drive to Stalingrad and the Caucasus.

For a long time it had been usual to pay weekly tribute to one or other of the Allies in a fifteen-minute programme before the nine o'clock news each Sunday night. The origin of this gesture had been the custom of broadcasting the French and Polish national anthems in the early days of the war. To these had been added the national anthems of Norway, Holland, Belgium, Yugoslavia, Greece and all other countries as they were overrun. When the number had risen to ten, and everyone had grown tired of humming the tunes, their place was taken by a weekly *Salute* to one or other of the countries, or to one or other of their wartime leaders. I had already written my poem *The Condemned*, broadcast as the BBC *Salute to Norway*. For the Sunday following the anniversary of the Russian Revolution, therefore, I was asked to write a *Salute to the U.S.S.R.* This I did with *Stalingrad*, a poem read for the occasion by Valentine Dyall, Joan Littlewood and the late Roy Emerton. Informed opinion in the Foreign Office, I gather, did not expect that city to hold out either; but as the siege was then at its height, the poem was well received by the listeners. Accordingly, I was asked, this time by Nicolls personally, in his capacity as Controller of Programmes—to write a companion *Salute to Marshal Stalin*, for the Russian's birthday the following month. I must admit, I was rather surprised by the request, but complied without any qualms: his leadership, by this time at least, was obviously an inspiration to all the Russian people. Hailing him in the characters of four of them—engineer, peasant, soldier and partisan—perhaps I was carried away by their fervour. At any rate, when the script was finished the Saturday before the broadcast, it was found to be over-enthusiastic! I was naturally somewhat irritated, and enquired what sort of salute amounted to a poke in the eye? Even so, the broadcast was called off, the space being filled by a repeat of my poem *Stalingrad*. A tactful announcement explained to the Marshal that his birthday was being honoured by remembering once more the gallant city which bore his name.*

On this occasion, the poem happened to be heard by Lord Beaverbrook, who promptly rang the BBC and asked for a copy of the text: he would like to run it, he said, as a centre-page feature in the *Daily Express*. Unfortunately, he had been forestalled, and when told by the BBC Duty Officer that the only available script had just been sent to the *Daily Worker*, his lordship hung up. When I heard the news next morning, I was somewhat irritated again—the more so since the *Daily Worker* had only quoted a couple of lines. I wrote to Lord Beaverbrook forthwith, respectfully pointing this out, and sending him a copy of the text. He replied in a friendly way, regretting that the psychological moment had passed. I have still never appeared on the centre page of the *Daily Express*.

Despite the many things I had done for them, I must admit the Russians were unusually unresponsive. I was constantly mounting broadcasts for which I needed their co-operation, but on no single occasion was it forthcoming; their Embassy was studiously polite, loaded me with hand-out material which I already had, but never came up with a single speaker to take part in a programme.

Since America had entered the war in December 1941, I had been called upon to produce more and more actuality shows for the North American Service. For one of these, *Christmas among the Allies*, I had gathered a body of soldiers, sailors, airmen, and the rest from the forces of all the Allied Powers represented in London. The Americans, needless to say, could not have been more helpful: I had only to say what I wanted and somebody was told to get on with it. But it was of the first importance, obviously, that the Russians should also be represented—if the BBC were not to be accused of discriminating against them. I repaired once more to the Russian Embassy, and once again they regretted their in-

---

* On this occasion, I found myself supported retrospectively by that arch counter-revolutionary, Val Gielgud. Unfortunately, when the crunch came, he was off duty for the weekend. The ban was imposed by Gilliam himself!

ability to assist me: no Russian personnel were in the country! This was patently absurd—I had only to point to the hat-rack in the Embassy lobby, which Red Army caps festooned like so many red stars on a Christmas tree. The Embassy regretted that the owners were all just leaving the country. This I refused to believe—and even warned them that if no Russian serviceman was present for the broadcast, I should be forced to explain to the listeners; and to the large audience in the theatre booked for the occasion—that they had refused to take part. Even to the Russian mind, this did not seem to be very desirable. They countered evasively by saying that even if any of their officers were available, none of them could speak English. I replied that they could broadcast in Russian, so long as they were there on the stage. At last, and very reluctantly, a Russian Admiral was produced: it was agreed that he should broadcast—in Russian—a message of goodwill to the world along with the others.

Perhaps Stalin was still annoyed about his birthday, but on the night of the broadcast, instructions were (apparently) received by the Embassy from Moscow; on no account must the Admiral speak—even in Russian! Perhaps because he was embarrassed, the Admiral accompanied his political adviser to the theatre and they delivered their ultimatum jointly, five minutes before the show went onto the air. Almost by force, I managed to persuade him onto the stage before the curtain went up; at least I wanted the audience to see his uniform. The theatre was bedecked with the flags of all the countries represented—the Red Flag being well to the fore—and enthusiasm on all sides was intense. Each of the spokesmen was loudly applauded, as Wilfred Pickles introduced him, and in time the turn came for the Russian. I had given Pickles his line: he proudly announced the presence of an Admiral of the Red Fleet who had taken part in the defence of Leningrad. The admiral stiffly rose to his feet and solemnly took a bow. He didn't have to say anything—he was cheered and applauded thunderously. Pickles shook him by the hand and, somewhat sheepishly, the Admiral sat down again. No doubt he had compelling reasons, but so far as my experience goes this was the only occasion on which anyone made an impressive broadcast appearance without so much as opening his mouth. Despite my distrust of Admirals, I hope that this one was not shot.

To be perfectly fair, while he remained in England, Maisky himself was always perfectly friendly and co-operative; and while it was not often possible to approach him direct, he could hardly be blamed for the boot-faced attitude of his staff.

On the occasion of Roosevelt's birthday in 1942, I was broadcasting *Greetings to the President* with yet another roster of assorted allied well-wishers. This time they were being introduced by Roosevelt's old friend Anthony Drexel Biddle, then the American Ambassador to the Allied Governments in London. Maisky, as Russian Ambassador, had agreed to record a message himself, but through somebody's mistake, the recording had not been made. The broadcast was due to go out at three o'clock in the morning— for broadcasting in the United States at ten o'clock New York time. It was midnight, London time, before the oversight was reported to me by S. J. de Lotbinière, then in charge of Overseas programmes. With what I considered great aplomb, he went round to the Russian Embassy in person at something after one o'clock in the morning. His Excellency had gone to bed: de Lotbinière insisted that he be wakened. This was reluctantly done, and in his pyjamas Maisky recorded his message, which was then rushed back to me in the studio. If by any chance he was listening, the President received it dead on time. But as Lobby stood about six foot eight in his shoes, and Maisky about five feet in his bedroom slippers, I always wished I had been there to watch the recording being made. For my money, they both of them rated a suitable decoration.

4

America

I HAD ALWAYS been interested in American literature and what I gathered about the American scene. During the thirties, this interest had been quickened by the years I had spent reviewing American periodicals for *The Criterion*. Every week, the *New Republic*, the *Nation* and the *Saturday Review* arrived in my letter-box, accompanied by a rising flood of American literary monthlies and quarterlies. Some of them, like *Poetry* and the *Modern Monthly*, printed my work occasionally, but it was the new school of so-called proletarian writing which interested me the most in *Partisan Review* and the other left-wing magazines. In that I found the American scene reflected as it appeared to writers of my own generation, men who were hitching their way by truck and box-car from one end of the country to the other in search of work. Steinbeck's *The Grapes of Wrath* merely marked the end of a grim decade for me.

So far as radio was concerned, America was less interesting. Eliot's brother, Henry Ware Eliot, had done his best to put me in touch with the sort of American producers who might be interested in my work. But I was already on the staff of the BBC before America's National Broadcasting Company asked for a special production of *The March of the '45* in 1937. From then on, I was far too busy at home to think about the American market. It was not until 1939 that I was asked by the same network for another programme—the British poster-programme for the opening of the New York World's Fair, *Calling New York*. Also carried by the BBC, there was nothing of special interest about it, apart from the fact that Lord Halifax took time off from entertaining Ribbentrop to give it a sober peroration.

It was only with the start of my work for the North American Service in 1941, that I seriously began to think about being heard in the United States again. Week after week, I found myself writing and producing programmes about the British war effort with the American audience chiefly in mind. After Pearl Harbour, of course, I was called upon to do far more for them. And I certainly got off to a lousy start.

My first Anglo-American hook-up, on New Year's Eve 1941, proved to be the only disaster I ever had in broadcasting. I had lined up Iceland, North Africa and places all round the British Isles to tie up with small-town groups all over America. The joint programme opened in the Mid-West, where a farmer whose people came from Treorchy in Wales told the CBS announcer that he wondered what life was like in his old home town under total war. This was the BBC cue to go over to Treorchy for greetings from some of those who remembered the farmer's family. But the farmer—and CBS—could not have been half so appalled as I was by the uproar that appeared to answer his question! For when we faded up the Treorchy channel on my London control panel, a couple of hundred lit-up GIs came bellowing in from the American Eagle Club in Piccadilly. (Actually, they were warming up for what was to have been the final sing-song which climaxed the programme.) We hastily faded the channel out, but by some awful mischance of radio engineering, the same unholy uproar was on every channel we had to draw upon—even John Snagge the announcer's and Reykjavik and Cairo!

I had more to worry about, however, than the wreck of a mere programme. The boisterous GIs were roaring out all their popular songs, many of which (as I happened to know) were banned from the American air by a dispute between the networks and the American musicians' union. If one of those banned numbers had accidentally been broadcast, CBS would have found itself caught up in a million-dollar lawsuit—in which they would promptly have involved the BBC. I had no option but to take my entire end of the programme off the air until the fault in the hook-up wiring had been found and put to rights. By the time that this was done, transmission time had run out: CBS was left with a total fiasco to explain to a peak-hour listening audience all over the United States!

Full responsibility for the mistake was accepted by the BBC Engineering Division—but that was small consolation to me. My big American moment had hardly proved a big success! The BBC North American Director, Lindsay Wellington (later to be knighted, but not for that night's work), happened to be a friendly sponsor of mine; and along with him in the New York office, he also had my friend John Salt as his Assistant Director. However red their faces were, when apologising to CBS, they both made it clear for the record that such a *débâcle* had never happened before in the history of British broadcasting. Even so, it was not until the following summer that any American network agreed to another live hook-up with Features Department in London.

When they did, it was the NBC who were anxious to have us mount for them a star-studded series of impressions of life in war-time Britain. The task of producing the first of these, and setting the pattern for the whole thirteen, was handed over to me. The series was called *Britain to America*, and to narrate the shows Gilliam and I agreed to call in Leslie Howard—then at the peak of his popularity as a result of his fine performance in the film version of *Gone with the Wind*. The London Symphony Orchestra was booked, special music composed for it, and a large and illustrious cast led by Margaret Lockwood was laid on to play the various dramatic scenes which I used to illustrate my theme—a Sunday afternoon in wartime Britain. Having nothing at all to guide me, and a hundred different ways of doing what I was trying to do, I was naturally somewhat anxious about the reception of such a costly experiment. The story I had to tell was a moving and evocative one, and having at least by now a hazy idea as to what the American audience liked, I wrote it as honestly as I could, crossed my fingers and sat back nervously to wait for the response. The sudden deluge of ecstatic cables which poured in shortly from New York was a great relief to me: apparently I had struck the appropriate note.

The rest of the series were mostly written by other members of Features Department, the best of them being *Where do we go from here?* by Louis MacNeice. As co-editor with Gilliam, however, I was closely associated with all of them. In the course of the work, I enjoyed a very friendly relationship with Leslie Howard, who was not merely a gifted actor and sincere narrator, but also quite one of the most likeable people I ever met. His personal secretary, to whom he was devoted, was an utterly charming girl who regularly attended him to the studios. Finding them in the BBC canteen together one afternoon, I noticed that she looked rather unwell, and was told that she was suffering from a blinding headache. As Howard was shortly due on the air, I took her back to my office where she could rest, and gave her some aspirins. A few days later, I was dismayed to hear that she had died of meningitis. As I had feared, Howard was so desperately upset by her death that he cancelled all work for the next few months. He finally agreed to do one more broadcast with me in 1943, shortly after which he left on a trip to North Africa. Shot down by a German fighter on the flight back from Lisbon, his own tragic death was an even sadder personal loss to me.

Impressed by the success of *Britain to America* in the States, the Columbia Broadcasting System decided to carry a similar series of their own. To handle the programmes for them, they sent over Norman Corwin, one of their most talented writer-producers, whom the BBC was happy to provide with all production facilities in London. As a general thing, American radio had little to teach us. But from the days of the old Columbia Workshop productions,* CBS had built up an impressive record of imaginative radio—and Corwin himself was undoubtedly one of the most gifted writers who ever devoted himself to the medium. He had made radio history in America by writing his own series of radio fantasies, *Thirteen by Corwin*, in which he had been virtually

* Two of their productions, *The Fall of the City* by Archibald MacLeish and *Job to be done* by Pare Lorentz, had been broadcast by the BBC during the thirties. *Job to be done* in particular impressed me as a splendid piece of social protest, such as I despaired of getting the BBC to let me write about unemployment nearer home.

given the freedom of the air to write whatever he chose. Only Orson Welles, perhaps, had as much to offer as a producer—and that was never on offer for thirteen weeks consecutively.

Corwin's series *An American in Britain* was a sheer delight to everyone who believed in radio writing as a creative art. Unlike *Britain to America*, which had gone out on the Overseas Service, the series was broadcast in both countries. The ironic humour of the writing, and the keen observation behind it, were particularly appreciated over here. They made the American viewpoint infinitely more sympathetic to those who had known it previously only at second hand. All who were lucky enough to work along with him on the programmes had the highest admiration for Corwin's gifts. It was a sad day for all of us when Hollywood took its inevitable toll, and offering him infinitely more for doing infinitely less, deprived radio everywhere of one of its most accomplished craftsmen.

Shortly after Corwin had returned to America, I again found myself at odds with the BBC over one of my scripts. This time, the cause of the trouble was a play I had written for New Year's Day 1943. It was called *The Builders*, and was another modern morality in the same tradition as *Aaron's Field*. It was actually inspired by the Beveridge Report, whose recent publication had been received with no marked enthusiasm by Winston Churchill. In effect, the play was a cautionary tale: it showed the sort of stagnation into which the post-war world could sink, unless some sort of forward planning was brought to bear upon it. The hero of the play was Jack, the last soldier to return from the war, sometime in the future. To his dismay, he found himself back in the sort of hopeless twilight-life that we had known back in the thirties. The same old economics of scarcity prevailed, and with all the techniques of the modern world available, they still could not build him a decent life. As he was obviously not wanted, a plot was hatched up between the Politician and the Economist to wall him up where he stood, so that he could be tactfully forgotten. This they were in process of doing when, just in the nick of time, Jack's pre-war sweetheart—now the woman next door—raised a revolt of the neighbours to put a stop to the game. If that was the best they could do for him, she suggested, why not wall up the Politician and the Economist, until such time as they thought out a rather more helpful plan? The neighbours were only too happy to do so, and the play ended with two muffled voices desperately trying to be constructive.

All this was apparently regarded by the BBC as likely to spread such alarm and despondency that the troops might well lay down their arms and surrender: nothing was going to be done for them —the BBC had told them so! I replied that if nothing was going to be done, the news had certainly not come from me: all I had tried to point out was just how necessary it was that something *should* be done. But in those enlightened days, of course, anything like a Welfare State was regarded as quite out of the question—Beveridge Report to the contrary notwithstanding.

On this occasion, Basil Nicolls took me severely to task. As a policy censor myself, he told me, I ought to have known better. I said that while I was always ready to use a blue pencil in the interests of national security, I didn't intend to write with one to the detriment of national intelligence. I begged leave to doubt whether the public was quite so stupid as the BBC supposed, and this time I demanded a ruling in the matter from the Director-General himself. Ogilvie having resigned earlier that year, there were now two of him: Sir Robert Foot was in charge of the business end of broadcasting, and Sir Cecil Graves, the nephew of Lord Grey of Fallodon, was looking after programmes.* After Graves had read the script, he came down on the side of Nicolls; but his reason for doing so was really so disarming that I had perforce to accept it. "I'm only a simple sort of a chap," he explained, "and I didn't quite get the point. If *I* could misunderstand the play—not being used to poetry and all that—I'm afraid that other

---

* When the joint appointment was announced, it proved less popular than John Cheatle's dictum that the BBC had now one foot in the graves.

Robert Foot came to us from the Gas, Light and Coke Company. After taking over sole control, when Cecil Graves retired through ill health, he left us again to join the Mining Association. His task with them was reputed to be the staving off of the nationalisation of the mines. His failure to do so was celebrated in my ballad-opera *Johnny Miner*.

people might do so too." Surely, I suggested, the point could be made crystal clear in the opening announcement. But no, he didn't think that it could—not to chaps like him. Seeing my disappointment, he offered me a palliative. "As a matter of fact," he said, "we're thinking of sending you over to New York . . . So try and look on that as some sort of compensation."

The Builders was never heard in this country, and the publishers who bought it went out of business while it was still only in proof. Australia, being far ahead of us in forward thinking and social legislation, broadcast it more than once without alarming so much as a kangaroo. By the time the war was over, Nicolls himself had relented: he referred the play himself to the new Director-General, Sir William Haley. Alas, it was held to be no longer topical: the Welfare State had arrived! At least I could not be blamed for having helped to bring it about . . .

Rumours of my proposed attachment to the staff of the BBC's New York office had reached me before Sir Cecil Graves had mentioned it. Lindsay Wellington, I knew, was anxious that I should join him there with a view to my writing up the wartime scene in the United States. But meanwhile, I had another series of programmes to think about.

CBS had again suggested an Anglo-American collaboration—this time a programme alternating weekly from our end and from theirs—each being broadcast simultaneously in the BBC Home Service and over the CBS network. The programmes were to reflect the way of life of the two peoples, and to show how both were fighting substantially for the same things. The title suggested for the series was *Transatlantic Call—People to People*. I was to write the opening show from Britain, and act as general editor of the others: the first show from America was handed over to Norman Corwin.

In *Britain to America*, NBC had asked for a galaxy of British stars, but CBS made no such stipulation: what I did with my first show was entirely up to me. The London representative of CBS at the time was Edward R. Murrow, perhaps the most influential and courageous broadcaster of all time. His nightly newscast

Above left: 5. Alan Lomax

Above right: 6. Ethel Waters
in *The Man who went to War*

Left: 7. Val Gielgud

8. Recording with the Maoris

9. D. G. Bridson with Jane Russell and
Nicholas Ray in Hollywood, 1951

This is London had brought the horrors of the Blitz vividly home to every American listener; and no one had done more to win their sympathy for the British stand, before or after Pearl Harbour. Murrow was a man that I much admired and liked enormously. I told him of my plans for *Transatlantic Call*, and that I proposed to open the series with an actuality show from the North of England. The top CBS news announcer Robert Trout happened to be in London at the time, and Murrow agreed to release him so that he could handle the interviews for me. As for our going up to the North, Murrow was delighted with the idea: he knew how much of a novelty plain North Country voices would be to American listeners—irritated as they often were by the typically London accents of the BBC announcers.*

He also assured me that actuality programmes, such as he had heard me produce, were something quite unknown in the States. Radio there was strictly for the professionals: if any misguided man in the street was inveigled into the studio, it was only to hear himself gonged and laughed off the air in some such sadistic show as Major Bowes's *Amateur Hour*. The idea of building a broadcast entirely around ordinary people was something American radio had not yet thought of doing.

Once again I went back to Oldham for a good sharp earful of Lancashire talk and opinion. Three days before the broadcast, Ed Murrow and Bob Trout joined me there. I had already chosen and scripted my speakers: all that was necessary now was to put them through their paces. For the next two nights we did so, going from blacked-out house to house, rigging the microphone up on the kitchen table, getting everyone used to working with the first American most of them had met. This was a new insight into radio production for both of them, and one which thoroughly intrigued them. This time, moreover, we had a theme: what sort of a life did the people of Lancashire want after the war? Whatever they might have thought about *The Builders*, this was something that all my Lancashire friends felt strongly about: they wanted

---

* Twenty years later, the Beatles were to be hailed in America for the same North Country vowels.

something a damn sight better than what they'd got from the pre-war mess and muddle. If their industry was going to survive, it had to be modernised and production would have to be properly planned. A couple of hundred years ago, Lancashire had given the Industrial Revolution to the world: now they were out to give it something better. The vigour with which the people expressed their views on the air hit the American audience like a bomb.

To say that CBS in New York were surprised by the show would be an over-simplification. At first, they roundly accused the BBC of having cheated: nobody, they claimed, could speak so trenchantly at the microphone unless he was a professional—and the BBC had claimed that these were none of them actors, but all real and everyday people! Murrow immediately put them right on that: he had met them all in their homes and had been with them in the studio when the show went on the air. The people were real, all right—the only professional thing about the show was the way they had been produced. A similar group of speakers, he promised, would soon be coming up from towns all over Britain—with just as much to talk about.

Once convinced on that point, CBS went suddenly wild with a new enthusiasm: if that was what actuality meant—then that was what all America had apparently been waiting for! This was something new to them, and the programme heads at CBS could think of nothing they wanted more. Corwin came up the following week with an excellent programme on New England—but that was a far more literary script, using professional actors and making no bones about it. Normally, this would have been taken for granted, but after Lancashire in the raw, CBS decided that they also must have the real thing—and not, as the press unkindly put it, 'a reasonable facsimile'. The real thing they got the following week from Wiltshire, in a show produced by Jenifer Wayne.*

---

* The show innocently included one of the funniest lines I have ever heard in a broad-cast. Suitably encouraged by Bob Trout, an octogenarian carpet-maker was remembering his varied life in the craft. "Oi've laid 'em in palaces," he mused, "and Oi've laid 'em in cottages. And if Oi look *very carefully*, Oi could tell you the year Oi made 'em!"

The statement excited no comment in Wiltshire, but I gather that howls of delighted laughter could be heard from Brooklyn all the way to San Francisco.

This time it was a lively bunch of countryfolk from Wilton, and just to give it good measure, she threw in a real live English Earl as well. No Earl could have been better chosen to delight American ears. Any attempt at feudalism on his part, his lordship claimed, and his tenants would chuck him into the river. "So what?" he insisted upon Bob Trout replying, with nicely detached amusement.

Wiltshire was followed in turn by a jaunty piece of Cockney humour, worked out with the people of Lambeth Walk by Marjorie Banks. This was a part of London which lived a life of its own, with housewives jostling round the stalls, children playing in the bomb-ruins, and local beauties buckling to with oxyacetylene welding gear. As Gilliam happened to be over in the States at the time, he was even able to lay on Charles Chaplin direct from Hollywood, with a message for his erstwhile neighbours.

From then on we had it all our own way with the series: the pace and pattern of the shows had been set. *Transatlantic Call* ran weekly in Britain and America for the next three years. In the States, it was carried by up to a hundred and eighty stations in the network.

In June 1943, I found myself in America for the first time. Crossing in the old *Queen Elizabeth*, then doing service as a troopship, I had my first view of New York early one summer morning as we drifted into the Narrows. The walls and towers of Manhattan were an unforgettable sight, rising out of the mist like another vision of Kubla Khan. I had only to see it there, riding above its busy harbour, to know that the city was right for me.

My first view over the whole island from my thirty-third-floor office in Rockefeller Centre was even more unlikely. The tall grey spires of St. Patrick's Cathedral ended floors below me, and the brightly coloured cabs crawling along Fifth Avenue looked like a variegated army of ladybirds. Indeed, it was the light and colour of the city which probably surprised me most:

what I had seen of the world looked positively drab beside it. Glass flashed from the Chrysler Building and chromium shone from the Empire State; the RCA building next door reared up past my window for another thirty storeys again—a golden slab of my native millstone-grit.

As for the jostling streets, threading my way along them was an exercise in rediscovery: the wild profusion of goods in the shops, food in the restaurants and drink in the crowded bars was something that wartime London had long forgotten. So was the blaze of lights after dark, though the city was still proud to insist that this was a war-time dim-out. The nightly blare of car-horns, subterranean rumble of the subway, howling wail of occasional sirens and nasal drawl of passing voices blended into a strange music, only to lose itself again in the pounding jazz which surged up out of the nightspots. My first two days in New York were almost a psychedelic trip.

Tearing myself away from it all, I caught an early plane for Toronto, my first week's commitment being to produce for the Canadian Broadcasting Corporation a Dominion Day feature, *Canada at War*. The script was written as a collaboration with my Canadian friend Gerald Noxon, whom I had known in London when he worked on documentary films with Grierson and others. The show was colourful enough, no doubt, but much like a hundred others that either of us had written—a series of wartime vignettes that ran the gamut from the Maritimes to the Far West and Vancouver. At least it gave me a chance to adjust myself to the New World by degrees, for Toronto was rather more easy to assimilate than what I had so far seen of New York.

The feeling of Montreal was pleasantly French by contrast, and Ottawa genteely bureaucratic, but all three towns were built on a scale to which I felt more accustomed. It was only after I had crossed Canada by train that I felt the scale of the whole to be rather excessive. As for what I saw of the endless wastes laid open by the Alaska Highway, a depressed Negro had said it all: "nothing but miiiiles and miiiiles of nothing but miiiiles and miiiiles." The only thing which bothered me about Canada, in fact, was its emptiness—an almost boundless extent of country flickered across by the Northern Lights. But spending a pleasant holiday with the Noxons by Lake Ontario, I might have been back in Westmorland, if it hadn't been for the fire-bugs and the mosquitoes. Also, of course, if I could only have seen fifty miles across to the far shore of the lake . . .

I got back to the States in time for Independence Day, which the American end of *Transatlantic Call* was celebrating from Philadelphia, and this I was invited to attend. After his first three shows, Norman Corwin had fallen sick and been forced to retire from the series. His place had been difficult to fill, and with their new insistence on nothing but actuality, CBS were hard put to find any producer with the right experience.

By the time the show reached Philadelphia, they had found him—one of the few people in America who had spent his life recording actuality speakers (or rather singers) all over the States. This was Alan Lomax, whose collection of American folk-songs—recorded along with his father John A. Lomax—had formed the basis of the famous Library of Congress archives in Washington. Their work in the field has been honoured by every folk-singer since, from Ewan MacColl to Pete Seeger and Bob Dylan.

Alan Lomax was a Texan, a large, powerfully built man with a great zest for living and for his work. He was very much a singer in his own right, apart from the folk-songs he had collected, and a compulsive mixer. In the first of his *Transatlantic Call* productions, American actuality came alive: he spoke the same language and sang the same songs as Americans everywhere. More to the point, he was able to help them speak that language into a microphone, and to get the full flavour of their characters across. The shows that he handled came over with the same American impress as the prose of Thomas Wolfe or the poetry of Whitman. He could interpret America because he was so American himself. My meeting with him in Philadelphia was a lively and hilarious experience: it was also the start of a long and valued friendship. I never knew any American who more fully embodied the virtues—and the more engaging vices—of all his country-men.

Alan Lomax soon introduced me to the sort of young Americans I had always wanted to know—the young liberals who stood for Roosevelt, the W. P. A. and the New Deal. Apart from Alan's own family, there was Nicholas Ray, then working for the Office of War Information with Louis Untermeyer as a documentary radio producer. Nick was keenly interested in my own methods of actuality production, and he soon became one of my favourite drinking cronies until he went out to join John Houseman in Hollywood. There he quickly established himself as one of their most gifted directors with an avid post-war following among the *nouvelle vague* in France. Burl Ives was another of our circle, then making his name on CBS as the Wayfaring Stranger—an enormous twenty-stone bull of a man with a nature as gentle as a girl's and a tenor voice as pure and sweet as a choir-boy's. Otherwise, he was Gargantua—eating his pounds of steer at a meal and drinking his wine by the quart flagon: my only drinking boast was to match him one evening, level-pegging on bourbon. Over the years, both in the States and around the British Isles, I was to work with him on some of my jolliest shows.

With Alan and Burl, I soon made many friends among the Negro folk-singers then to be found in New York. There was the almost legendary Leadbelly—Hudy Leadbetter—whom Lomax's father had found singing in a Southern penitentiary after killing a man in a brawl. He was then singing at the Village Vanguard, where he had come to rest after killing another man who had annoyed him. Luckily for me, I never did—and the songs which he recorded for me were a quite inimitable delight. At Downtown Café Society, I also grew friendly with Josh White—already well to the fore in the long struggle for Negro integration. Josh was a fighter for whom I had great respect, a man with a sense of humour who could still be as tough and mean as he sometimes had to be.

The violence of American life was something I gradually came to accept. I had seen men knocked out in bars, and on Christmas Eve was to watch the police club a Negro through the window of

Dempsey's Restaurant, while the loud-speakers filled Times Square with the strains of *Holy Night*. In Café Society one night I was eating peacefully with a party of friends and talking to Josh over our steaks. Sitting next to me, Alan Lomax suddenly jumped to his feet, seized the man at the next table and knocked him clean across his supper. Waiters rushed over, but saying nothing to Alan, threw the body into the street. I asked, in some astonishment, what the hell was going on? "He annoyed me," said Alan, sitting down again. Five minutes later, the man came lurching back, protesting that he wanted to apologise. With a vigilant waiter on either side, he approached our party again and held out his hand: Alan rose, prepared to shake it. "I didn't mean to offend you," said the man, "I only said that I didn't want to sit at the next table to a goddam nigger." Alan hit him again, before the waiters could drag him away. But this time, like everyone else, Josh had heard the remark. He froze in his chair, then slowly rose to his feet as his hand reached for his pocket. Three or four girls at nearby tables rushed to pinion his arms to his side. The body was thrown out again without Josh being able to draw his knife—and the bevy of his admirers subsided back to their suppers again. He was obviously a very popular folk-singer . . .

Perhaps the only song more scarifying than Josh's own *Hard Time Blues* was Billie Holliday's *Strange Fruit*, then to be heard at the Onyx on 52nd Street. But splendid singing and jazz was still to be found all over New York. Down in Greenwich Village, around Times Square or up in Harlem the bars and nightspots were crammed each evening with American servicemen on leave, and the town was there to please them. Ethel Waters, Maxine Sullivan, Hazel Scott, Pearl Bailey and Mary Lou Williams—these were only the best of the women I loved to hear. And the dancing of Katherine Dunham and Pearl Primus was equally good to watch. As for the great jazzmen—that was still an age to remember, with Louis Armstrong, Fats Waller, Art Tatum, Eddie Condon, Sidney Catlett and Red Allen, Lionel Hampton and Red Norvo. All were there to enjoy nightly, often enough for the price of a couple of drinks at a crowded bar.

I had been welcomed into American radio as a pioneer of actuality shows, but I was not at all anxious to be known as that alone. There were far too many other things that I enjoyed being equally well. Having my cordial relationship with NBC no less than with CBS, I wanted to get back again to the sort of scripted and acted shows that I was no less fond of doing. After a quick look round the Middle West, I settled for one in which I could give my own impression of Chicago, still notorious as the stronghold of Colonel McCormick's *Tribune* and the Middle West isolationists. NBC gladly offered me all facilities for the programme, and in due course I came up with *An Englishman looks at Chicago*. I found the city a very pleasant and invigorating surprise. In Grant Park and Lake Shore Drive it could claim one of the finest prospects in the world; it had a great tradition in the arts, and many other things that I admired but hardly expected to find there. Most of all, it was the people that impressed me, their directness and honesty and the strong sense they had of their own identity. Where New York was metropolitan, Chicago was utterly and completely American. As everyone kept explaining, it was the hub of the continent—New York was merely an accident somewhere on the perimeter. In many ways, Chicago's local pride reminded me of Manchester . . .

There were, of course, many sides to the place which nobody wanted to talk about. The ghastly blood-bath of the stockyards, the squalid ghetto of the South Side, the violence and the brutality were there for all to deplore; but these were only the sleazy side of the picture. The zest and forcefulness of the place, the friendliness and the driving energy were more than enough to offset them. Chicago *was* America, and this was what I principally stressed in my broadcast—a fact that came over loud and clear, I gather, to listeners in Britain. The interest and enthusiasm of all who helped me to put it together was plenty in itself, but the praise that the show won in America was even more encouraging.

Even *Variety*, that hard-boiled showbiz organ which normally hadn't a good word to say for the BBC, went out of its way to be complimentary.* And with that to cheer them on, NBC were only too happy to give me the network coast-to-coast for anything else I wanted to do.

The American insistence on judging people solely by results was a very welcome innovation for me. Whereas in the BBC who you were would often decide how high you went, the American networks had only one criterion: Can he do the job better than anyone else? If so, he had nothing further to worry about—till somebody showed up who could do it better still. As for the money paid—that was vastly more than the BBC had ever paid for anything. My opposite numbers in the networks were all far better paid than I was, and enjoyed a far more lavish standard of living. That I was prepared to accept, so long as I was judged by professional ability and not by my style of life. I found that I mostly was. There was certainly nothing on American radio more complicated technically than the shows I managed to do.

The Chicago show, for instance, had drawn upon all the resources of radio that I normally liked to employ—a large cast, specially recorded effects, an original score and good musicians to play it. The same were made available to me when I went on in due course to San Francisco. If Chicago had been a pleasant surprise, the Capital of the West Coast was all that I had hoped it would be. The staggering beauty of the setting, with the two great bridges thrown like red and silver rainbows across the water, the crazy gradient of the streets, the exotic fun of Chinatown, the food to be had on Fisherman's Wharf, the drag and the strippers on all that was left of the Barbary Coast—these were attractions one expected. But the great upsurge of industry in the

---

* "It was a glowing full-dimension picture of a lusty city and, particularly in the poetic closing tribute, was more courteous and sympathetic than many Americans might have drawn. It was an outstanding broadcast . . . and it reveals Bridson as a scripter-director with something to say to American audiences, one whose work should be heard more frequently."

Variety, 15 September 1943.

Bay area, the aircraft plants and the refineries, the unbelievable output of the Kaiser shipyards—these were something indicative of California's future.* Most exciting of all to a European, perhaps, was my first sight of the Pacific, pounding in through the Golden Gate, and the sudden realisation that the enemy over the water here was not Germany but Japan. Out of these three contrasting themes, *An Englishman looks at San Francisco* was easily put together.

In Chicago, I had had to import my Englishman from Canada in the person of Hugh Sinclair. But in San Francisco, I was able to call on the very distinguished group of English actors then in Hollywood. By great good fortune, Herbert Marshall was free to come and join me, and so began yet another delightful friendship. In his drily amusing way, he was almost the true quintessence of Englishness, and after the show had gone out, I returned to Hollywood with him virtually as his guest. It was certainly an exhilarating interlude. The kindness of Ronald Colman and all the others of the English colony, the presence of Norman Corwin at MGM and of Jack Houseman at Paramount, the daily lunches at the Brown Derby and the nightly dinners at Mike Romanoff's, with Hitchcock, the Bogarts and everyone else milling in and out; whatever it did for one's liver, it did a great deal for conversation. There too I met up with James Hilton, enjoying all the comforts of his air-conditioned Shangri La, and a fellow Lancastrian after my own heart. Our habit of lapsing into derisively broad Oldham dialect at fashionably British cocktail parties was a source of distress to Sir Aubrey Smith and the older school of Southern English gentlemen. Equally, the sight of everyone from Alan Mowbray to Dame May Whitty faithfully playing their favourite character parts was a source of infinite amusement to us.

As for Herbert Marshall himself, he was among the most

---

* In the Kaiser shipyards, 4,000-ton Liberty Ships were being built and launched in as little as four and a half days. A woman welder at the yards told me Bing Crosby's latest crack: "They gave him a bottle of champagne and told him to christen a Liberty Ship. He said O.K., but where was it?—*he* couldn't see any ship. So they said, 'Start swinging the bottle, brother—it'll be there!'"

amusing raconteurs that I ever knew.* Enjoying the respect and rewards of an Elder Statesman in Hollywood, he still yearned nostalgically for the fogs and discomforts of wartime London. He was a man of such charm that I even enjoyed the whisky that he woke me up in the small hours to come and drink with him (as a nightcap) on the other side of town! One place or another, we continued to see a lot of each other: now that he is no longer with us, I wish I could meet his like again . . .

Back in New York in the winter of 1943, I decided to stage one actuality programme for NBC. They lent me the theatre in the RCA Building where I could mount the show before an audience. Then with Hyde Partnow as my interpreter, I crossed the Bridge into darkest Brooklyn. There I found life even more boisterous than I had been led to suppose. For as Lambeth is to Westminster, so Brooklyn is to Manhattan: they are neighbours only separated by a river and a million miles. But quite unlike Lambeth, Brooklyn is sensitive about its phonetics—from Sand Street and the Navy Yard to Toity-toid Street or Coney Island. Indeed, I was roundly attacked by a Brooklyn taxi-driver for only wanting to do the show in order to raise a laugh out of the Brooklyn accent. On the contrary, I assured him, I only wanted to give the Borough a chance to laugh at mine—and that it certainly did.

As for the Brooklyn speech-pattern, that I found more colourful than anything I had heard in American before. By way of an example, I cannot do better than quote the following, transcribed from the soliloquy of my lunch-counter proprietor: "Wise guys! I open up the doors at six o'clock in the morning. One day I'm making coffee. A maniac comes in. 'Hey, jerk,' he says, 'gimme a cuppa coffee.' Jerk! You're not in business to fight, right? A physical altercation can spoil the nickels. 'Derelict,' I

---

* He told me that at a theatre *première*, the man in front of him had suddenly broken wind rather noisily. To cover his embarrassment, he had turned and looked accusingly at his neighbours. Sitting behind him, Bart had leaned forward and tapped him on the shoulder. "It's no good, you blighter," he whispered, "I saw you tilt!"

says, 'don't disturb my equanimity.' So again he insults me—a
hollow hulk like that! So I say to him: 'Your idiocy is very refreshing.' So he gets sore and wants to fight. So I say to him nice
and polite: 'Hey, bum,' I said, 'stop knocking yourself out. The
door's open. Beat it!' "

But most irrepressible of all was the bunch of Dead End kids
that I picked out of a Brooklyn school—as near to embodied
mayhem as anything I met in my life. After a day listening to
their cult vocabulary, I wrote the best of it into a cross-talk act—
with me at the wrong end of the ribbing. I then went back to the
class-room, and with only the master to protect me invited them
to play their parts. Butch I cast as Bud, and Fink I cast as Hob-
binol—to see how they projected and how the best of them
shaped up. Seeing that none of them had acted before in their
lives, they all shaped up remarkably well, whichever parts they
played. Then, of course, came the sixty-four dollar question:
which of them could play me? They all had a go at that—mimick-
ing my accent and everything about me as a Limey. I can only say
that, in comparison, a caricature by Gerald Scarfe would have
been distinctly kind . . .

But it was back at the studios, rehearsing the final production,
that they really came into their own. Riding the elevators, hanging out of the dizzy windows, pulling plugs and flinging the
switches, they nearly wrecked the Rockefeller Centre and drove
even the Brooklyn engineers half out of their minds. Only the
thought that rival gangs might never get to hear them saved the
RCA transmitters. As for playing it up before a studio audience,
that was what they were really waiting for; and the roar of delighted applause that the audience gave them on the air—that
might well have wrecked the transmitter also. It made me realise
once again how little American radio had done with the people
it was trying so desperately to woo—with soap. *An Englishman
looks at Brooklyn* might well have been written about Abyssinia,
without appearing more strange and stimulating to a typical New
York audience. Yet Sidney Kingsley's *Dead End* had played on
Broadway at least eight years previously!

With my last American production, I decided to break entirely new ground: in the event, I came up with radio's first ballad-opera. My respect for the American Negro dated a long way back—in fact, to the time when Florence Mills had twice enchanted me in *Blackbirds*, when Cochran brought the revue to Manchester in 1927. Since I had been in New York, and had had a chance to hear Negro music at its best, my respect had vastly increased. I wanted to produce a Negro musical, written around a war theme, which could give lively expression to the Negro character, his humour and his supreme artistry. I realised that the script would have to be a collaboration, unless it was to run the risk of striking a false note—the very last thing that I wanted. And I had no doubt at all who my collaborator should be.

I had first come across the work of the Negro poet Langston Hughes back in the early thirties, and had been much moved by his lyric *Christ of the South* which had appeared in the Carolina review *Contango*. I sketched out the story line of the show I had in mind, and wrote to ask Hughes whether he would be interested in working on it with me. He came down from Harlem to discuss it, we spent an uproarious evening together, and he agreed.

My plan was to write a simple sort of folk-tale round the lives of a man and his wife in a town like London during the war. But though their story would be London's own, the town itself—like the man and his wife—would not be English, but Negro. The man joins up and goes to fight the war with his friends; his wife goes to work in a war factory and suffers all the terrors of the Blitz. The man is badly wounded; he is worried about his wife and child at home and becomes delirious. He dreams that he meets up with God, and asks him a few hard questions. Reassured, he recovers—enough to be sent back home on leave. His wife begs him to desert, but the man is now determined to go on fighting until their cause is finally won.

By turning London into Harlem, two things became possible: firstly, we could give wartime London a look at itself through Negro eyes; and secondly, we could give it a chance to imagine the Negro's own struggle. Finally, we could let it hear the best of the Negro music, with which the struggle was actually being waged.

We called the story simply *The Man who went to War*, and scene by scene we worked over it together, I creating the situations and Langston translating them into his own terms and idiom. The action developed themes which we could illustrate in song—sometimes in comment between the scenes and sometimes rising naturally out of the dialogue. The music, of course, was folksong—and this Alan Lomax helped us to choose. When the job was complete we were left with a ballad-opera much in the eighteenth-century tradition of John Gay and Henry Carey.

So far as casting went, there was no lack of available talent: all I had to worry about was the money that it would cost. And that, by New York standards, was something impossibly far beyond my budget. Ethel Waters was a natural choice for the wife and Canada Lee for the husband; the part of God, of course, was built to measure for Paul Robeson. But Canada Lee was Hollywood material: he had just made *Lifeboat* with Tallulah Bankhead for Alfred Hitchcock. Ethel Waters was playing in New York cabaret at a couple of thousand dollars a week. And whatever he earned for that, Robeson was starring on Broadway in *Othello*. There was only the one course open to me: explaining my idea to them, I invited all three to make the ballad-opera with me as a gesture of Negro friendship for the people of Britain. News had been coming back from Britain of the warm reception that the Negro troops had enjoyed there, and the thought of making such a gesture appealed strongly to the three of them. They promptly accepted the job at a token fee of a hundred dollars each. Josh White took over the singing narration, William Vesey, Brownie McGhee and Sonny Terry had singing parts of their own. As for the choral numbers, these were taken over by the Hall Johnson Choir from *Green Pastures*, who nobly got to work on the songs and spirituals which had to be rehearsed. By the time auditioning was over, we had gathered together the most expensive Negro cast yet heard in a single broadcast—British or American. But this one was to be heard only in Britain: union rates prevented its being carried by an American network for less than about ten times the money that we could afford to pay.*

The impact of the work in performance was incredibly moving. Ethel Waters' parting from her husband and her singing of *Sometimes I feel like a motherless child* almost stopped the show in the studio. The performances of Canada Lee and Paul Robeson, the rousing songs in the troop-train, *We're gonna move into Germany* and *Keep your hand on the gun*, the eerie spiritual *City called Heaven* sung in the air-raid shelter as the bombs came whistling and crashing down, William Vesey's *Let my people go!*, Josh White's sung narration, his *How Long?* and *Sally don't you grieve*, the final inspiring chorus *Walk together, children*—these were only the high-spots that I remember.

As a gesture of friendship from one people to another, *The Man who went to War* was probably unique. As a prophetic echo of the Negro's post-war struggle for Civil Rights, it might have been a timely warning. Either way, it was quite one of the most popular broadcasts I ever had on the air, being heard in Britain by nearly ten million listeners on its first transmission alone.

I could not have wished for a happier start to my long friendship with Langston Hughes, who twenty years later was again to collaborate with me in editing my Third Programme series *The Negro in America*. He was among the most stimulating companions I have known, and I never found myself in New York without spending at least one evening with him in his beloved Harlem. His poetry was matchless, his plays a delight in the theatre, his output of books and journalism prodigious, and his fight for the Negro cause unremitting. But it was mostly for his ebullient good humour that his friends remember him. No matter how heated the disputes in which he found himself caught up, his gurgling

---

* Even so, the recording was promptly destroyed after its second broadcast by some fool of a BBC administrator who decided it was too expensive at £500!

It was many years later that Alan Lomax discovered the only surviving set of discs in America. He took them into the BBC New York office for copying onto tape that could be sent on to me in London. Instead of being copied, the actual discs were freighted to me —and as they were wartime stock, cut on a glass base, they reached me in a thousand fragments.

And that was the end of *The Man who went to War*.

hiccupy laugh would break in whenever the argument over-reached itself and became absurd. And for all the indignities to which he had been subjected himself, there remained absolutely no bitterness in his nature. His whole life was devoted to making the world a better place for his people to live in. The world would not have been so good as it is for anyone if Langston Hughes had never been a part of it.

5

War's end and after

RETURN TO THE austerity of wartime London was much like going bankrupt, or re-living the privations of one's penurious youth. It could have been depressing, if the war had not been so much nearer to keep life interesting; and my first heavy air-raid for a long while greeted me as my train pulled in to Euston. To the whistle of the descending bombs, I began once more to taste the metallic sharpness of the fillings in my teeth.

A few days before my return, Sir Robert Foot had resigned as Director-General and been succeeded by W. J. Haley, later to be Sir William. He had previously operated as the BBC's Editor-in-Chief, having joined the staff from Reuters, of which he had been a director. Although I had not known him at the time, he had shared my own formative years in Manchester, where he had worked for the *Manchester Evening News* and ended up as joint Managing Director of the *Manchester Guardian*.

He was in many ways a remarkable man, largely self-educated, a first-class organiser, and possessed of a well-read interest in literature and the arts. He had indulged in a spell of book-reviewing in his Manchester days under the pseudonym of Joseph Sell—which presumably he found in *Lavengro*. In later years he was to write pleasantly bookish essayettes for *The Times* (of which he became Editor) under the pseudonym of Oliver Edwards.

Unlike some of the Directors-General under whom I served, he was keenly interested in broadcasting, and must have spent a fair amount of his time listening. Even so, he remained completely unknown to most members of his staff, many of whom

did not even know him by sight.* This may well have been because he was rather a diffident man, who appeared to find conversation difficult with strangers. Perhaps it was also why he was
described by a well-known novelist as the only man he had ever
met with *two* glass-eyes . . .

On my return to London, I was invited by Haley to give my
impressions of American radio to a meeting of senior programme
staff. I gave an enthusiastic account of my work with the three
networks, and contrasted the esteem in which broadcasting personnel were held in New York with the comparative disregard
which they rated here in London. I also pointed out how largely
competition was responsible for this, where everyone was worth
as much as his talents would fetch in the open market. Finally, I
commended the way that professional pride was built up among
American radio-writers and producers by the valuable awards
and prizes with which their work was frequently honoured. I
wished that something similar could be done for them over here.

At the end of my account, Haley enquired with some irony
whether I got the impression that American producers were in
the business because they were fond of radio, or because they
were fond of making a lot of money. I replied, with what I hope
was equal irony, that I got the impression they were in it because
they were fond of both. I pointed out that while I was with him
in Hollywood, my opposite number Norman Corwin happened
to be earning twenty-five times my own salary, and seemed to be
very fond of radio indeed.†

When I got back to my desk, I had a great deal of work to

* The story went that on his departure from the BBC in 1952 he toured Broadcasting
House saying his goodbyes. Down in the canteen, he solemnly shook hands with two
ladies dispensing the evening meal. "Who on earth was that?" asked one of them. On
learning that it was the Director–General, she was suitably impressed. "Well," she said,
"*there's* a nice friendly gentleman! Not like the Director–General who's just left, Sir
William Haley!"

† Though his $2,000 a week came from MGM for film-scripting, it was his work for
radio which had won him the contract. He continued to write occasional radio scripts
for the next few years, of which his celebration of the end of the war, *On a Note of Triumph*,
was an outstanding example.

cope with, much of it being a hangover from my nine months' stay in the States. I had left another ballad-opera lined up with Alan and Elizabeth Lomax in New York, a production which I had been loth to relinquish. This was *The Martins and the Coys*, a family-feuding comedy from the Apallachians in which the Nazis became even more acceptable as a target than everybody's next-door neighbours. Once again, the cast was outstanding—the roster this time including Burl Ives, the fabulous Woody Guthrie, the young Pete Seeger, Will Geer from *Tobacco Road* and Lily May Pearson of the Coon Creek Girls. Roy Lockwood, BBC's resident New York producer, made a lively occasion of it all, which luckily survives in one commercial recording.

My first assignment in London was a nostalgic look at America as a whole, which was easy enough to cast even in London, with so many American troops there waiting for the coming invasion of France. I had a crateful of my American folk-song recordings to put on the air, as well as taking over the editorship of *Transatlantic Call* again, for which I was soon busy writing a lot more shows. There was also renewed demand for another series of *Billy Welcome* programmes, which took me up and down the country. These were now such established favourites that when I staged one experimentally at Rochdale in the local theatre, the queue for the performance stretched all round the block. I was glad to be able to arrange a special item for it with Gracie Fields in Hollywood.

All this was well enough, but far too reminiscent to be really interesting. D-Day was now imminent, and a vast news coverage of the landings and the whole campaign had been lined up during my absence in America. We already had many correspondents in the field in Italy, of course, who had followed the fighting all the way through North Africa. These included old friends of mine like Wynford Vaughan-Thomas, Reginald Beckwith, Denis Johnston, Michael Reynolds and Godfrey Talbot. But these were soon to be joined on the Western Front by a far larger team which included many more—Robert Barr, Richard Dimbleby, Frank Gillard, Alan Melville, Robert Reid, Michael Standing,

Colin Wills and Chester Wilmot among them. The Americans
Ed Murrow, Larry Leseur and Eric Severeid, and the Canadians
Matthew Halton, Stanley Maxted and Stewart MacPherson were
also ours to draw upon as needed. When the invasion came, *War
Report* was to be on the air nightly with the best of all available
despatches from all the active fronts, cut into a fast-moving commentary on modern warfare such as the world had not yet heard.
The editors of the programme were Laurence Gilliam and Donald
Boyd, and once again I stood in frequently as Gilliam's deputy, a
duty which I keenly enjoyed. Meeting the correspondents as they
flew in every so often from the fighting, one needn't have had a
clearer reminder that the war was quite literally an hour's flying
time away.

To remind one of the fact more persuasively, the Germans
began to launch their flying-bomb attacks on London. My first
sight of the V1s was from the roof of a BBC building in New
Cavendish Street, where I was spotting the second night they
came over. They could be seen almost as soon as they crossed
the south coast—not by their exhaust-flames, but by the streams
of crimson tracers shooting up at them from all sides in
what appeared to be endless garlands of rambler roses. It was
only when they roared in through the barrage to the West End,
that their fiery tails and staccato rattle identified them for
what they really were. But fascinating as they were to watch,
the buzz-bombs were a maddening irritation to any radio
producer.

I was busy writing a big programme for American Independence Day when they built up to their full climax. It had long
seemed to me that little as the Americans knew about the English
point of view in the War of Independence, the average Englishman knew still less about the American. To remedy this, I
wrote *The Spirit of '76*, declaredly in the announcement to present the American viewpoint as it appeared in all their textbooks.
Its heroes were the minute-men of Lexington and Bunker Hill,
the army of Washington freezing at Valley Forge or crossing the
Delaware, and the author of the Declaration of Independence,

Thomas Jefferson.* The villains of the piece were the myopic George III and his Hessian mercenaries. As all too often in history, the long-suffering British soldier was out in front as a cover for other people's bigotry and ill-considered policies at home.

In view of the constant shower of buzz-bombs, I was denied the suite of studios that I needed at Maida Vale, as these were rightly regarded as far too open a target. After a long battle, I finally settled for the Concert Hall on the lower ground floor of Broadcasting House. Though this was far less exposed, it was a very poor substitute from my point of view, and could hardly have been worse for the production: for with everyone crammed into the one studio, it was impossible to balance speech at all audibly against symphonic background music. As it was also impossible in such an echoing barn to get any good outdoor acoustics, I was forced to pre-record my shouted outdoor dialogue over in Regent's Park.

I had a large cast of American service-men, led by Sergeant Henry Sweet, who had just made a big success of his part in the film *A Canterbury Tale* with Eric Portman. Together we all went in search of peace and quiet in the shrubbery, waiting for suitable lulls in the distant grind of the city traffic. The order "Don't shoot till you see the whites of their eyes!" was duly roared out for me by the sergeant, upon which the Revolutionary Army hurled itself to the ground as yet another buzz-bomb came clattering in low overhead. If the Redcoats had been there to advance at that particular moment, Bunker Hill would have been taken without a shot.

As it was, both Bunker Hill and Trenton were lost to the London Symphony Orchestra, which Muir Matheson whipped into such a pitch of revolutionary fervour that he drowned out my narrator almost completely. In view of my wartime studio difficulties, I was hardly consoled by the critic in *The Observer* who

* The part was obligingly played for me by a Vice-President of NBC, Davidson Taylor, who happened to be in London at the time. He had been very helpful in getting me network facilities in New York.

complained that the producer "had only himself to blame if listeners heard less than they should." Even so, he paid high tribute to the programme, which he chose to call "a major occasion in broadcasting," and even suggested that "the whole generous and sensitive spirit of the thing should do more to advance Anglo-American understanding than a wilderness of politicians' speeches."

Robert Graves was of a different opinion. In an angry letter to *The Times*, he deplored the programme as historically inexact—rather lessening the impact of the rebuke by giving a wrong date for the skirmish at Lexington, a howler which delighted all his American readers. (His *Sergeant Lamb* novels, of course, were committed to selling the British side of the story, so perhaps he was not entirely impartial.) But his chief complaint was that any such tendentious broadcast could only sow dissension among the British and American troops in Normandy—supposing that any of them had had time to spare for listening . . .

By an odd chance, General Eisenhower read the letter, and demanded an immediate enquiry.* He had not heard the broadcast himself, but if this was the British reaction to it—whose idea had it been? He promptly despatched General Walter Bedell Smith, one of his military aides, to Broadcasting House to find out, declaring that "if an American officer arranged this programme to be broadcast in England . . . he would send the man home if it was within his power." Sir William Haley duly assured the aide that the idea had been mine alone—adding, perhaps, that if Ike wanted to send *me* back to the States, no doubt I should be delighted. As it was, he explained, the broadcast had the full support of the BBC. I hope he also made it clear that the British were not so naïve as to take exception to any statement of the other side of an Anglo-American dispute quite so ancient—a fact that was well borne out by our own Audience Research Report a few days later. *The Spirit of '76* was almost as well re-

---

* The story was told in the War Diary of Captain Harry Butcher, U.S.N.R., who was Naval Aide to General Eisenhower at the time. I was happy to set the General's mind at rest by sending him the Audience Research Report when I caught up with the story.

ceived by listeners as my other anti-Hanoverian diatribe, *The March of the '45*, revived a month later.

With the approach of VE-Day, I was asked to write the BBC's tribute to the American service-man, for broadcast during the Victory Week celebrations. It took the form of a dramatic poem, *This was an American*, and told the story of a typical GI killed in Germany. The script was much liked by Ed Murrow, who promised to get me the best available American star to play the lead for me. Much to our astonishment, the American Army for the first time declined to co-operate: in the opinion of their Public Relations Division, it would be wrong for them to appear to be paying tribute to themselves! Douglass Montgomery, the star of Anthony Asquith's fine film, *The Way to the Stars*, was luckily available at the time. Though an American citizen, he had volunteered for service with the Canadian Army before America entered the war. I could never have hoped for a more moving and sincere performance than he gave in the leading role.

With the return of peace to Europe, I began to receive news of my radio friends in Norway, and shortly flew into Oslo to report on the country as I found it after five years of occupation. Never has it been my luck to be in on such a bonanza! The Wehrmacht's stock of wines and spirits for an expected two-year last-ditch stand had been captured by the Resistance and handed out to the jubilant Oslo people. Most of it was still being carried round the streets in bulging pockets and even ruck-sacks: I had only to speak a word of English for bottles to be warmly pressed upon me. Rumour had it that the Red Berets, who had just flown in to join forces with the Norwegian Resistance, had blown the safes at the Gestapo headquarters and flung armfuls of captured currency down to the cheering crowds in the streets. A number of courts martial were regretfully thought to be pending, but if the rumours were true, I hope the German capture of sterling after Dunkirk was remembered in mitigation. In any case, as one of the first British civilians seen in Norway since the liberation, I personally enjoyed more alcoholic hospitality than I could readily cope with. It was only the unvarying diet of boiled lobster at the Hotel Bristol which helped to remind me how very much else was still in desperately short supply. For once in my life, I would gladly have swopped a lobster for half a loaf of non-ersatz bread . . .

My tour through Norway in a commandeered German truck, and using commandeered German recording gear, was something of an experience in itself. The country was still completely occupied by the Wehrmacht, which was still very much under arms. All the troops had been expecting to fight on, and many of them bitterly resented the surrender of their High Command. Driving up to their armed camps with one Norwegian officer for an escort, barking out orders at them while they clicked their heels and saluted, demanding tankfuls of their petrol and having it instantly supplied, was an experience that I much enjoyed. The fire-bombs on Manchester and the buzz-bombs on London had left me in a very demanding mood. I expected—and I received— the best and most punctilious service.

My Norwegian programme also gave me my first experience in the use of tape recording. A German wartime invention, *magnetophon* tape had effected a quiet revolution in mobile recording techniques. For here was something which completely outclassed either wire or disc or film recording as I knew them, both in quality of reproduction and in the ease with which the tape could be cut and handled in the studio. When I returned to London, there was only the one captured *magnetophon* machine on which my tapes could be played. But a single day's practise in editing them, snipping away with a razor blade, was all that I needed to convince me how obsolete all other mobile recording systems had become. I loudly sang the praises of tape recording to the BBC administration, only to be told that it failed to come up to the exacting standards of BBC engineering! It was no use asking people to listen to better quality than they wanted to hear: the BBC preferred to stay with the disc recording that they had always used. Despite the pleas of everyone who came to use tape recording abroad, it was not for a number of years that

Broadcasting House was persuaded to change over to the new system. Tradition dies hard in Portland Place, particularly among the administrators who never made a recording or even entered a studio in their lives.

Luckily, my work over the next few years was to take me out of the studios and send me half around the world. It has to be remembered that since the start of the war, firm news from most parts of Europe had been virtually non-existent. For the five years of the fighting, news had come from the battle-fronts, or it had come from the home-fronts of Britain and America. But what had really been going on in Poland or Czechoslovakia or Greece or Jugoslavia was mainly a matter for speculation. Few reliable stories had filtered through even from Resistance sources. How were people living in the vast areas that had been fought across? What was being done to make life tolerable for the millions of the displaced and dispossessed?

As an ex-newsman, Haley himself was interested in such questions, and realised that radio was in a unique position to supply the answers graphically. It was partly due to Haley's initiative that the War Reporting Unit had been set up, and now that the war was over, he was anxious that the excellent coverage of News Division and Features Department should be carried over into equally lively reporting on the many problems of peace. News was now available everywhere, and there were BBC correspondents reporting from every capital in Europe. But hard news was only a part of the need: there was also background to the news—news coverage in depth—and that was what feature writers had always been in business to provide.

During the war, in fact, the feature programme had come of age. It had developed new techniques and was drawing on new resources in the way of mobile recording gear—though not yet upon tape recording. Feature producers had followed the armies, flown with the planes, sailed in with the ships, and had brought the new immediacy of sound to the impact of war reporting. They had dealt with every aspect of the war, and had brought to the microphone thousands of people whose personal stories had been an integral part of the war effort. No war had ever been reported and made real to a world audience in such vivid terms before, and a vital part in the process—emotional involvement of the listener by colourful re-enactment—had been played by the feature programme.

But over and above its achievement in imparting information, the feature had also proved its ability to engross and entertain. It had been developed notably as a medium for creative writing of a new order. From early successes like Stephen Potter's *The Last Crusade* and Robert Kemp's lyrical *Cutty Sark*, it had moved over into the province of radio drama with Louis MacNeice's *Christopher Columbus* and Edward Sackville-West's re-treatment of the story of Odysseus in *The Rescue*. As an instrument of social satire it had assumed new overtones in the work of Jenifer Wayne, Nesta Pain and Stephen Potter's series *How*—in which he tried out the first ploys which led on to Lifemanship.* In the field of the documentary proper, parallel with the work of the Crown Film Unit, it had been splendidly developed by Francis Dillon, Robert Barr, Leonard Cottrell, Marjorie Banks—and most notably of all—by Cecil McGivern. Historical documentary ranged over the whole retrospect from the classical world to the recent past, and had scored one of the first great successes of the war with *The Shadow of the Swastika* series, scripted by A. L. Lloyd and Igor Vinogradoff, and produced in Manchester by Laurence Gilliam.

The wide variety of feature styles and feature material was one of the most impressive aspects of the form; and in the course of the next few years, it was to be widened still further. For shortly after the end of the war, many new feature producers had been

* The *manship* suffix has taken on new overtones which would have surprised Dr. Johnson or Sir James Murray. When Adlai Stevenson was in England, Potter was introduced to him at a cocktail party. "I was delighted when you used *Brinkmanship* to describe the Dulles foreign policy," he grinned. "I really can't claim originality for that," said Stevenson. "It stemmed from *Lifemanship* and all that—invented by that very amusing English writer . . . I can't remember his name."
A better example of One-upmanship it would be hard to imagine.

taken onto the London staff—R. D. Smith, David Thomson, John Bridges, Alan Burgess, Joe Burroughs, Rayner Heppenstall, Farquharson Small and Thomas Waldron being among the earliest of them. Over the next decade, they were to be joined by many more.

At the end of 1945, Features Department was given a new and independent status. As I have mentioned, throughout the war, Features and Drama had been a joint department under the control of Val Gielgud. Working to him had been his two Assistant Directors: Moray McLaren (and later, Howard Rose) had been in administrative charge of radio drama, and Laurence Gilliam had been responsible for the feature programme output. Resources had been pooled between the two halves of the department, and producers had been available for helping out with work for either. There had been something to recommend the scheme, as it had helped to break down the rigidly watertight departmentalism so dear to the tidy BBC mind. But it was obvious that with a vast expansion of radio pending, separation was necessary; and by 1946, Gilliam had assumed the sole responsibility for feature programme output in the domestic and overseas services. With the coming of the Third Programme later the same year, that output was to be increased again.

My own position in the new dispensation was still that of Gilliam's deputy: I was not officially appointed Assistant Head of Features till later on. But in the autumn of 1945, we were both very much concerned with getting back feature stories from all over Europe. The coming of peace had opened up new possibilities of travel, and the new emphasis on international reporting was reflected in the series *Window on Europe* which I inaugurated.

My Norwegian programme had set the pattern, but this time I was to visit a country entirely new to me. In September 1945 I had written another dramatic poem for Douglass Montgomery, in which he played the part of an American soldier who fell in love with a young concert pianist from Prague. The part of the girl pianist was played by Hedda Ippen, a young Czech refugee in London; and reading up for the script, I found myself with an urge to visit Czechoslovakia. If only as a reader of the *Manchester Guardian*, I had been outraged by the shameful betrayal of Munich, and was anxious to know more about the country which had been first to fall under Nazi domination. The R.A.F. transport plane which flew me in to Prague was delayed by bad weather, and I arrived a day late on expectation. As a result, I found that the room which had been booked for me at the Alcron Hotel had been handed over to the Red Army. Indeed, Russians were everywhere: the streets were still paraded by them, and no accommodation was to be had in the entire city. I had only one potential friend in the place, to whom I had been recommended by Leonard Miall, who had recently found her in charge of Foreign Press relations. Her name was Alena Bernaškova, and she happened to be laid up with influenza somewhere in the outer suburbs. No taxis were to be had, the only available transport being the crowded tramcars, clanking around in almost total darkness. Standing in Wenceslas Square, and not at all sure of my direction, I shouted out to the milling crowds on the sidewalk, "Does anyone here speak English?" A dozen voices immediately answered "Yes," and I knew that I had fallen among friends. Once they had guided me to her, Alena's parents kindly found me a bed.

Even in those days, Czechoslovakia was a country of confused loyalties. Traditionally, she had always aligned herself with the West—but the West had abandoned her at Munich. Mostly, the country had been liberated by the Red Army, but the wild excesses of some of the Soviet troops had not endeared them to many people. In Prague, the Red Army officers were smart and well-behaved, apart from occasional outbursts of high spirits. But the earlier armies that had taken Slovakia and Moravia had fought their way across from the steppes around the Caspian, and some of them might have belonged to the Golden Horde of Genghis Khan. One still saw them around—slit-eyed Kirghiz and Kalmucks who had followed the war out of Asia—faces I was to see again years later, crossing the Khyber Pass with a string of Bactrian camels. Troops like those could hardly be expected to

observe the finer points of behaviour when they found themselves victorious in Central Europe.

As for the local politics, much as the middle-class people of
Prague and Brno might long for closer ties with the West again,
most of the peasantry had probably more in common with the
way of life in the East. The workers of the big industrial plants
were certainly largely Communist in their sympathies. Indeed,
the largest Communist parade that I have ever seen took place on
May Day in Wenceslas Square, shortly before the elections of
1946.* The vast square was blood red with the banners of the
marching comrades as they came down fifty abreast. I was not
surprised to hear that the Party had won the largest number of
seats at the polls—though still too few to form a government.
Nor was I surprised to hear that their guns had won control in the
coup d'état two years later . . .

But even back in 1945, the stories that I gathered in Czechoslovakia were nearly all of them ugly. Ever since the assassination
of Heydrich, the country had been at the mercy of the S.S. and
the Gestapo; and evidence of their methods was there for all to
see. I had been appalled in Norway to find the mass-produced
instruments of torture upon which they relied—the precision-
finished thumbscrews and kneecap-smashing vices. Somehow, I
had rather imagined that torture was a matter of sadistic improvisation. Not so with the S.S. and the Gestapo! With them it was
an exact science: their tools and instruments were carefully manufactured, with the same German efficiency as dentists' drills or
surgeons' scalpels. And the only gas that was *not* manufactured for
their convenience was any form of anaesthetic.

In the Pancrác Prison (now, of course, at the disposal of the
Russians) the Czechs showed me the only guillotine that I have

* A Czech friend from Bush House, by then in charge of news on the Czech radio, got
me a ringside seat for the occasion. It happened to be on the tribune of the Communist
Party high command, facing up the square. There I found myself taking the salute for six
hours along with Gottwald, Zapotocky, Slansky and the others.
I was a trifle embarrassed to see the newsreel cameramen taking shots of us all, and
imagined the surprise which my appearance in such company would arouse in the BBC
if I were recognised. Actually, I was not even introduced to Slansky, soon to be liquidated
for Western sympathies.

ever operated. It was installed in the Execution Suite, along with all the other necessary paraphernalia of death. I recorded a walk from room to room, illustrated by all the appropriate sounds. Here the sentence of death was pronounced . . . Here through this curtain in the next room (note the clinically bathroom acoustic of the tiled walls) the sentence was immediately carried out. If you were only a Jew, you mounted these wooden steps . . . Above your head was suspended this steel rail, which runs all round the walls . . . Just like the curtain-rail in your sitting-room, only stronger . . . Runners are on it, too—just as on *your* curtain-rail—you hear them? A noose was placed about your neck, then hooked onto the nearest runner . . . Then you were shoved off the steps—and carried off in the wake of your friends, to die kicking in slow strangulation . . . Up to fifteen minutes it sometimes took —but hear how *smoothly* the runner carries you off . . . Only if you were an Aryan—a Czech political hostage, perhaps—were you granted the privilege of being beheaded, over here in the centre of the room. This is the guillotine: you can hear them slowly winding the heavy blade up on its ratchet . . . You were strapped down on the bench, here . . . Your head now lay on this block . . . All that one had to do was just to jerk the trigger—so.

I like to think of that hundredweight blade crashing down in every comfortable sitting-room in Britain . . . Also the diminishing series of crashes as it bounced up four or five times on its heavy spring buffers—just to make sure that it severed any stray remaining sinews. All that they didn't hear was the thump of the head in the basket, and the blood gurgling down the drain to make fertiliser for Nazi crops—in the Reich that Hitler boasted would last for a thousand years.

For Gilliam's first post-war Christmas Day hook-up programme, I went on to Lidice. There I arranged a Christmas party for the few child survivors of the Lidice massacre: they had somehow been traced and brought back to new homes with friends near the razed village. They were all far too young to remember anything about the tragedy: some of them had been taken as far away as Germany, as so much potential slave labour.

The party was a huge success with all the children except one: he was much too young and scared to play with any of the others. They told me he had been used for medical experiments, and apart from his foster-father, I was the only one he would allow near him without crying. No doubt he recognised in me the only other person present who couldn't speak the Czech language—which he had still to learn . . .

From Czechoslovakia I went on to Jugoslavia, which I had seen before the war and wanted to visit again. There, the destruction and war chaos was worse than I had ever seen. Belgrade was still largely a shambles from the bombing attack of 1941, the ruins looking charred and blackened by contrast with the snow which lay over the whole city. I was well received by the Jugoslav authorities, being one of the first British radio men they had seen since the war. I was installed in due state at the Moskva Hotel, one of the few buildings in the entire city that was heated. I was followed there shortly after by Randolph Churchill who was writing a series of anti-Tito articles for an American newspaper syndicate. Hearing that I had a telephone in my room, he demanded one for himself. As no more telephones were available, he kindly had our Embassy suggest to the management that somebody should be moved . . . Arriving at the crucial moment, my guide and interpreter Dr. Vuksan went into battle in a way that left the Embassy in no doubt as to whose side Marshal Tito was on! "I told them," said my fiery Serb, "that there was no telephone in the room where Churchill was held prisoner during the war till the Partisans liberated him." I was no less grateful for the moral support than I was that night for my first square meal—when a friendly head waiter quietly slipped me a pound of *paté* wrapped up in a page of *Pravda*.

The patriotic fervour of the Jugoslav people during the first dark days after the war was truly memorable. An almost frenzied activity was to be seen on all sides, as they toiled day and night to get their country back on its feet again. Every morning I was wakened by singing parties of Partisans tramping off in the dark to some heavy task or other; and desperately bad as things were all over the country, nothing could withstand their tireless energy. No country in Europe had suffered so heavily in the war: a million and three-quarters of her people had died—or nearly an eighth of her total population. No country had been more fought over: the ruins of one village I visited had changed hands forty-five times in the course of the fighting—with German Nazis, Serbian Chetniks, Italian Fascists, Croat Ustachis and Tito's Partisans driving each other to and fro from one campaign to the next. The railway tracks of the entire country had been torn out with huge grapples, the rails sawn into short lengths, and every tunnel and bridge blown up by the retreating Germans. With virtually no equipment at their disposal, every re-opened sector of line was something of a national triumph.

They finished rebuilding a railway viaduct at Lašva while I was still in Belgrade, and I was duly invited to drive in the first train across it. Along with hundreds of cheering young Partisans, I made the trip out one Sunday in a special train emblazoned with a galaxy of red stars and waving banners. The viaduct crossed a narrow gorge, its two steel spans supported by a towering stone pier in the centre. Rebuilding the stone pier had been easy, but running a couple of thirty-ton steel spans out to it from the sides of the gorge had been rather more difficult. No cranes of any size were available, nor even a ready means of moving the spans out from the steelworks where they had been built. It was from the engineer responsible that I heard the story of how it had been done.

A locomotive tender is built to carry a load of ten tons, he explained: therefore three empty tenders had been adapted to carry each thirty-ton span, thus saving him twenty-five days waiting for heavy equipment from Croatia. By building great wooden trestles between the pier and the sides of the gorge, a temporary line had been run out across it. By halting the tenders and the load over the first trestle, the span could be anchored in the right position—and by taking the trestle away, and letting the tenders fall into the gorge, the span had been lowered onto its pier and buttress. A similar operation over the second trestle had

WAR'S END AND AFTER

completed the job in record time. And there I was, crossing the new viaduct in a train to prove it.

Anything less like orthodox engineering methods I couldn't imagine, but the bridge had certainly carried me safely over. I congratulated the engineer on his powers of improvisation, but asked him what would have happened if something had gone wrong. He gave me a rather pitying smile: "If something had gone wrong," he said, "I should have been shot, of course." I asked whether this didn't seem a trifle drastic, but apparently it didn't. "In the new Jugoslavia we can't afford to make mistakes," was his only comment.

I was to see more of the Partisans on a trip through Bosnia, where they were still under arms pending the final surrender of the last few Chetniks still in hiding. I was travelling by jeep with a girl from UNRRA, and suffering from a bad attack of flu, for the weather was sub-arctic. Our jeep finally ended up stuck in a deep snowdrift from which it was impossible to pull out. There we were soon discovered by a Partisan patrol, who quickly dragged us back onto the road. As the road itself was impassable, they offered to put us onto the night train for Belgrade, jeep and all. This we gladly accepted, but as there were still some fifteen hours to go before the train was due, they said that a party was necessary. Rustling up some food and a couple of gallons of slivović, the Partisans proceeded to throw one, singing, dancing and drinking the time away with us. Their leader told me that during the war he had operated a secret radio, passing messages over to the R.A.F. in Italy. His first duty had been to inform them whenever German supplies were halted in the marshalling-yard at the nearby Bosan-sky–Brod junction. For months there had been no heavy traffic, but at last the day had arrived: the yard was filled with German guns and equipment. He joyfully tapped out his code message, and waited for the coming attack. The very next night, it came: the sky was filled with the roar of the planes. They dropped their load of bombs—boom, boom, boom, boom—a wonderful thing to see! Unfortunately, they missed the marshalling-yard completely, but blew the Partisan's house to smithereens. To hear his roar of

129

laughter, and feel the slap on the back that he gave me, it might have been one of the funniest things that had ever happened to him. The British R.A.F. . . . ? They were wonderful!

With these sort of stories and many more that were less amusing, I was rather proud of the broadcast material that I brought back to London with me. I was the first BBC feature writer to report back from beyond the Iron Curtain, and I was only too anxious to get my story onto the air. Before writing my script, however, I decided to take out a little insurance. I went to my Controller (who shall be nameless) and asked for policy guidance. I pointed out that as Jugoslavia was a Communist country, anything that I said to her credit would run the risk of being denounced as Communist propaganda. My Controller looked rather worried: if I even said that the trams were running again in Belgrade—that would be Communist propaganda too . . . ! It might be called that, I conceded, and the trams certainly were. My Controller sucked at his pipe for a minute or two. At last a happy smile spread over his face: "Do you think," he enquired hopefully, "we really need to broadcast the programme at all?"

As it had been firmly agreed that I should make the trip; as it had taken a month to gather the material; as I had nearly frozen to death in the snow; and as it had cost a certain amount of money to bring me back alive, I was more than a little exasperated. I assured him that the programme *would* be broadcast, and suggested that someone had better look over my script before it was. In the event, the task fell to Sir William Haley again: as nobody else seemed anxious to accept the responsibility of passing judgment on it, the buck stopped on his desk. I was happy to learn that he wanted no more than half a line cut from my thirty foolscap pages; and as that represented only one unsubstantiated opinion, I accepted the cut without argument. I was happier still, after the transmission, to receive a cable of congratulation from my intrepid interpreter: the broadcast, he said, had been much appreciated in Belgrade.

During my tour of Jugoslavia, I had seen a great deal of the excellent work being done in the field by the medical teams of UNRRA—the United Nations Relief and Rehabilitation Administration. The inevitable aftermath of the war had been misery, poverty and disease, starvation and homelessness: UNRRA had gone in after the armies to try and cope with them all. Apart from the millions to be fed, the displaced and dispossessed had to be clothed and housed; medical supplies had to be distributed, clinics and rehabilitation centres set up. Industries which had been destroyed or had ground to a halt during the fighting had to be restarted, a task which called for the importation of millions of tons of machinery. Agriculture had to be made possible again in land which had been ruined or had been neglected and run to waste. All this was the duty of UNRRA, whose army of young helpers were scattered all over Europe making the work possible.

I was offered facilities to visit some of the places where work was being done, and glady agreed to tell over the air the story of what they were achieving. Starting in Holland, I made a forty-hour journey by truck convoy to Prague, with a cargo of frozen fish donated to Czechoslovakia by the people of Iceland. The drive took me through some of the shattered cities of Western Germany, where the utter devastation left by the bombing was a sight I am unlikely to forget. From Czechoslovakia, I went on to Vienna, still under quadripartite occupation by British, American, French and Russian troops. There the poverty and the hunger were rather more genteel than some I had seen in other places. Even the Red Army was in far more genial mood, and I spent amusing evenings drinking with them in the Russian sector. When I toured the Displaced Persons' Camps at Salzburg, on the other hand, I found the Polish, Baltic and Ukrainian nationals far from anxious to be sent back to new homes under Soviet rule.

From Austria, the journey took me by plane to Italy, where the damage and destruction left by the war was a sad reminder of all that civilisation can be made to suffer. I remember the hordes of orphaned children living in incredible squalor up in the caves above Naples and Carrara. I walked in the ruins of the monastery up at Montecassino, destroyed so needlessly in the assault on the

Gustav Line—along with the refugees who had taken shelter within its walls. By comparison with scenes like those, Rome was a haven of comfort, apart from the unemployment, the poverty and the hunger again. Florence had been far more badly damaged in the fighting, and there the tale was rather worse. But it was over in the slums of the Giudecca, the island across the canal from Venice, that I found the worst poverty of all. I well remember the wizened old woman whose last meal had been 'a walk round the table', but who was gratefully looking forward to her next. A butcher had given her one or two bones which she was getting ready to boil—bones which in England, as I remarked, would normally be given to a dog . . .

There were sad and demoralising things to report from Europe during the first years of peace. It remained my duty—sometimes a very sad one—to report on many infinitely more tragic than any I have mentioned here.

6

Southern hemisphere

IN 1947, I exchanged the rigours of life in post-war Europe for a pleasant interlude in Lotus-land, being sent by the BBC to write background features to the Royal Tour of South Africa by King George VI and Queen Elizabeth. One can have little idea of the creature comforts enjoyed by the wealthier citizens of classical Greece and Rome until one has seen what is still to be had in an even kinder climate and thanks to the servitude of an even larger labour force of helots. Unfortunately, though it is dotted with swimming-pools, Afrikanerdom has produced little else of cultural importance. Few people, I fancy, would ever describe Johannesburg as the Athens of the South. Most of its inhabitants were proud to describe it as Little New York, though to my way of thinking it was far more like Little Atlanta or Little Dallas.

Even so, as a place to visit, the then Dominion provided a very pleasant nirvana, and the generous hospitality that I enjoyed there was of a kind that had been impossible in Britain since before the war. As the guest of the South African Broadcasting Corporation, I was looked after particularly well and found myself in what must have been the most congenial company I could have hoped for.* Much interest was expressed in the sort of programmes I was out there to produce, their own work in the feature field having only just begun; and one of the tasks for which I was inducted was to act as adjudicator for a features competition which they arranged during my stay.

But by far the most interesting man that I met was Hugh

* The most talented of their own staff writers was Denis Mitchell. A few years later he came back to England, and I managed to get him appointed to my old job of Features Assistant in the North Region. He was soon to make a name for himself with an outstanding series of television documentaries.

Tracey, the African musicologist. He was almost the only white South African who seemed to be vitally interested in the remarkable culture of the African people themselves. He was a pioneer in the recording of African music, his work in the field being now recognised as highly important. It was to him that I owed what little insight I acquired into the wonders of African music and dancing, and his respect for the Bantu peoples was in strange contrast to the indifference or contempt in which they were held by almost everyone else.

The racial situation in South Africa, indeed, was something which I found very hard to accept. Nor have I ever been in a country where I had to think so carefully before I expressed an opinion on racial matters. To have spoken out honestly would have involved me in endless arguments with my hosts, if not in downright brawls. As neither was likely to be constructive, I eventually decided to concentrate on what I was supposed to be doing, until such time as I could do something better more effectively. The fact that I disliked a great deal of the political thinking even of Smuts's moderate government was neither here nor there so long as I had more urgent things to write about: I was quite prepared to cope with it later on. Meanwhile, there was much that was colourful and remarkable to be enjoyed, and my six-months' visit passed all too quickly. As the Royal Family probably agreed, South Africa was a fascinating country—for us.

My assignment did not tie me down to regular daily reporting: that was the business of the BBC news correspondents Frank Gillard, Wynford Vaughan-Thomas and Robert Dunnett. My own task was to keep ahead of events and come up every so often with large-scale feature programmes to focus attention on some of the more impressive high-spots. As one comical Afrikaaner mayor explained it to his dorp, I was there "to forestall the Royal Tour."

My first commitment was to arrange yet another unusual item for Gilliam's round-the-world Christmas Day programme. This I did with a team of incredible Bantu dancers from the compound of one of the Rand gold mines—my first initiation into the excitement of African tribal dancing and the Mchopi orchestra. It provided a strange contrast to the Christmas party the previous year at Lidice. After that, I was free to travel the Union on my own account, gathering the material for my curtain-raiser to the Royal Tour, *This is South Africa*. The programme did not have to be very remarkable to emerge as the most elaborate production yet mounted in the Johannesburg studios. By the time it was broadcast from London, I was again down in Cape Town waiting for the arrival of the Royal Family.

The landing itself I watched from the roof of a skyscraper block in the city centre, with a wide panoramic view over the harbour. At first one could see nothing but the morning haze, for white mist lay over the sea like the long cloud upon Table Mountain. One simply knew that somewhere out there lay H.M.S. *Vanguard*, latest and most powerful battleship in the world. I had already been in radio contact with Frank Gillard who was on board, but waiting for the first sight of her was still intriguing enough. Slowly a shadow gathered amid the whiteness, and emerging like the Flying Dutchman—only in almost un- bearably slow motion—the giant ship hove into full view and eased in silently to the quayside. Looking back on that splendid sight, it is ironic to remember that *Vanguard* has long since been broken up for scrap, without having fired a shot in anger. As Ezra Pound once pointed out—like fruit and vegetables, battleships are perishable commodities. At the time of writing, at least, the Royal Family is still with us; and the young girl that I watched stepping ashore is now Queen Elizabeth II.

Apart from such parties and gatherings as I felt like attending, I was spared the boredom of following in the wake of the royal progress, and quickly flew on to Durban, where I could get to work on my next production. I had already been out and about with one of the BBC recording trucks, and had cut a number of highly interesting discs in what was then Basutoland. But the recordings that I now went on to make in Zululand were more unusual. The country proved to be rolling grassland, the valleys planted with mealies and the hillsides dotted with copses of wattle.

Here and there were the Zulu kraals, their beautiful beehive huts round and neat as upturned wicker baskets, fenced in with protective hedges of cactus and bundu thorn. The Zulus themselves—the people of Heaven, in their own language—were tall and muscular, a nation of born warriors who still lived a tribal and patriarchal existence in their own territory. I was received regally enough at the Royal Kraal by the Zulu Chief Nkantini, who traced his descent from Umpande, the brother of the Zulu King Dingaan, whose massacre of Pier Retief and his party was avenged by the Boers at the battle of Blood River. He was an oldish man, grey haired, heavily built and run to fat in his riding breeches and leggings. I made him a gift of blankets, and my praises were sung by the royal bard. The recital went on for twenty minutes, which rather astounded me, until I learnt that I only rated the first three lines, the rest of the poem being devoted to Nkantini himself.

Even so, he gave me permission to record the songs of the womenfolk of his household and the play-songs of his naked children. During this performance, he sat and drank his beer from a huge earthenware jar, surrounded by his obsequious warriors: it was beneath his dignity to take any interest in the proceedings. Without his knowledge, however, I had recorded some of his conversation; and in due course I invited the assembled company to hear it played back over our loudspeaker. At the sound of their master's voice, the whole gathering burst into shrieks of laughter. At first, the Chief failed to recognise himself, but when at last he did he was equally amused. As one more useless example of white man's magic, recording at least appealed to the Zulu sense of the ridiculous.

Only one little incident upset the royal equanimity. Our recordings were cut on acetate discs, and the thread grooved out by the cutter head had soon coiled up on the ground like so many small bundles of shiny black candyfloss. As these were highly inflammable, and children might play with them in the heat of the sun, our usual practice was to burn them before they burnt up anyone else. This the recording engineers, Lew Lewis

and Bob Wade, punctiliously proceeded to do. A blaze of flame
shot up, and an acrid cloud of yellow smoke blew over and en-
veloped the Chief. Coughing and spluttering, he leapt to his feet
with a murderous glare of anger: his royal dignity had been insulted! His warriors leapt to their feet as well, and for a moment
there was high tension in the air. The fire died down again, the
smoke drifted away and profuse apologies were offered by the
three of us through our interpreter. Perhaps it was just as well that
Zulus were no longer allowed to carry arms except on cere-
monial occasions: an assegai might have done me no good that
morning . . .

But it was the Royal Dance at Eshowe that provided the
climax to my Zululand excursion. Thirty thousand people had
converged on the town for the *Indaba*, at which they were to see
their King and Queen for the first time. The dance itself, the
Ngoma Umkosi, was only performed on royal occasions. It had
been danced before Chaka, founder of the Zulu nation—the so-
called Black Napoleon for whom over a million warriors had
cheerfully laid down their lives.

To watch the dance, the crowd had assembled at first light,
thronging around the open arena in their thousands. The night
before they had feasted upon three hundred head of cattle,
donated by the Union Government, in a wood outside the
little town. The blaze of hundreds of fires among the trees, the
growling song of the crowd, the bellowing of the cows waiting
to be slaughtered, the carnage and the smell of burning flesh in the
darkness was something reminiscent of Dante's Inferno. But out
there in the sunlight, wearing their full war-dress, the Zulus were
a truly magnificent sight. Hemmed in by the vast crowd, they
advanced upon the royal dais from the far end of the arena, their
piebald oxhide shields a moving wall of white and black and
brown against the dark sepia of their bodies, their ostrich plumes
and sakabula feathers tossing amid a bristle of waving knob-
kerries. Their dance was a slow, rhythmical stamping of feet
woven about the ground bass of a growlingly intoned chorus.

After the men, it was the turn of the women, and to them the day really belonged. They flooded onto the field in so many dark waves, their bodies bare to the waist, their necks festooned with white and coloured intricacies of beadwork, their loins gay with beaded aprons. As they came on, the field rang with their shrill cries, their glistening breasts bounding and slapping against their bodies in a staccato accompaniment to the prancing of their feet. By comparison, the stately dance of the warriors seemed stumbling and half-hearted.

Finally, as the women retired, the impis gathered for their charge—the *ukuqubula*. Their ranks drawn up behind their shields, their weapons raised in a shout of battle, they charged headlong towards the royal dais. The earth rumbled under the flailing of a thousand feet, and the shields clattered as they came racing on. Stopping dead in their tracks a few yards before the Royal Family, they shouted their *isaga*—the war-cry of the Zulu. They gripped their shields and beat them with the shafts of their assegais, and the noise was like a volley of gunfire. Raising their shields aloft, they shouted out their royal salute—*Bayete! Bayete! Bayete!*

All this made for some exciting recordings, but for me, the most memorable figure of the day was an old Zulu warrior that Wynford and I saved from being trampled to death by the crowd. He must have been ninety years old, and having waited in the heat of the sun for upwards of four hours, at last could stand it no longer. Squatting down on the grass, he was suddenly engulfed in a frenzied scramble of bare legs as the crowd surged forward to catch a glimpse of the royal arrival. Seizing him by his arms, we managed to drag him back onto his feet and fought our way through the crowd with him to the barrier. Exhausted as he was, he was a man of great natural dignity; his cropped hair was iron-grey under its circling head-ring, his beard was stubbly and grizzled, his brown body as wrinkled as the bark of an oak-tree. In his fist he was still clutching his shield and knobkerry, as we held him up at the rail for a ringside view of the slowly approaching cavalcade. Standing erect and resplendent in their open car, the King and Queen passed within two or three yards of us, and the old man's eyes glazed in silent wonder. Later, a Zulu police-man told us that he had fought against the British at Isandlhwana. He had walked thirty miles from his kraal to pay respect to the throne whose armies he had defeated sixty-eight years before.

Like those I had made in Basutoland, the recordings for my programme *The Zulus* were unusual and fascinating. Those cut that day at the Eshowe *Indaba* were irreplaceable, for the *Ngoma Umkosi* will never be danced for a British sovereign again, if it is ever danced at all. But by order of some BBC administrator, all the recordings were again destroyed—with the exception of some 30-second extracts which served merely to remind one how irreparable was the loss of the remainder.

My admiration for the Zulu race did not prevent me also admiring the pioneer achievements of the nineteenth-century Voortrekkers. The story of their withdrawal from British rule in the Cape Province during the eighteen-thirties, to found their Boer Republics of the Transvaal and the Orange Free State many hundreds of miles to the North, was a subject for radio treatment after my own heart. Before leaving South Africa, I wrote it up in my verse feature *The Great Trek*, a programme which sought to catch the spirit of the adventure. Set against the background of the Karroo, the Drakensburg and the High Veldt, it echoed to the crack of rawhide whips and the lumbering exodus of the tented ox-waggons. Retelling the story of the massacre of Retief at Umgungindhlovu and the victory of Andries Pretorius at Blood River, it made colourful listening. That the national epic of the Boers should be written up for them by an Englishman appeared to surprise and gratify the Afrikaners. I gather that after I had returned to London, the programme became something of an annual event in South Africa and has been repeated many times over the last twenty years.

But whatever my admiration for the Afrikaner's fight for national survival in the nineteenth century, I had none at all for his refusal to move on into the twentieth. Although there was no *apartheid* policy under the government of Jan Smuts, this was obviously coming with the first return to power of the Nationalist Party of Dr. Malan. As it was, the plight of the Bantu people in the Union was bad enough, to say nothing of the Indians and the Cape Coloureds. Their wages were scandalously low, they were harassed by the Pass Laws and forced to live in the labour compounds or in the disgraceful shanty-towns that went by the name of 'locations'. They had no share at all in the government of their own country or the social amenities which their own labour provided. With a view to calling attention to all this, on my return to London in the summer of 1947, I wrote an account of South African racial policy for the documentary series *Focus*. In that programme I stated the relevant facts as I had been quietly collecting them during my stay in the Union.

In order to obtain some statistics that had not yet been published, I applied to South Africa House. The figures were duly supplied, but I was asked why I required them. When I explained that they were needed for a broadcast, I was politely asked for a copy of the script. Although under no obligation to show them one, I certainly had nothing in it that I wanted to conceal, and sent one round to them forthwith. I can only describe the result as in the nature of a mild explosion.

As I refused to discuss with them the propriety of writing such a programme, explaining that BBC policy was decided by other people and that my job was merely to conform to it, an official deputation arrived at Broadcasting House led by the Assistant High Commissioner in person. Demanding to see the Director-General, they were received by Basil Nicolls in his capacity as Director of Programmes. Before receiving them, however, Nicolls had asked for my assurance that the broadcast was in every way factually correct. I told him that to the best of my belief it was: I had been particularly careful to check every fact that had gone into it. In any case, I willingly agreed to accept any corrections of fact that South Africa House could give me. At the same time, I very much doubted whether accuracy was the real point at issue.

It wasn't. The only object of the visit was to get the broadcast taken off the air entirely—due to go out as it was the same evening. With Haley's full support, this was a request that Nicolls was not prepared to meet. The broadcast, he said, was a matter of public interest: factual accuracy was all that he was prepared to discuss. The main objection lay, of course, in their knowledge that the broadcast *was* factually accurate: what they were hoping for was a discreet suppression of the facts. On this point, Nicolls stood quite firm. The only concession that he was prepared to make was to include—at equal length—an attempted rebuttal by the High Commissioner of my quote from Mrs. Pandit's blistering indictment of South Africa's racial policy before the General Assembly of the United Nations. This I was only too happy to include.

The deputation finally left after uttering a quite remarkable threat: as the Prime Minister himself was out of the country at the time, they proposed to approach his Deputy, Herbert Morrison, and ask him to instruct the Postmaster-General to take the BBC transmitter off the air in the interests of Commonwealth solidarity! They were told, rather coolly, that they were quite at liberty to do so.

The news of this development reached me while my rehearsal was still in progress, and added a certain piquancy to the proceedings. When the show came up for transmission that evening, I was still unsure whether or not it would be heard. So, apparently, was the Director-General, who had admitted that he would be listening with equal interest! I am happy to report that the broadcast went out without interruption. But I was later informed that the ensuing correspondence between the Union and Downing Street had gone on—also without interruption—for some time. Even so, at no stage was my statement of the facts challenged in any way. Nor was I once blamed for having stirred up such an unholy ruckus.

My next major production was rather less controversial. In November 1947, the BBC celebrated it twenty-fifth birthday, and a week of celebratory broadcasting was planned. The honour of opening the festival fell to me, with a feature tracing the growth of radio from the early days of Savoy Hill to the high point of popularity which it then enjoyed. I had myself been broadcasting regularly for over half the period, so had no lack of experience to draw upon. The previous year, the Third Programme had been inaugurated and the BBC Television Service had been resumed after its wartime suspension. All in all, there was much to celebrate, and such as they were, the BBC Sound Archives were there to draw upon for recordings. My programme *Mirror of our Times* was nostalgic and proved to be unusually popular. So far as I was concerned, its most outstanding ingredient was the ironic and beautifully spoken narration of Robert Donat.

Donat did many programmes with me before his far too early death, and was one of my most valued friends. Unknown to either of us at the time, we had grown up quite close to each other in Manchester, even using the same local in Lapwing Lane, West Didsbury. We came to address each other as Cousin Geoff and Cousin Bob and shared the same affectionate remembrance of the North. Before I grew my beard, there was even something of a resemblance between us—in build and colouring, at least— and both took very kindly to John Glyn Jones's remark that our mothers had probably known the same man.

Donat was a superb reader of poetry, and there was more warmth and sensitivity in his performances than in those of almost any other actor with whom I have worked. There was nothing which he could do for me that he ever willingly refused, though his long battle against asthma prevented him from doing as much for anyone as he wished. Towards the end, he came to the studio looking so ill that I sometimes could hardly recognise him. But the good humour was always there, and the stories he used to regale me with remained as amusing as ever. Just as it was always well to the fore in his affections, Manchester was always somewhere there at the back of his voice: we could neither of us get drinking together for long without becoming broader and broader in our accents. Indeed, some of the greatest roles that he played were North Country character parts; and his

dialect anecdotes were among my happiest memories of him.*
I followed up my birthday tribute to broadcasting with something a little more polemical. I had long wanted to write another
ballad-opera, and building upon the theme of life in the coal
towns that I knew, I sat down to write *Johnny Miner*. The hero of
the work, Johnny himself, was an archetypal figure—the essence
of pitmen everywhere—and his story followed the fortunes of the
miner from the bad old days of the early nineteenth century up to
the recent nationalisation of the mines. The scene was set in the
Durham coalfield that I knew best, and the show was played and
sung in the good rich Durham dialect. The selection of the folk-
tunes was made for me by A. L. Lloyd, the arrangements being
by the Hungarian composer Matyas Seiber; the songs were sung
by Owen Brannigan, Marjorie Westbury and others, the choruses
being taken by the Opera Group of the Workers' Music Association under the leadership of Alan Bush. It was a lively, rumbus-
tious show and despite its Geordie gutturals was well received
by the listeners. It was not nearly so well received by the ex-coalowners and their friends, however, who were still carrying on a
rearguard action against the nationalisation issue. They initiated
another long correspondence against me with the BBC, in which
my ex-Director-General Sir Robert Foot may or may not have
participated. At least, I again had the support of my then Director-
General, and correspondence notwithstanding, the programme
was soon repeated. It was also staged by the Workers' Music
Association in the London Steiner Hall, but by then I was out of
the country again.

At the end of 1947, I was sent out to Australia and New Zealand, where I was to work for the next eight months. Another

* I particularly enjoyed the story about his landlady at the theatrical digs in Ackers
Street, where he liked to stay when returning to Manchester on tour. Bringing his breakfast up on a tray, she pulled back the curtains and gazed out bleakly from his bedroom
window. All that could be seen was the roof of the Church of the Holy Name, grey with
sooty snow. After a long silence, she turned away with a weary shake of her head. "Come
day, go day," she mused, "I've etten as much rice-puddin' in mi time as ud *cover* yon
church!" She marched out of the room, leaving Bob to make what he could of the
thought.

Royal Tour was in the offing,* and this time I was given a chance
to stockpile my background features before it actually began. The
Australian Broadcasting Commission were themselves preparing
to form a Features Department under the direction of John Proud,
and it was thought that I might be able to help in setting a few
patterns and coming up with occasional advice.

Australia was a country to which I found myself warmly
drawn from the start. I liked the dry humour and the independent
spirit of the people, their hearty don't-give-a-damn attitude to
life and the sheer gusto which went into everything they did—
particularly eating and drinking. Sydney, where I spent most of
my time, had one of the loveliest settings of any city I had visited.
It was also one of the liveliest places that I knew outside America,
and I soon had a wide circle of friends. Even the BBC's Australian
Representative, Neil Hutchison, was an old pre-war crony of
mine from our days together in the North Region. In due course,
I moved in with him and his wife at Double Bay, after sharing
Dick Bentley's flat with the actor Gordon Chater, while Bentley
was over in London with Jimmy Edwards in *Take It From Here*.

The parting words in London from my Controller, Richard
Howgill, had been a quiet hope that I wouldn't annoy the Australians as much as I had annoyed the South Africans.† But this
I proceeded to do with my very first programme, *An Englishman
looks at Sydney*—at least, I annoyed a few of them. Liking the
place as I did, I still reserved the right to take the mickey out of
it now and again; and there were many things in Sydney which
exasperated my friends there no less than they exasperated me. I
disliked not being able to entertain my girl friends in the public
bars. I disliked still more the habit of closing all bars at six o'clock
in the evening, as they then did. With so much wonderful food
to cook, I rather deplored the passion for endless mutton chops

* This had to be postponed on account of the illness of King George VI the following
year.

† He was still involved in correspondence with them over the *Focus* programme.
Correspondence with the ex-coalowners was apparently being coped with by Lindsay
Wellington, by then the Controller of the Home Service. I was happy to be a party to
neither activity.

and steaks embellished with fried eggs. I didn't like tea with every meal, and with so much excellent Australian wine to be had, I couldn't understand why so few people appeared to drink it. I was irritated by the way that Australian waiters asserted their independence (which I liked) by taking it out on the diners (which I did not), especially if the diners happened by any chance to be Pommy bastards. Just because it was warm and sunny, I didn't see why Australian girls should spend most of their lives on their backs—at any rate, on Bondi Beach. As for Australian commercial radio, I disliked its fatuous jingles as much as I dislike the jingles on commercial television in Britain today. Apart from which little quirks, I liked life in Sydney enormously—and said so loud and clear in my broadcast.

My friends, of course, shared most of my quirks with me, and enjoyed the programme accordingly. But commercial radio's high priests—naturally enough—took grave exception to the mock jingles in doubtful taste with which I peppered it at their expense. Rather more unexpectedly, the Australian Minister for Immigration personally complained to the ABC's General Manager about my skit on truculent service at some of the Sydney restaurants: this, he averred, was likely to cause a falling-off in the needed flow of British immigrants to the Dominion! It apparently never occurred to him to complain to the restaurants direct . . .

I was on safer ground with my next programme, *The River*. To gather material for it, I had to travel some three thousand miles— by plane and train, by motor-coach, on horseback and by river steamer. The programme traced the course of the Murray River from Mount Kosciusko and the headwaters of the Snowy, along the borders of New South Wales and Victoria, across the sandy wilderness of the Mallee and down to the open sea in South Australia. Although it was largely concerned with all that irrigation was doing to open up the country, *The River* also gave me an opportunity to attempt a panoramic impression of the Australian landscape. From the screaming parrots of the gum-forests in the mountains to the huge white pelicans down by the estuary, it also dwelt on the vividly exotic wild-life of the continent. The strangely evocative scene-painting of the special music composed for the programme by John Antill was one of its major pleasures for me.*

My stay in Australia happened to coincide with the making of Harry Watt's film, *Eureka Stockade*, for Ealing Pictures. The script of the film should have been written by Cecil McGivern who had recently joined them; but on his declining the assignment, it was taken on by another early friend of mine, Walter Greenwood. Although I just missed Walter, I saw a good deal of Harry Watt, whose recent success, *The Overlanders*, had probably been the finest film made in Australia up to that time. *Eureka Stockade* proved to be disappointing by comparison; but as Harry Watt was the first to admit, he far preferred directing cows to directing actors and actresses. Even so, I much enjoyed the time that I spent with him on location at Singleton, where he was shooting. There I found Ralph Truman, Jane Barrett and other radio friends from London. There also I met up with the gaunt and incomparable Chips Rafferty, and a young actor called Peter Finch.

Although he had only a small part in the film, Finch was already well respected in Sydney, where he was heard regularly on the air. Indeed, he won the radio award as actor of the year while he was still filming. He was also to be seen playing in his own productions at a theatre club where he was discovered by Laurence Olivier. In due course he was to play the lead for me in both *Australian Rhapsody* and *Ballarat*, the two Australian shows that I most enjoyed writing. Back in London, we soon became good friends.

My play *Ballarat* told the story of the Australian gold-rush of 1851, and the effect that it had on the lives of two young immigrants who got caught up in the gold fever. In a very different way, it covered much of the same historical ground as *Eureka*

* Antill and I later collaborated in mounting my verse programme *Australian Rhapsody*, his brilliant score for which was the best thing of his I had heard since his *Corroboree* suite fascinated me in a Promenade Concert at the Albert Hall.

Stockade, the pitched battle for which provided it with its climax. While he was shooting the cavalry attack on the stockade, Watt allowed me to cut sound for my own production—a facility much appreciated by the galloping Aussie troopers, who finding me crouched in the grass with my microphone as they thundered past, playfully took a swing at my head with their sabres. All in all, with another platoon of soldiers digging up acres of ground for me, with stockmen cracking their whips, bullockies driving their waggons and miners cradling pay-dirt, *Ballarat* contained some of the most evocative sound that I ever cut. The programme was liked in London for its wholly Australian authenticity, and praised in the *New Statesman* for conveying (as I had also tried to do in *The Great Trek*) the colour and movement of an American Western, "than which," their critic declared, "I can imagine nothing more difficult to do in the medium." Difficult or not, it was something that I enjoyed attempting.

In all my Australian productions, I was much worried by the fact that programme engineering work was handled for me not by ABC personnel, but by casual staff from the Post Office. This was apparently accepted as part of the Australian way of radio life, but was rather unnerving to anyone brought up on the far stricter standards of programme engineering in the BBC. The handling of the dramatic control panel is of vital importance to any major feature production, and calls for long experience in interpreting the producer's instructions. Music, speech and sound have to be blended with the utmost sensitivity, or the dramatic effectiveness of the whole production can be thrown off balance and ruined.

I was alarmed, therefore, when my first Post Office engineer (I think he was normally a telephone operator) came in to my rehearsal, examined the control panel, and asked me how it worked. As the whole show was to be carried by him, this was to my mind rather like being asked by the pilot how to fly an air-liner. After I had shown him what was involved (and suffered agonies correcting his mistakes) I was more alarmed still when he left immediately before the transmission, having handed over to his cobber who was just coming on shift! In the nature of things, even a highly trained BBC panel operator requires a couple of dress rehearsals before he can be sure of controlling a complicated show correctly. On this occasion, as there was no time to do more than give the new engineer a marked script, I looked forward to having a month's work completely wrecked and a few hundred pounds' worth of programme budget poured down the drain. Although it was some six years since I had operated my own control panel in London, my old feel for it was luckily somewhere in reserve. As the engineer was as scared of the job as I was of leaving it to him, we finally handled it between us—in defiance of every union regulation. To my agonized relief, we got the programme onto the air without any major disaster.

Apart from such little hazards, my spell with the ABC was a very enjoyable one. Their General Manager, then Colonel, now Sir Charles Moses, was by far the most companionable top executive that I have worked along with. He had a magnificent physique, his favourite hobby being tree-felling. Indeed, he was the only head of a broadcasting organisation that I have ever known to keep a lumberman's axe in his office sharp enough to shave the hair off his fore-arm. Our tastes in food and wine and cigars were very much the same, and we spent many long nights indulging them. As a visiting fireman, I was able to help him persuade his Commissioners to agree to the ABC building up a Features Department in Sydney on the same lines as our own in London. During my stay in the country, I was thus able to hear many good programmes put out by the new school of Australian radio writers. Two of the best of them, John Thompson and Mungo McCallum, were later to join us in London for a year or two.

The night that I had arrived in Australia, the ABC had broadcast a new production of *Aaron's Field* to welcome me, and, by an odd coincidence, Third Programme had revived it a couple of days after I set out. At both ends, it still appeared to be wearing reasonably well. What was more encouraging still, the ABC asked me to follow it up with my own production of *The*

Builders, which they had already broadcast when the BBC had taken it off the air. This was a project to which I was looking forward with some enthusiasm. A jinx was still haunting the play, however, and at the critical moment I went down with a bad attack of mumps, my only consolation being that I contracted the disease in the nicest possible way. Retiring to bed with the collected works of Henry James, I waited for my swollen face to assume its normal proportions again. Viewing it in the glass every so often, as the stubble spread into a gingery and inverted halo, I finally decided to keep the best and throw away only the sideburns. Apart from one short interlude, I have worn a beard ever since.

When I first emerged with it, I must admit that my beard passed without much notice. Every actor in Sydney had grown a larger one for a bit-part in *Eureka Stockade*; casting for which, they told me sarcastically, was now complete. At least I was able to wear it to the final rehearsal of *The Builders*, production of which had been taken over for me by the ABC drama producer, Paul O'Laughlin. I can only say that he made as good a job of mounting the show as I had hoped to do myself; and I much enjoyed the belated pleasure of hearing it on the air for the first time.

Along with such legendary stalwarts as Sid Deemer and Cyril Pearl, two of my closest friends in Sydney were Wilfrid Thomas and Bettina Dickson. I spent most weekends with them at their summer place on Pitt Water, where Chips Rafferty and others of the film colony were to be found. It was there that I first ate rock-oysters and barbecued steak with Joe Fallon, whose cooking, as I learn from the newspapers, is equally dear to the Duke of Edinburgh. When I left Australia for New Zealand, Wilfrid Thomas accompanied me on the tour, broadcasting his weekly letter back to the ABC in his capacity as the Australian Alistair Cooke. We were handsomely received in Wellington by the NZBS (as it then was) who took it upon themselves to show us all over the Dominion.*

* Our guide was the genial Gilbert Stringer, who is now the Director-General of the New Zealand Broadcasting Corporation.

After the dried-up vastness of Australia, New Zealand proved to be rather more English in its appeal. Indeed, everything had been done to make it so, even to the extent of importing English sparrows. Unfortunately, they had not imported the best features of the English weekend, their own being quite the driest and dullest that I ever experienced. But if the odour of sanctity was a trifle overpowering in Wellington, Christchurch and Dunedin, the Dominion could be delightful elsewhere. Once one had crossed the South Island by the spectacular Arthur's Pass and begun to explore the fjords and glaciers of the west coast, one found oneself in a new Norway. But this was a Norway buried beneath a riot of tropical vegetation and tree-ferns. The spectacular had taken on a new strangeness, and I can remember no scenery anywhere which had more to offer by way of the exotic, and the almost impenetrable. It was a fit setting for Butler's *Erewhon*.

But it was among the Maoris of the North Island that I found the most dramatic radio. Theirs was a new landscape again, one shaken by earthquakes and volcanic eruption, and bursting out incessantly in geysers and boiling springs.

Physically, the Maoris are among the most handsome people in the world; their dignity and courtesy are inimitable, their friendliness engaging and their culture magnificent. In little over a century they have made the jump from the stone age of Polynesia to the age of nuclear physics; they have produced their own statesmen, scientists, artists, poets and scholars from a total population of no more than sixty thousand. After the Maori Wars of the last century they have settled down in perfect harmony with the white New Zealanders—the *pakeha*—and live with them on terms of equality. New Zealand may well be proud of her racial policy, for she has never had one. None has ever been thought necessary.

I was entertained by the Maori farmers around Rotorua at a *hangi*★ feast laid on by thirty or forty of them, and the same evening

★ The meal was cooked in *hangi*—pits dug in the ground in which fires were kindled. Large flat stones were left in the fire until they were red hot, then damped down with wet flax mats and ferns. Meat and *kumara* were laid on the steaming heap, covered over with ferns once more, then finally sodded over and left to cook in the trapped steam for a couple of hours.

a special dance was arranged for me to record in the Maori Meeting House at Ohinemutu. The beautiful blood-red building, its vast gable carved and glittering with *paua* shells, was itself a notable example of Maori architecture. As for the crowd inside, both men and women had come in their traditional dress: huia feathers, kiwi cloaks, flax kilts and pui pui skirts. The brown bodies and gaily coloured costumes made graceful patterns against the scarlet and white and black of the decorated walls.

The Maori *haka* or war-chant I had first heard as a boy, performed by the All Black rugby team when Nepia was in his glory. But roared out there that evening in the echoing hall, the *haka* was far more menacing. With bare feet stamping, eyes bulging out of their sockets and tongues curling half-way round to their ears, the kilted Maoris whipped themselves into a frenzy, the whole building shaking to the pounded and shouted rhythm. I was reminded of the old Icelandic berserkers, who gnawed half through their shields in battle anger. Perhaps the resemblance was not too fanciful either, for the trans-Atlantic voyaging of the Vikings and the trans-Pacific voyaging of the Maoris were equally far-ranging and equally incredible.

The Maoris, indeed, provided a fitting climax to my happy discovery of the Southern Hemisphere, and were featured in two popular broadcasts. I can only wish once more that the fascinating recordings they made for me were still in existence to be heard, but administration triumphed again. As it was, I was proud to accept blood-brotherhood with them that evening, and the Maori tiki I brought back with me I am still wearing after twenty years.*

---

* There is only one finer tiki that I know in London, which belongs to my Maori friend, Inia Te Wiata, whose rich bass voice is well known to Covent Garden. After our Maori broadcasts together, he gave a most poignant performance as Enkidu in my verse drama, *The Quest of Gilgamesh.*

7

Round and about

ON MY RETURN from New Zealand, I went to stay with
Laurence and Marianne Gilliam in Highgate. We had been close
friends for a long time, and my marriage having just broken up,
I was temporarily without a home of my own. All of us finding
the company congenial, I found myself living with them for the
next three years. Marianne kept an excellent home and Gilliam
himself was devoted to good living: I was only too happy to
enjoy my fair share of both to the full. In any case, the arrange-
ment was convenient from the point of view of BBC work.
Gilliam was due for attachment to the Television Service, which
he was later expected to join. In his absence I would be running
the Features Department for him, and we should have many
things to talk over in the evenings.

Cecil McGivern, who had worked with me in the North and
then joined me in London, had just returned to the BBC after his
short sojourn with Ealing Studios as a scriptwriter. His couple of
years there had not proved very fruitful: in fact, he had written
virtually nothing for them at all. But his experience in the film
world had given him some insight into the running of a visual
medium. At Basil Nicolls's instance, he had been offered the job
of Controller of BBC Television—which he had gladly accepted—
and over the next few years, his great gifts as an organiser were
to be much in evidence. While television was still being run on a
shoestring, McGivern succeeded in laying the real foundations of
the BBC Television Service as we know it today.

Why Gilliam failed to join him permanently in that task is one
of those mysteries which I never managed to solve. I gathered
from Gilliam himself that he was not over anxious to serve under

someone who had lately been on his own staff. I think it equally likely that McGivern was rather chary of embarrassing himself with such a forceful and capable back-seat driver: no doubt he felt that their roles might shortly have to be reversed. The fact remains that Gilliam's marriage with television was never consummated, and was finally annulled. After kicking his heels around Lime Grove for a year, he returned to his favourite hobby of energising radio features.

Gilliam's work for radio during and immediately after the war had been outstanding. His flair for initiating ambitious and costly projects would seem to have been uniquely right for a new and expanding medium like television. He was a man born to be lavish; he had grown up in a rapidly expanding market, and one which could always afford to indulge imaginative planning. But in 1949, television had not yet reached that point; it had not even begun to pay its way. It may well have been felt by the BBC that someone rather more cautious was needed there for the moment, and in Cecil McGivern that caution and painstaking attention to detail could certainly be found. Radio, on the other hand, was still very much at its peak: there was yet plenty to be done for it on the scale which Gilliam understood. Even so, he returned to his old job with obvious disappointment.

Despite the administrative chores with which I found myself saddled during his absence from the department, I had continued to write and produce my normal quota of programmes. And for Christmas 1948 I wrote my modern nativity play *The Christmas Child*, in which I returned nostalgically to the Northern scene. The story was that of a typical family in one of my favourite Cotton Towns, and the scene was set on Christmas Eve. Joe the husband and Mary his wife are anxiously expecting the birth of their first child. Lizzie and Zachary have been in to wish them well after supper, and while Joe is seeing them off, Mary falls down in a fainting fit. She dreams that she is the Virgin Mary at Bethlehem and that her child has just been born. She is visited by Tom Shepherd, Billy Spinner and Johnny Miner, who sadly remember how their own sons have all been killed—by malnutrition during the Depression, by an accident in the pit, or fighting in the last war.* Three Wise Men—the Statesman, the Economist and the Sociologist—all remind her what life might be like in a properly regulated world; but the Voice of Herod breaks in with news of an even more deadly Bomb, and the dream turns to nightmare fears of another massacre of the innocents. Even so, as she comes to again, Mary forgets her fears in the happiness of knowing that her child is going to be born on Christmas Day.

Some time after the script of *The Christmas Child* had been circulated, I was suddenly rung by Lindsay Wellington, then the Controller of the Home Service. More in sorrow than in anger, he reproved me for having caused him a lot of trouble; even so, he said, I should be glad to know that the play could go out after all. As I had not been aware that there had been any question about this, I was much surprised by the news, and said as much. He told me that there had been a great deal of discussion on the subject, at a suitably high level. I said I was even more surprised to hear it. I had really been asking for trouble, he said, by loading the dice so heavily. I wondered in what way I had loaded anything. "You know perfectly well what I mean," said the Controller. "By making your Joe and Mary a *poor* family, to begin with . . . !" As I had merely modelled them on the Holy Family, I was much intrigued by his argument; apparently I should have made Joe a contractor in a fair way of business. But dangerously Christian though it was, *The Christmas Child* went out, for better or worse.

The excessive timidity of the BBC Higher Command in the early post-war years is truly ludicrous to remember, especially in the light of what was seen and heard on the air in the permissive sixties. But the fact remains that until the advent of Hugh Carleton Greene as Director-General in 1960, the BBC Home Service had never regarded itself as a pacemaker for public opinion. Its role, as the BBC saw it, was to reflect the most respectably orthodox

* As *The Christmas Child* was set in Oldham, it was played with a Lancashire accent. I was severely taken to task by the Durham pitmen—who complained that every fool knew Johnny Miner was a Geordie! It seemed that my archetypal character had taken on a new life of his own.

opinion as it already existed—and that way lay conservatism of the pre-Macmillan kind. As a maker of programmes, on the other hand, I always regarded myself as being in duty bound to instigate discussion; and *The Christmas Child* was no doubt all part of the process. Even so, and despite its rather dramatic reminder of Britain's share in the Bomb, I cannot think that the play was desperately subversive!

My next programme, *End of a Dictator*, got me into trouble with some of my listeners. It told the story of the last days of Mussolini, from his fall in 1943 to his ignominious end in the last days of the war, strung up by the heels in Milan. I had friends among the Italian Partisans who captured him, one of whom had been decorated for organising the escape of twelve hundred British prisoners of war, who were being hunted down by the German S.S. Partly with their help, and with a lot of research on my own part, I was able to tell the story of the last days of the ex-Dictator in some detail. And a shabby tale it proved to be. The last throw of this so-called Leader—cutting and running for the German frontier with some millions of pounds in stolen loot —was undoubtedly dramatic, but hardly high tragedy. So far as I was concerned, it was the story of a cowardly and posturing criminal vainly trying to avoid the penalty for his crimes, and as such I treated it.

As the Partisans closed in on him at Dongo, I expressed no sympathy for the hunted quarry: on the contrary, he was roundly charged with all the disasters he had brought upon his people, and held up to the contempt in which I personally held him. By all who hated Fascism as much as I did, this rough handling of Mussolini was loudly applauded. But the well-known sympathy of the British for any sort of under-dog incited others to rise in protest. Any such kicking of a man when he was down was held to be unethical! And who did I think I was, thus to set myself up in judgment?

The answer to that was simple enough: I was the man who had written the programme. I was not trying to write dispassionate history: I was expressing my own point of view about a man who

had once asked Hitler to let him share in the honour of bombing
my friends and me in London. The Duce had had his say then: I
reserved the right to have my own. I had become a writer simply
because there were things I wanted to say—and somewhat to the
embarrassment of the BBC, say things I occasionally did. As a
writer, furthermore, I have had no more than the one prayer to
utter: may I never be reduced to seeing both sides of any question.

Even when Gilliam returned from his abortive spell in television, I still found myself caught up in a great deal of administrative work on his behalf. For this I was getting no proper
recognition from the BBC, and certainly no extra salary. Although
Val Gielgud had always had his Assistant Head of Drama on the
payroll, no Assistant Head of Features to Gilliam had ever been
appointed. I at last decided that this was hardly good enough, and
let it be known that if I was expected to go on filling the role indefinitely, I insisted upon being given the proper status officially.
Otherwise, I suggested, somebody else should be given the job,
and paid for doing it. In this, Gilliam backed me up completely.

It was typical of the administrative mind that the BBC should
retaliate by advertising the job, while I continued to do the work.
Naturally enough, I put in for it myself, along with many others.
When filling in my application form, I came upon a space in
which candidates were invited to make "a statement of their
qualifications and experience which will emphasise their suita-
bility for the post in question." I took some pleasure in stating
that my only qualification for the job consisted in having done it
for the last four years. Again thanks mainly to Gilliam, I was finally
appointed Assistant Head of Features in 1950.

One reason for my raising the issue had been Gilliam's increasing preoccupation with a private project of his own. In the course
of dispensing Marshall Aid to Europe, the Americans had created
their Economic Co-operation Administration, or ECA, with a
Public Relations office in Paris.* Naturally enough, they were

* The ECA had been set up in 1948. In 1951 its work was taken over by the Mutual
Security Agency, or MSA. The radio programmes were carried by MBS in 1949-50.

anxious that the excellent work the ECA were doing in Europe should be fully appreciated by the American taxpayer who happened to be paying for it. They were accordingly planning to mount a large-scale series of documentary radio programmes—to be carried in the United States by the Mutual Broadcasting System—in which the story of American Aid could be told. Realising that the BBC was admirably equipped for producing such a series, they suggested a joint project in which the ECA should provide the budget and the BBC should provide the programme facilities. As it happened, the BBC was unwilling to carry so many programmes on a subject of mainly American interest. But they agreed to lend their studio facilities, and Gilliam was given permission to act as producer of the series as a spare-time extramural activity.

Mounting such an ambitious and expensive amount of radio could hardly be spare-time work for anyone: for Gilliam it rapidly proved to be a whole-time intramural headache. The total budget had been made over to him as a lump sum—which could not be exceeded, but which was sufficient to pay for the whole operation and leave him a clear profit of some two or three thousand pounds at the end of it. Unfortunately, the operation was rather more complicated than he had realised. Writers had to be hired and sent on assignments all over Europe, producers had to be made available (and paid for) outside their normal duties, large casts had to be booked, composers and conductors and orchestras contracted for, BBC studios and equipment made available, and outside clerical assistance brought in to cope with the vast amount of paper work. Gilliam soon found himself engulfed in all the troubles of a spare-time impresario.

Apart from my normal work for Features Department, I wrote some half a dozen shows for the series as paid work in my evenings off. I had an up-to-date knowledge of post-war conditions in most of the reconstruction areas and rehabilitation zones. The ECA had merely taken over where UNRRA had left off, so that I had a certain amount of information to draw upon without being under the necessity of going out to look for it. The series was called *This is Europe*, and my first script for it dealt with post-war problems here in Britain. I had just been out to Turkey and Cyprus for the BBC and had brought back a number of interesting recordings, so that another three shows were written around American aid in Anatolia. In one of them, *The Road*, the lead was taken by Richard Burton, an actor of whom I was to see a good deal more later on in America. I took a couple of weeks' accumulated leave to visit Portugal and Norway, but though the first of these trips proved everyway successful, for the first time in my experience Norway had to be written off: the local branch of ECA in Oslo was feuding with their central office in Paris and refused their co-operation! As I was taking my 1950 summer leave in Italy, however, I added an extra week to cover a further story in Trieste, where no such feud existed. The programme which I came up with, *Oil for the Lamps of Europe*, was the last that I had time to write for the series. While I was writing it, I had the pleasure of meeting up with James Joyce's brother Stanislaus, whose reminiscences would have made a programme far more important.* As it was, I had a date to keep in Venice with another Joyce, and before I could revisit him a year or two later, Stanislaus was dead.

Many BBC feature writers helped Gilliam with the ECA series, among them Alan Burgess, who was one of the most successful documentary writers that the BBC ever had. Unfortunately, Gilliam had always shown a marked preference for trying out new writers where old and competent ones would often have served him better. On nursery slopes, where a tight budget and rapid turnover were not important, the habit was well enough: with the BBC to subsidise it and carry the inevitable losses, it had often paid off handsomely—good new writers had been

---

Our evening rambles round Trieste were particularly interesting, and took us from Joyce's old classroom at the Berlitz School of Languages to his favourite haunts and the flats that he had occupied. It seems that each night he walked home through one of the city's traffic tunnels, and we followed in his footsteps. The tunnel's curving length re-echoed with the deafening roar of heavy traffic. Its walls were entirely lined with the dirty white tiles found normally only in Gentlemen's Lavatories.

I still wonder whether this nightly pilgrimage was not partly responsible for Joyce's anal fixation, as observable in the fourth chapter of *Ulysses*.

discovered. But where the subsidising was strictly at Gilliam's own expense, it proved highly unfortunate. Many scripts had to be paid for, and promptly written off. Others had to be re-researched and rewritten before they could be used, which meant the paying-off of actors booked for cancelled rehearsals. All in all, his lavish and somewhat extravagant approach to production served him ill on this occasion. Despite the months of work which he had put into *This is Europe*, he found himself very badly out of pocket at the end of it all.

While Gilliam was coping with his private headache, the BBC was beginning to suffer one of its own. Headed by Lord Beveridge, a committee of investigation descended upon us in the course of making recommendations regarding the renewal of our Charter. I had the highest respect for Beveridge as the architect of the Welfare State, but was surprised to find him rather less impressive as an investigator of matters which concerned me personally. One of his *obiter dicta* I shall always remember as a perfect example of official thinking on the subject of the arts. At a gathering of feature and drama producers, Gielgud and I were asked to retire so that they could unburden themselves to Beveridge of their complaints and grievances. As they were all deplorably underpaid at the time, they drew his attention to the fact, pointing out that even junior administrators were paid far better for work infinitely less valuable to broadcasting. Much to their annoyance, they got no sympathy at all from his lordship. It was right, he maintained, that administrators should be better paid than creative people, because their work was so much less interesting! It would be some consolation, perhaps, if—like Bufo before them—they helped to bury whom they helped to starve . . .

My second experience of Beveridge as investigator was no more reassuring. 1950 happened to mark the centenary of Wordsworth's death, as 1949 had marked the bicentenary of Goethe's birth. As a Wordsworthian himself, Beveridge suddenly expressed acute dissatisfaction with the scale on which the BBC had celebrated the Wordsworthian anniversary. Goethe had been far more handsomely served, his commemoration including

Harding's fine production of Louis MacNeice's translation of *Faust*. By comparison, Wordsworth had fared less well, one of the main tributes being my own *Rothay Revisited*, in which I traced the survival of Wordsworthian echoes in the daily lives of the Lakelanders today.

A special meeting of Controllers and departmental Heads was called at Beveridge's instance to consider the matter fully. He there proceeded to take Third Programme direction severely to task for neglecting local genius and overselling alien. As Third Programme Controller, Harman Grisewood was virtually accused of anti-British activities, a charge which he rebutted with his usual good humour. I was personally commended for my own pro-British efforts on the Home Service (although he had not heard the programme, Beveridge had been informed that it was well enough in its way) but one swallow couldn't make a summer; and what had Third Programme done for Wordsworth on its own account? Various programmes were cited, but none was deemed sufficient.

At last the reason for his onslaught began to emerge more clearly: Beveridge's own Memorial Address at Grasmere had been completely ignored! His animadversions on the fact lasted for the next hour or two. One might have supposed that a man in his position . . . Being acknowledged on all sides as a scholar of some note . . . Could a more typical instance of Third Programme arrogance be imagined . . . ? If this was responsible direction of a national programme service . . . And so on, and *da capo*.* I almost wondered whether the BBC Charter was not about to be revoked forthwith. Perhaps it might have been, if other members of the Beveridge Committee had not been a trifle more objective in their thinking! Luckily, most of them were, and Lady Megan Lloyd George in particular endeared herself to all of us. But then of course, Lloyd George's centenary did not come up for another thirteen years . . .

* Grisewood's comment on the incident in his autobiography *One Thing at a Time* is charmingly terse: "It was the most prolonged exhibition of pique and vanity which I have ever witnessed."

Above: 10. Wyndham
Lewis, a drawing by
Michael Ayrton
January 1955

Right: 11. Ezra Pound
a drawing by
Wyndham Lewis

Above: 12. D. G. Bridson
with Robert D. Graff,
producer of *The Valiant
Years*, New York, 1960

Left: 13. Laurence Gilliam

In 1951, the position of Head of Television Documentaries was advertised. I was surprised that it had not automatically been offered to Gilliam, even though he might have declined to accept it. In turn, he suggested that I should put in for it myself; but I told him that I had no ambitions that way at present—I liked life where I was. It then emerged that Paul Rotha was in the running, and strongly tipped to get the job in view of his wide experience in documentary films. Gilliam suggested, therefore, that I should at least show willing by putting in an application. This, he thought, would be showing the flag for Features Department; and, as he would be sitting on the Appointments Board himself, he could guarantee that I should not be selected accidentally! Accordingly, I sent in my application with some ironic amusement: it is always pleasant to make a play for something one does not remotely want. But a few days later, news came through that Rotha had just taken a job elsewhere; and to my dismay I found myself suddenly become hot favourite for the post after all.

McGivern and Gilliam were the two most influential members of the Appointments Board, and by now Gilliam was firmly convinced that I ought to take the job anyway. I was far from happy at the idea, but could hardly withdraw at this late date. I determined to hold out for certain conditions that I was pretty sure McGivern would not accept. This I did, only to have them all agreed in principle. I was much alarmed to think that I was now in a fair way to being selected in spite of myself.

I was not. Friendly as we had always been, McGivern made it clear enough that he was no more anxious to have me working for him than he was to have Gilliam himself. Gilliam pressed my claims hard: McGivern backed the claims of one of the other candidates, whose qualifications were apparently not so good as my own. Gilliam was much incensed, and threatened to refer the matter to the Director-General unless I was appointed. This I dissuaded him from doing: I was certainly not going to move into television against McGivern's wishes. In any case, I was having too much fun in radio to ask for anything better at that time. In the event, no appointment was then made at all. A year later, Rotha's other work being finished, he was duly appointed to the post. After he had resigned it, the post was quietly abolished.

One of the reasons why I had been so diffident about the whole business was that I had just been offered by the State Department a four-month tour of America as their guest. I had long been hankering to return there, but dollar shortage had always prevented the BBC from sending me. This was an opportunity not to be missed, and after clearing it with the BBC, I had accepted the offer for the following month. My sponsor had been the American Attaché for Cultural Affairs, to whom I had been introduced by my friend Derek Patmore. A full itinerary had been drawn up for me, my plane reservation had been made, and I was just on the point of applying to the American Consul-General's office for my visa. The television job having been disposed of, this I was now free to do—and there I presented myself. I was ushered into the presence and handed over my passport. The gentleman examined it carefully, and handed it back to me. He said he was sorry, but a visa was out of the question: I had been behind the Iron Curtain—Jugoslavia, Czechoslovakia, Bulgaria—and was thus debarred from entering the United States under the terms of the McCarran-Nixon Bill.

I pointed out, with some annoyance, that I was not asking to visit America: America was asking me to do so. Who was asking me? he wanted to know. The State Department? What branch of the State Department? Cultural Affairs? "Hell!" said the gentleman, "*they'd* ask anyone!" That was as it might be, I said: but they had just asked me, and the following week I was expected for various appointments in Washington. I also let it be known that I should make a lot of noise if I wasn't there to keep them. I had been behind the Iron Curtain—what of it? As a radio man I was expected to go everywhere, even to America. And as a radio man, I should know where to publicise the fact if I didn't get there. The gentleman said he would cable Washington for further instructions. I was asked to raise my right hand, solemnly swore, was fingerprinted, and told I should be contacted in a day or so.*

My visa was quickly granted, though I was told that the Consulate could not guarantee its being honoured by the Immigration Department at La Guardia Airport. With a pocketful of hammers and sickles, I had visions of ending up on Ellis Island, which was still kept open for subversives. If this was life under McCarthyism, I thought, it had little to say for it. Even my beard would be weighed in the balance against me: after all, Marx, Engels, Lenin and Trotsky had all worn beards before me. More to the point, it occurred to me that a beard would probably get me beaten up in the bars: I well remembered the American fondness for starting up fights over ideological issues. As a conciliatory gesture to the Senator from Wisconsin, I decided to play safe. A party was organised at which, in the presence of a staunchly antired Wyndham Lewis, my beard was shaved off by the Turkish Press Attaché, Nejat Sönmez—who was not merely a NATO ally, but one of the few people I could trust with a razor. Thus made outwardly orthodox, and with no more than a neat moustache again like Stalin, I boarded my plain at Heathrow.

At La Guardia—with some misgivings—I handed my passport over to an Immigration Official as wide as a bulldozer. He leaned back in his chair chewing a pulped cigar, and slowly flipped the pages from front to back, then back again to the front. He looked up critically at length, carefully comparing me with my passport photograph. That was still bearded though I was not, a fact which he obviously noted. "So you work for the BBC," he observed. I agreed that I did. "The British Broadcasting Company?" I pretended that it was. There was a long and agonising pause. "Do you know a guy called Frank Phillips?" he suddenly enquired. Frank Phillips the announcer? I had been drinking with

---

* This ludicrous interlude was subsequently reconstructed in my programme *Return to the U.S.A.* I was told at the American Embassy that it had been heard "with great pleasure by *somebody very high up indeed.*" I rather gathered that this had been the Ambassador himself, who was probably no less embarrassed by the absurdities of the McCarran–Nixon Bill and the McCarran Act which followed it than ninety per cent of his staff. Both pieces of legislation, incidentally, had been passed by Congress over the veto of President Truman.

him a couple of nights ago! "That right?" he said with interest. "Say—I was on Omaha Beach on D-Day. We used to listen to Frank Phillips reading the noos on the radio. That guy was the only guy we could trust!" He stamped my passport vigorously, handed it back to me, and even shook me by the hand. "Have yourself a good time, Mr. Briddson," he said. "We're glad to have you with us." Even under McCarthyism, it seemed, America could still be friendly.

Oddly enough, it was not my Communist contacts that caused embarrassment in Washington. I asked the State Department for permission to visit Ezra Pound, then locked up in St. Elizabeth's Hospital, with charges of High Treason still hanging over him for his wartime broadcasts from Italy. This was obviously regarded as an improper request, and I was politely told that it would be better if I made my own arrangements in the matter. Through the good offices of Huntingdon Cairns, I had no difficulty in doing so.

Despite our correspondence in the thirties, which had been resumed again after his internment, I had never actually met Pound. After his arrest, I had called on his wife at Rapallo to pay my respects and ask for news of him. She had been out shopping, and it had been a sad experience waiting for her in his empty apartment, with Gaudier's great bust of him out on the balcony, Chinese ideograms on the wall and his books everywhere. It was sadder still to find him in America locked up like a caged lion, no matter how sympathetically he was treated by the hospital staff. I regretted the rather silly broadcasts that he had made from Rome during the war. But they were at least innocuous, and I could not identify him in any way with the viciousness of the Fascist régime. To me, Pound was still the greatest living poet, and one to whom I felt that I owed much.

It was a friendly interne who pointed him out to me, sitting with his wife under a tree in the warm sun. She came to spend every afternoon with him, and they both seemed strangely relaxed in a scene which seemed to me charged with unusual tensions. To find him, I had walked past a separate block in the grounds where wild-eyed women were clawing at the bars across their windows. Other inmates were wandering aimlessly around, muttering and gesticulating to themselves. After five years of living among them, Pound had come to accept them as part of his daily life. Even when they insisted on breaking in on his privacy —black or white—he was courteous and friendly to them all.

I had written to let him know that I would be calling to see him, and as I approached he leapt to his feet. He was still athletic and active, and his eyes screwed up into a quizzical stare as he mentally compared me with what I suppose he had imagined me to be. He gripped my hand and the silent scrutiny went on. Apparently satisfied, he turned and led me back to his wife: I was formally introduced and we all sat down to talk. I was glad to bring him news of many friends in the outside world, including Eliot and Wyndham Lewis. I should have been far more glad if I had known how much I was to see of him in the future.

From Washington I went on to Hollywood, where there were other friends to visit in happier circumstances. Nick Ray was now a fully fledged film director with a rapidly growing reputation. Herbert Marshall and his wife were a source of delight each evening: James Hilton, Norman Corwin and the others were all in excellent form. I was also glad to meet up again with Bill Robson and Irving Reis, two of the best producers of the old Columbia Workshop, with whom I had grown friendly during the war. Robson was still in radio, but Reis had moved into films and was currently directing Rex Harrison for Columbia Pictures.

Among other things, I was gathering material for two *Focus* programmes on the growing threat of television to the film industry, and consequently had much recording to keep me busy round the studios. At RKO I was also covering the shooting of Gabriel Pascal's production of *Androcles and the Lion*, in which the Canadian radio actor Alan Young was starring with Robert Newton, Jean Simmons and Victor Mature. I spent a fascinating day at the Walt Disney studios, where I was royally entertained and shown around by the Master himself, one of the most enthusiastic and dedicated craftsmen I ever met. At Paramount there was Bob Hope, Alan Ladd and the doyen of Hollywood directors, George Stevens; at Universal, James Stewart, the young Tony Curtis and Piper Laurie; and at MGM, John Houseman (then planning his film of *Julius Caesar*) and the Great Mogul himself, Dore Schary.

My session with Schary was almost an imperial occasion: he had just inherited the running of the MGM empire from Louis B. Meyer, and was very close to God. Remembering him as a gifted scriptwriter in his earlier days, I congratulated him upon the great fight scene in *The Big City*, which starred Spencer Tracey back in the thirties. Schary's face lit up with a rare delight: "Goddamit," he said, "that was the best scene I ever wrote—and you're the first man who has ever mentioned it." Turning to the obsequious squad of ever-present heyduks, "Give Mr. Bridson anything he wants on the MGM lot," he ordered. Unfortunately, apart from his own recording, there was very little that I did want—least of all a Hollywood job.

The saddest thing about Hollywood at the time was the almost panic fear which many people were suffering there. Television was far less of a threat to profits than the Un-American Activities Committee was to many people's livelihood. Day after day, well-known names were bandied about at the hearings. Directors, stars, bit-part players: all were bullied and grilled by the inquisitors in the name of national security. All too often they chose to pay for their own immunity by naming friends and casual acquaintances as "known Communists or Communist sympathisers." Few of these reckless allegations were ever checked: the mere citation of someone in the daily lists of "named subversives" was enough to destroy his career in films or radio or television for good. In the voice of anyone who defied the inquisitors, one could hear the anxiety of a man who knew that he was destroying himself. I was sickened by such a travesty of all that the law was supposed to stand for and protect.

A number of my own friends, of course, had left America in disgust until sanity returned. Many of them were over in England, like my closest American friend, Alan Lomax. Others had gone to Mexico, like Robert Heller, once the CBS producer of *Transatlantic Call*, who was then busy helping to build up Mexican television. Others again had stayed in the States only to be hauled before the Committee and forced to defend themselves as best they could. Not one of them, to the best of my knowledge, had been guilty of anything more than a firm belief in liberal ideals. But once the witch-hunt was on, to be accused of any ideals at all was enough to damn you in the eyes of a handful of bigoted demagogues. To be a thinking American at the time was an un-American activity in itself; and it was long before the fear stirred up by Senator McCarthy returned to commonsense.

My own better judgment on the subject of beards appeared to be justified by events. Even my accent marked me down for suspicion in certain feeble minds. "Gimme a cuppa coffee and a dozen eggs," was the order one evening from a drunk in an all-night diner. "Waddya wanna dozen eggs for, Mac?" asked the counter-man with equal truculence. "I wanna break 'em over that guy's hat," said the customer. Realising that mine was the hat in question, I asked the man what was wrong with it. "I doan like it," he said. I admitted that neither did I, it was just the best hat I could buy in New York. "That ain't an American hat?" said the man suspiciously. I passed it over for his inspection, a well-known American trade-mark inside it to prove my point. "Well, I'll be darned!" said the man: "Say, why doan we havva drink?" I said I'd had plenty of drinks already, but thanked him for the offer. He clapped me on the back and left me, swearing eternal friendship.

Meeting up with Burl Ives again, I was amused to find him wearing a perfect replica of the beard I'd left behind me. He asked me why I'd shaved mine off, for heaven's sake? I told him I didn't want it filled with egg, and told him what had nearly happened to my all-American hat. "That's crazy," said Burl, "nobody bothers about *my* beard." I told him I wasn't surprised to hear it: he still weighed over three hundred pounds, and the sleeves of his jacket I could have worn for trousers . . .

Nonetheless, for all normal purposes, I still found America as lively and stimulating as ever. Drinking parties with Burl and Josh White still went on with singing long into the night. Langston Hughes was still in Harlem, and Harlem was still good for folk-song and jazz in every bar along Lennox Avenue. Down in the Village there was Nellie Lutcher at Café Society and drinks with Muggsy Spanier, Darnell Howard and Rudi Blesh over at Nick's place. Out in Chicago there was Sidney Bechet at the Bluenote. ("If you spit you'll hit it," said the cop when I asked my way almost outside the door.) In San Francisco there was Wingy Menone with whom I discussed jazz on a television interview; and in New Orleans there was George Lewis and Barney Bigard. There too I was even called upon to compère the Dukes of Dixieland in a broadcast from the Famous Door in Bourbon Street.* Basin Street, on the other hand, proved a sad disappointment to me, with only the one sleazy dive still open. *Whites Only* said a sign over the door . . .

When I returned to London, I found Gilliam's marriage in process of breaking up, as mine had done four years earlier. Both Laurence and Marianne were friends of whom I was very fond, and I rather felt that it was time they were left to cope with problems on their own. I moved into a flat at Hampstead, and before very long found myself caught up in yet another large-scale travel project. A Commonwealth Broadcasting Conference had been called in London to consider the future development of Commonwealth radio and television. As I happened to be the only programme official who had worked in all four white Dominions, I was asked to attend some of the sittings.

There was much talk at the time about the so-called Colombo Plan for financing development in South-East Asia. What the

---

* Rather a tricky assignment, this one. The band (and I) were perched on a platform just behind the bar. As it was early evening, the customers were far more keen on drinking drinks than hearing music, and fought their way to the front almost under my feet. I was introduced to them by Bill Elliott of the local station WNOE as "the famous announcer from the BBC in London, England." "What else can he do besides talk?" shouted a large man just below me to the great delight of the crowd. "Not very much," I shouted back, "but at least I get paid for it." The economic factor appeared to satisfy him: dollars, after all, were very sacred cows. He kept politely quiet throughout the broadcast.

Five Years Plans had done for the Soviet Union, the Colombo Plan was to do for the Asian sub-continent—or so the story went. In view of the British aid involved, the BBC had agreed to give the Plan publicity, and I was asked to put up a scheme of coverage for consideration by the Conference. I worked out a treatment that consisted of three major documentaries, with half a dozen supporting talks of a rather more personal kind. I agreed to write and produce the documentaries, and the Australians agreed to make one of their talks producers available to go on the Grand Tour with me. The programmes were to be carried throughout the Commonwealth.

My interest in economic development anywhere was limited; and so, I suspected, was the interest of many listeners. Also, I was getting a trifle bored with the automatic feature coverage of every worthy subject which happened along. There seemed to me far more challenging subjects to tackle rather nearer home, but I looked forward to the trip with some interest as an exercise in pure sight-seeing. In the event, it turned out to be one of the most exhausting assignments I ever undertook, with almost daily plane trips, rail travel and car rides clocking up some thirty thousand miles in the three months. Best of the air trips were those made in the first ill-fated Comets, which had just brought in the excitement of jet flying.

So far as development went, much was indeed being achieved. But there is a limit to the enthusiasm which can be generated by hydro-electric schemes, and much of the second half of the trip was a matter of one damn dam after another, always in the most inaccessible places. So far as my private tastes went, I was far more interested in seeing what I could of the art and the antiquities, those of Ceylon being particularly fascinating. Looking at paintings has always been one of my personal pleasures, and the rock-frescoes at Sigiriya were in glorious contrast to anything painted during the fifth century in Europe.

In Singapore, I was joined by Loftus Hyde, my Australian fellow-traveller, and apart from occasional sallies, we made the rest of the tour together. From Malaya we went on by way of

Bangkok and Rangoon to Dacca; and whatever we had seen of them so far, up there in the Ganges delta the problems of development were infinitely more complicated. Transport anywhere was difficult, and many parts of the interior could only be reached by river boat. There was a strange dearth of roads in the country, and a lack of any stone with which roads could be built. I even watched them baking bricks in the hot sun, then smashing them into small pieces to make whatever road surfacing they could. Out in the jungle behind Chittagong, I was fascinated to find elephants helping to build a factory miles from anywhere. The engineers were thankful enough for elephants: there was precious little else around to help them.

In India, I watched them building bigger and better dams for a vast new hydro-electric scheme in the Demodar Valley. But these were dams built like the Pyramids, by vast armies of men and women who toted the filling up in baskets on their heads. Wearing their turbans and dhotis, saris and veils, jingling necklaces, anklets and nose-jewels—they swarmed up and down the towering walls like myriads of industrious ants. In a nearby resthouse, of all unlikely people, I came across the son of Rabindranath Tagore.

Whatever her industrial potential might be, it seemed to me that India's first need was somehow to defuse her population explosion. Until that could be done, development appeared to be something very like an academic exercise. Even the few Indians who were trying to cope with the problem were almost reduced to despair. One of them, an Indian student from Cambridge, told me how she had tried to start up family planning in the villages round Bombay. Returning to one of them shortly after the lectures and free distribution of rubber contraceptives, she found all the children happily playing games in the village street. Dutch caps and diaphragms were sailing like coracles in the open drains, and inflated sheaths were drifting through the air like dirigibles. She asked indignantly why the parents had not kept such things out of the reach of the children. Indian as she was herself, she had failed to realise that in a peasant's hovel there was nowhere to hide anything, let alone a cupboard to lock it in. The last I heard of her, she was gloomily waiting for the coming of the Pill, or voluntary sterilisation in exchange for a Japanese transistor set.

In West Pakistan it was much the same thing: devoted battling against insuperable odds. Millions of desert acres were destined for irrigation, but even back in Karachi the poverty was depressing. At least I enjoyed my trip up the Khyber Pass, where the camel trains of slit-eyed Tartars reminded me of my first discovery of the Red Army. As for the engineers of the Malakand power project, they were being sniped at by tribesmen from along the Afghan border—still apparently gunning for the young Winston Churchill or his descendants.

The story of this long trip was told in three documentaries, *Asia has a Plan*, which seemed to interest listeners rather more than they did me. What I had seen had certainly been impressive by reason of the tremendous effort that was going into it, and in that way at least the Colombo Plan could claim to be justifying itself. Crops were being planted where none had grown before, but even while they were ripening, mouths to be fed were multiplying like locusts. A quarter of the entire world's population lives in South-East Asia: in the eighteen years since I went there, that population has increased by another hundred and fifty million. Development in the face of such a growth rate is not a matter of raising low standards of living: the problem is rather a matter of desperately trying to maintain them.

By comparison with South-East Asia, my tour of the Near East in 1956 was almost in the nature of a rest-cure. Sir John Glubb had just been sacked in Jordan, Nasser was busy preparing to nationalise the Suez Canal, and the Palestinian refugees were spoiling for a chance to fight their way back into Israel. It was obvious that before much longer the Near East would erupt once more, and I was asked to lead a team of feature reporters into the area and mount a series of broadcasts on all the troubled countries concerned. In the course of a rather hectic month, I visited Iraq,

Egypt, the Lebanon, Syria, Jordan and Israel—but there at least, distance was no particular problem.

Unlike those of South-East Asia, moreover, the troubles were mostly man-made and not the outcome of natural processes. A certain amount was being done by way of economic development, but armaments have a strange way of swallowing up the money that might be better spent on raising standards of living; and whether you can tell butter or not, at least you can tell guns. The pity was that national prestige so often made them seem much more necessary.

Even before Suez—and as it has been ever since—the Arabs' sense of outrage in the Near East was obviously paramount. And the fact that Israel was making so much better a job of bringing new life to their old deserts was hardly likely to lessen it. For the plain fact remained that Israel was bringing a new fertility to every acre of desert that she could, and in contrast to her commando-run efficiency every Arab country I visited seemed hopelessly medieval. Nor did screaming Arab jets over Baghdad, Amman, Cairo and Damascus help to dispel the feeling.

Even so, one kibbutz is very like another. And in the Near East no less than in South-East Asia, it was the antiquities which fascinated me most of all. Whatever they did for the people who lived beside them, there had been more to remember in Polunnaruwa, the Kutab Minar and the Taj Mahal than there had been in most of the irrigation projects. Similarly with the Near East: Babylon and Baalbek, Jericho and the Dome of the Rock made a far more lasting impression than the still imminent threat of a battle over the head-waters of the Jordan. Even the most obsessive problems have a way of finding their own solutions. Particularly, of course, when they mostly concern other people . . .

The fact was that I had grown tired of acting as world feature reporter to the Home Service. For the last few years, I had been writing more and more for the Third Programme, where I was at liberty to do more creative work and follow my older interest in literary and cultural programmes. For the most part, the documentaries I should have preferred to write for the Home Service audience were still regarded as being too controversial or too political. And as the market went, so the producer was forced to meet it.

The Near East was a serious threat to world peace, and as such I was naturally interested to report on conditions there as I found them. But no less important to me, it also furnished material for one of my most successful treatments of an historical subject. I had long been fascinated by the strange story of the Dead Sea Scrolls, and while I was in Jordan and Israel I found time to make some unique recordings about their discovery. With Gerald Lankester Harding of the Palestine Archaeological Museum, I toured the ruins of the monastery of Qumran where the scrolls had been written, and clambered in and out of the Dead Sea caves where the best of them had been found. The interviews I recorded with Père de Vaux, who had excavated the Qumran site, with Father Josef Malik, John Strugnell, John Allegro, Yigael Yadin and all the others who had worked on the deciphering of the scrolls and fragments at Jerusalem, were subsequently combined with recordings made in Paris, Rome, England and America by the many scholars who had helped in their interpretation. No such gathering of experts had ever yet discussed the real implications of the scrolls in public. And I was glad when our Audience Research Department confirmed that listeners' reaction to the programmes had been among the most enthusiastic yet recorded for me. I found it no less encouraging that the audience was twice as large as that for our coverage of the Near Eastern crisis.

After all, one does not live by guns or butter alone—or even by news of them. There is a point at which one's interest in events begins to be outweighed by one's interest in more important matters: there would certainly be no literature or art or music in the world unless this happened to be so. And if programme planners were not so bemused by the noisy march of events—and the still more noisy cross-talk of those who profited by it—perhaps they might have realised as much by now.

As it was, around that time I was faced with a major decision to make as regards my own career in radio. The very nature of the medium had been changing rapidly over the last few years; and having grown up in an age of radio for the many, I suddenly found myself in an age of radio for the few.

PART TWO

RADIO FOR THE FEW

8

Third Programme

NINETEEN FORTY-SIX had marked a turning point in the history of British broadcasting. On 7 June, the BBC Television Service was resumed after its wartime suspension. And on 29 September, the Third Programme was inaugurated.

The effect of the sudden escalation of television viewing during the fifties was to cut the audience for the BBC Home Service down to about a tenth of its wartime size. And the effect of the creation of the Third Programme was to cut down the audience for the best listening of all to about a tenth even of that. The effect of both together was completely to change the pattern and function of radio in this country.

So far as my own affairs went, the coming of the Third Programme was soon to change the nature of my contribution to radio over the remainder of my time with the BBC. But before recalling some of the things that I wrote and produced for Third, it might be as well to remember how the programme came into being.

Back in the thirties, there had been two nation-wide broadcast programmes, the National and the Regional. The National Programme for the most part originated in London: the Regional drew its material mainly from the Regional services: North, Midland and West, and from Scotland, Wales and Northern Ireland. In addition to the two main programmes, of course, listeners in each separate Region had their own local variants.

With the start of the war, the National and Regional Programmes were merged to form the BBC Home Service, which for three months was the only programme broadcast domestically. In January 1940, however, a special Forces Programme was started up, designed for listening by members of the armed forces at home or over in France. It was a programme light and popular in its appeal, designed to be heard in communal quarters, and soon served as a link between the troops and their families at home.

In short, the Forces Programme was the first attempt by the BBC to cater for a particular *category* of listener.* By contrast, the Home Service continued to give the country a balanced diet of wartime listening. Symphony concerts were followed by plays and serious talks by variety or popular music. Before the war, balanced listening had been the policy on all wavelengths: the overall output had been so planned as to provide contrasted listening at all times. There had been no suggestion that the National Programme was more serious or the Regional Programme more popular in tone. By listening continuously to either, the full spectrum of entertainment and information could be enjoyed at every level. In other words, the two main pre-war radio programmes had been built on exactly the same lines as the two BBC television programmes of today.

There was a great deal to be said for this system of programme building, as indeed there still is. It provided a sensible alternation of light and serious listening. Programmes were not graded according to the tastes and supposed intelligence quotients of various sections of the public. If one wanted to keep one's listening light, one had merely to re-tune one's set when something too serious came along. All that could be urged against such planning was that it placed the onus fairly and squarely upon the listener of looking around for what he liked.

The creation of the Light Programme in July 1945 quickly put an end to all that. As the natural successor of the Forces Programme, the Light catered for those who wanted levity all the

---

* For troops in North Africa and further afield, the Forces Overseas Programme was later available. In June 1943 it merged with the General Overseas Service, which had succeeded the pre-war Empire Service.

time, purely for background listening. If that was all one wanted, re-tuning one's set was no longer necessary: one stayed tuned to the Light Programme hour by hour and day by day. Discriminating listeners, of course, continued to shop around; but the large audiences which serious listening had drawn during the war quickly began to melt away. No longer was it necessary to take evasive action if one wanted to *avoid* the first-rate: with the coming of the Light Programme, it could be virtually guaranteed that, except in the lighter forms of entertainment, the first-rate never came one's way. In other words, the BBC had been partly won over to the accepted standards of commercial radio, as broadcast before the war on Radio Luxembourg.

It seemed to me at the time that the only excuse for the creation of the Light Programme had been the fact that it left a greater proportion of time on the Home Service free for the carrying of outstanding and exceptional material. Much that is broadcast is bound to be ordinary, in the same way that much which appears in the daily press must also be ordinary. What saves the ordinary from becoming a bore is the proper admixture with it of something that is more than ordinary. And once the lighter content of the Home Service output had been hived off onto a separate wavelength, it seemed all the more necessary to liven and heighten the import of what remained. This, however, was only partly attempted. Instead, a third wavelength was given over to all that should be most challenging and enlightened in radio—presumably on the principle that it was much too good to be tried out on the masses. Home Service output remained the basic diet of everyday listening, but the leaven of excellence had been withdrawn from its daily bread.

Sir Basil Nicolls was not alone in his opposition to the creation of the Third Programme. Nor was Lord Reith the only one outside the BBC who was critical of it when it came. Many others were opposed to it in principle also, some of them with far more experience in planning radio than Sir William Haley, whose love-child the Third Programme was. The very verb 'to broadcast' means to disseminate widely; and it seemed to many people that to confine the best in radio to one exclusive wavelength could only result in disseminating it most narrowly. It was clear to everyone that such a programme could never attract more than a minimal audience: indeed, the success of the Light Programme had made that only too certain. In view of the smallness of its audience, any such eclectic programme would necessarily be uneconomic to run, and therefore economically vulnerable. It would monopolise a potentially valuable wavelength, and the cost of maintaining the service—by reason of its very excellence— would be disproportionately high. It was argued by Haley, on the other hand, that the wavelength was available, that the BBC could afford the extra expenditure, and that the prestige which such a programme could win would more than justify its cost.

All that was true enough. The question really came down to whether it might not have been wiser—by spreading a balanced output over the three wavelengths—to keep the audience for each roughly equivalent. By grading its output as it did, the BBC ensured that only one of its programmes was heard to reasonable capacity, one was heard a great deal less, and one was heard by only a very small minority audience.

In terms of pure prestige, there can be no doubt at all that the Third Programme paid off handsomely; and for what it brought onto the air, its record was unrivalled anywhere. Third Programme listening was the finest listening in the world. But it should not be forgotten that somewhere among its programmes the BBC had *always* offered the finest listening in the world. Toscanini's Queen's Hall concerts were heard on the National Programme before the war: so were many other hundred programmes which would now be automatically broadcast only on Radio 3. So far as creative writing goes, Louis MacNeice's best works, *Christopher Columbus* and *The Dark Tower*, were both broadcast on the Home Service before Third Programme was in existence. His later plays, broadcast on Third exclusively, were heard by vastly smaller audiences. I think that this was a pity.

Nevertheless, the Third Programme rapidly introduced an entirely new style of radio writing, for it made possible the broadcasting of much which would never have been acceptable to a larger audience. And while I believed in working to the larger audience in principle, the fact remains that over the next twenty years more of my work was heard on Third Programme than anywhere else. Whatever one's theories as to the best way of attracting audiences for the best listening, the simple fact remains that Third Programme always had more to offer the thinking listener than any other radio service. If too few people were able to make that discovery for themselves, the rest had merely themselves to blame.

In any case, it was not by the mere size of its audience that the Third Programme had to be judged. Though it never increased over the years, far more significant is the fact that its audience never substantially shrank. Where the rise of television during the fifties decimated the audience for the Home Service, the number of listeners to Third Programme stayed virtually the same. By definition alone, the Third Programme was never intended for popular listening: the fact that it was able to maintain its original appeal—despite all competition, and however limited it may have been—is the best indication that it met an existing and continuing need.

Much good radio that was heard only on Third Programme *might* arguably have been broadcast to larger audiences elsewhere, but that is only one factor that has to be considered. There were other factors that were infinitely more important to a writer. Most important among them was the fact that *without* Third Programme, far more of our finest radio would never have been heard on the air at all. I am not referring to matters purely of programme duration: even the five-hour version of *Hamlet* could always have been accommodated somewhere else. Even the most controversial material could have been made acceptable to larger audiences, as it has been on television. But it was precisely because the Third Programme audience was small that it was found possible to broadcast regularly on its wavelength experimental work that would otherwise have found no outlet. Indeed, this was always the strongest argument for keeping the Third Programme in being: it soon established itself as the pace-maker and trend-setter of radio. Without its encouragement, the work of the *avant garde* in literature and music would have been far slower to find a national audience. The fact that their radio audience was small certainly did no disservice to such work: a larger audience would have greeted it only with incomprehension and derision. The best audience anywhere for experimental work has always been small, and discriminating. Played to such an audience, experimental work can be fairly judged—it can get itself talked about until it is generally accepted. It was hardly an accident—and certainly no bad thing—that one of Harold Pinter's first plays was performed on the Third Programme.*

The success of any radio venture depends upon the initiative and the judgment of those responsible for its direction. And having worked with all four of the Third Programme Controllers, I could hardly have a higher opinion of any one of them. A great deal of credit for shaping the programme in the first place must go to George Barnes, who was later knighted for his work as Director of Television. Barnes was placed in control of the Third Programme while it was still in the planning stage. In those days it was thought of merely as Programme C, and various names for it were canvassed. 'The Arts Programme' was wisely rejected as being not merely misleading, but also too limited in its appeal. When Haley invited Sir Desmond MacCarthy to address the senior staff on what he thought that the programme might try to achieve, one had even heard a rumour that it might be cursed with the title of 'Minerva Programme'. Luckily, Mac-Carthy got an assurance that no such owlish label would ever be pinned upon it. Third Programme it duly became, and under

* *A Slight Ache* was put up for the Third Programme by Donald McWhinnie, the Assistant Head of Drama, against the recommendation of Val Gielgud. As P. H. Newby, the Third Programme Controller, could not make head or tail of it, he referred it to me for a third opinion. After I had enthusiastically backed McWhinnie, the play was accepted and broadcast.

George Barnes's control it quickly established the pattern to which it adhered as long as it lasted.

Barnes was a tall, sandy-haired charmingly diffident man who was much liked by all who worked with him. His humour was as dry as a good martini, and he even had the ability to see the funnier side of himself. He was related to the Bloomsbury set, and enjoyed the friendship—as also no doubt the advice—of E. M. Forster. There may have been something a trifle pedagogic about his interests, but he never allowed it to interfere with his keen appreciation of purely creative work. He firmly resisted the temptation to make the Third Programme merely an instrument of higher education, though he went on ultimately to leave an honoured name in the field at Keele. He was actually in charge of the Third Programme, while it was on the air, for no more than five months, being then promoted to the newly created post of Director of the Spoken Word. He managed to retain his sense of humour even under that apocalyptic title, with its overtones from the Gospel according to St. John. (God, it was realised, could only be Sir William Haley.)

In view of heavy commitments to the Home Service and my long spell in South Africa, my only production for the Third Programme during the Barnes régime was an adaptation of both parts of *The Compleat Angler*, with Robert Farquharson in the role of Izaak Walton. The sadistic relish with which he impaled his lob-worms and grasshoppers and slit the bellies of his black snails threw an amusing side-light on that mildest and most lovable of sportsmen. The exquisite setting of the songs for these productions was one of the earliest pieces of composition that Antony Hopkins did for me. There were to be many others.

Harman Grisewood had been brought back to the BBC (after his post-war resignation from Talks Department) to act as George Barnes's personal assistant. In February 1947, he took over the controllership of the Third Programme, bringing in as his own assistant the writer Christopher Sykes. Grisewood was a man for whom I had always felt the most cordial regard. He belonged to the same generation of Oxford intellectuals as

Archie Harding, though himself a Catholic and a staunch Conservative. He was a man of impeccable taste, a friend and admirer of David Jones, and one to whom Third Programme owed a great deal over the next five years.* I had first met him in Manchester even before I joined the staff: as one of the most accomplished of the London announcers, he had been imported by Harding to narrate my feature *Tunnel* with Ewan MacColl. I can only say that this clash of Oxford overtones with militant Salford undertones made an interesting speech pattern. He liked to remember the gruelling scramble I led him through the lesser intestines of the still unfinished Mersey Tunnel in search of understanding. He also remembered a poem of mine, written out on the back of an envelope, which Harding had given him to read by way of an introduction. He repeated *Aaron's Field* on Third Programme in 1947, but it was not for another two years that my travel allowed me the time to work for him on Third to any extent.

My first really amusing production for him was Dean Swift's *Polite Conversation*; and as all will know who have enjoyed the work, it made scintillating listening. The cut and thrust of its small talk is vigorously vapid, the lechery pleasantly direct, and four-letter words used only for occasional shock therapy. Indeed, to anyone brought up in the Reithian odour of sanctity, the new Third Programme permissiveness came as a great relief. Not only were many of the old taboos removed from candid and uninhibited discussion; but the air was at last laid open to some of the finest writing we possess. Particularly was this true of all the plays and adaptations which would previously have been debarred on the grounds of subject matter or over-free vocabulary. Over the years, this emancipation has brought a bevy of neglected masterpieces before the Third Programme audience. In a more trivial way, it has also given rise to some of the funniest bawdy I ever heard on the air. And though Mrs. Whitehouse might not

* His autobiography *One Thing at a Time* is one of the few good books ever written about a successful career in the BBC. The firm stand that he subsequently took with the Government over the Suez Crisis is a notable incident in BBC history.

be amused, Swift and Sterne and Rabelais and Aristophanes have just as much right to a hearing as Jane Austen or Matthew Arnold.

Louis MacNeice had already produced his own adaptation of *The Golden Asse* for the Home Service, in which the part of Lucius the gullible provincial was played by a cheery pipe-smoking American friend of mine called Eddie Birnbryer—the nearest I could offer to genuine Eddie Bracken. But it was not until the coming of the Third Programme that Louis was able to match it with an adaptation of *The Satyricon*, for which I suggested Wilfred Pickles as an excellent Trimalchio. It happened that I was entertaining a rather staid Australian Controller of Programmes from the ABC while rehearsals of *Trimalchio's Feast* were in progress. Hearing that this was a typical large-budget Third Programme production, he asked me to take him along for a private preview. I remember with pleasure the look on his face as I ushered him into the control booth. As we came through the door, the booming voice of Dylan Thomas was coming over the monitor in unusual mock-pansy delight: "Oh, what a *beautiful* piss-pot!" the voice hiccuped incontinently, and for once Australia was cowed. "We could never say *that* on the ABC," he whispered apologetically. As he gradually overcame his fear of laughing out loud in church, he was able to join in the general roar as Pickles pulled the chain for the lavatory music composed by Alan Rawsthorne.

It should be explained that *Polite Conversation, Trimalchio's Feast,* Douglas Cleverdon's *Candide* and all other feature productions were the responsibility of the Entertainment Division of the BBC, to which Features Department belonged. Direction and planning of the Third Programme were Harman Grisewood's affair, but programme content remained the sole responsibility of the producing department concerned. On all questions of bad taste, political bias or any other policy matter, the producer himself would always be taken to task for any lapse of which he had been guilty on his own authority. If he was not quite sure of his competence to decide in the matter, the producer was under strict orders to raise all points for consideration with the head of his own department—in the case of Features Department with Gilliam, or in Gilliam's absence with myself. If either of us was equally doubtful, the onus was on us to refer the matter to our Controller. And if he was not prepared to give a ruling on his own initiative, he in turn could refer to the Director of Sound Broadcasting—who could himself, at a pinch, refer to the Director-General.

As I have suggested, with the coming of the Third Programme the wind of change began to blow through the stuffiness of Broadcasting House, on the Third Programme wavelength at least. I had an enjoyable instance of just how far it had blown by 1951. I was mounting my own production of Norman Cameron's translation of François Villon's *Grand Testament*, and seeing how literally he had translated *Les Regrets de la Belle Heaulmière* (whose breasts were too withered to appear in *The Radio Times* even singly), I rang up our own Controller, Richard Howgill. He rejoiced in the exquisite title 'Controller of Entertainment', but being a man of infinite entertainment in his own right, I had no hesitation in asking him what was the BBC's attitude to twat? After a careful pause, he enquired, "Twat in what connection?" I explained it as a word used by Cameron in his translation of Villon. "Third Programme, of course?" he mused. I told him that was the case. He then enquired whether I thought the word was a *fair* translation? I said that it seemed to me to be eminently fair—in fact, I could think of only one word that would be fairer. (We both dismissed that one.) "We can't tamper with the classics on Third Programme," he agreed after some discussion. So the word was duly passed as suitable for limited consumption.

As Gladys Young had just been awarded the O.B.E. for her services to radio, she was the obvious choice to read *Les Regrets*, in which she could catalogue her vanished charms in a well-cut tailor-made suit and a Henry Heath hat. This she proceeded to do at rehearsal without batting so much as an eyelid, to the convulsed amusement of the rest of the cast.

Shortly before transmission, I was summoned to Howgill's

office. He had been thinking the matter over, he explained, and
had finally discussed it with Harman Grisewood. Harman, it
seemed, had never heard the word—though Howgill had heard
it frequently during the First World War. Well, the long and the
short of it was . . . Well, suppose some old country parson was
listening—in Kent, say—a decent old boy, interested in poetry . . .
Harman felt that the word—presuming, of course, that he understood it . . . Well—he might be distressed, you know. It was all
very difficult—he could see that—as the word was actually a
rhyme: it rhymed with—how did it go?—Oh yes, 'Within its
handsome garden plot . . .' One couldn't upset the rhyme—he
could see that also—and one certainly couldn't omit the entire
stanza . . . It really *was* extremely difficult . . .

Having enjoyed the difficulty to the full, I finally took my Controller off the hook: I confessed that Cameron had left us an alternative version. By describing it as being 'Within a graceful garden
set,' we could get rid of the offending word, and describe the
disputed part as an 'amulet' instead—thus preserving even the
rhyme. Howgill was delighted. 'By Jove,' he said, 'that's damn
good—an amulet! And you know what? It's actually more
poetical!"

I am happy to report that Gladys Young was able to collect
her well-deserved O.B.E. without further unpleasantness.

It was early in 1951 that I finally got around to one of my most
cherished projects for Third Programme. I had first read Wyndham Lewis's brilliant fragment *The Childermass* back in 1932,
before I had yet begun to interest myself in radio. Even so, I had
been struck by its great dramatic possibilities as pure theatre; and
the second half of the book, of course, is written in strictly dramatic form. Played out under the towering walls of the Magnetic
City across the river, its gates and battlements rimmed with their
circle of smouldering volcanoes, the huddling mass of emigrant
souls in the foreground patiently waiting for admission to what
they believe is Heaven—the setting of the drama is only to be seen
convincingly in the imagination. It was that fact, when I re-read

The Childermass in 1950, that had assured me the work would make magnificent radio.

Shortly before I saw my way clear to mounting an adaptation of the book for Third Programme, Wyndham Lewis had finally lost his sight. He announced the fact in a hauntingly memorable article for *The Listener* called *The Sea Mists of the Winter*, one of the most remarkably objective pieces of writing that even Lewis achieved; and its appearance made a deep impression on me. I was already at work on my adaptation, and immediately got in touch with him to discuss the idea. He was then living in a flat near Vauxhall Bridge, where I met him for the first time. He agreed to the radio production that I suggested, provided that my adaptation seemed to him adequately to reflect the style and spirit of the work. After it had been read over to him, he declared himself perfectly satisfied. Indeed, as he had not re-read the book for many years, it gave him a lot of pleasure to be reminded of its funnier passages.

Once the production had been agreed upon, the first question that arose was proper casting: who was to play the part of the Bailiff? The part called for a truly *bravura* interpretation, of tremendous range and splendid virtuosity, for the whole production would stand or fall by that one performance. I had no doubt in my own mind that the part was custom built for Sir Donald Wolfit. I suggested, however, that it might be a good idea for Lewis to discuss the characterisation with him before we finally decided. Wolfit already being a friend of mine, this was agreed upon; and he made the trip out with me to Vauxhall Bridge one day for tea. Lewis and he got on extremely well; and in the course of discussion, Lewis casually gave the one clear key to the part that we had all been waiting for: "The Bailiff," he mused, "was rather a George Robey sort of character."

Wolfit's subsequent playing of the part was one of the most remarkable radio performances that I remember. He gave anything but a George Robey interpretation to it (excellent as he had been, Robey could never have approached it) but the occasional inflection, the waggish vulgarity, the playing to the gallery and the sudden confidential aside, each were a part of the Music Hall tradition that had made Robey what he had been. As one of the radio critics remarked at the time, Wolfit's Bailiff was "as nearly three-dimensional in effect as an evocation of broadcast sound could well be."

I like to think of the first production of *The Childermass*, broadcast by the Third Programme on 18 June 1951, as a memorable event in radio history. It was hailed as "a superb piece of radio writing," which carried "the impact of one of the few original minds of our time." Lewis himself was delighted with it, both in performance and in its reception. Whatever it meant to him, it had proved a great exhilaration to me; for it had proved once again what an imaginative medium radio can be. In no other medium at all, I think, could *The Childermass* have emerged so vividly, in all its frightening other-worldliness. For only in sudden stimulation of the mind's eye can we really frighten ourselves.

In view of the critical acclaim which had greeted it, I reminded Grisewood that *The Childermass* was still no more than a fragment, the first part only of a trilogy projected as far back as 1928. I suggested that it would be an excellent thing if the BBC could see its way to making it possible for Lewis to write the other two parts of the work. Lewis had told me that he was anxious to get down to writing them (after he had finished *Self Condemned*, on which he was then working) but that this would only be feasible if he could be assured of an income until they were finished. He estimated that the work would take about a couple of years to complete.

It says a great deal for Grisewood's imaginative direction of Third Programme that he agreed to the suggestion immediately. Lewis came in to discuss the details with us at Broadcasting House; and although it was understood that the work could not begin that year, half the money was advanced forthwith.* It was

* Grisewood could not have been more appreciative or encouraging. He told Lewis that he hoped he would always feel free to come and address the Third Programme audience on any subject he chose. Lewis thanked him, courteously but noncommitally. Did he listen regularly to the Third Programme? he was asked. No, said Lewis, he was afraid not. Had he at least got a radio set which received it clearly? Grisewood enquired, obviously

agreed that the two unwritten parts of the trilogy (now known as *The Human Age*) were to be conceived and written as novels, for publication as such. Before their publication, however, they would be adapted for radio presentation by Lewis and myself jointly. Finally, the whole trilogy would be produced twice on Third Programme before publication, and once thereafter: that would more than repay the total sum advanced by the BBC without any claim upon publication royalties. Any further radio repeats would be paid for at full rates.

Despite the difficulties imposed by his blindness, Lewis began work on *The Human Age* in 1952, and it took up most of his time over the next three years. Only on completion of the second section, *Monstre Gai*, was I given a sight of the manuscript. And it was not until the end of 1954 that the last part, *Malign Fiesta*, was also finished. As I read the whole work through to the end, I was again excited by its dramatic potential. Though conceived as narrative, it was once more easily translatable into dramatic terms; and the scale of the action, the imaginative depth of the setting and the sharpness of the characterisation again boded well for adaptation.

As the dramatisation finally emerged, two and a half hours were taken up by *Monstre Gai* and two hours by *Malign Fiesta*. Added to the hour and a half devoted to *The Childermass*, that made six hours broadcasting for the full trilogy. Despite this unusual amount of time, it was decided to broadcast all three programmes during the one week. They were accordingly scheduled for 24, 26 and 28 May 1955. Control of Third Programme had by this time passed to John Morris, who cleared air time accordingly. It was also arranged that each programme should be prefaced by a short critical introduction. I had been able to record an appreciation of *The Childermass* by I. A. Richards after I had played the first production over to him and Archibald MacLeish at Harvard

---

prepared to arrange for the loan of one if not. "Oh yes," said Lewis gravely, "I have a wireless set, but perhaps I had better get it *filled*."

I am glad to say that once he had acquired the habit of listening, Third Programme became one of his greatest pleasures in his blindness.

in 1951. T. S. Eliot agreed to record for me a piece that he had originally written for the American *Hudson Review*; and Graham Hough recorded a special assessment of *Malign Fiesta* under the auspices of P. H. Newby.

Critical reaction to the broadcasting of *The Human Age* was immediate and enthusiastic, many of the critics particularly commenting on the novelty of such a major work by a major writer making its first appearance over the air. "Last week was a great occasion in broadcasting and contemporary writing," wrote William Salter★ in the *New Statesman*, and he went on to say:

"The BBC has given us nothing from a living writer to touch *The Human Age*, nothing that even begins to approach it in its imaginative grandeur, power of writing, the evocation of terror and awe, and, I believe, in comic genius. Last week we heard the 'lonely old volcano of the Right' in full eruption: it was magnificent, and in the purest sense, dreadful, as Swift, for instance, can be dreadful . . . We are now more heavily in Mr. Lewis's debt than we have ever been before; and we are heavily in the BBC's debt too, for having elicited these long awaited books from Mr. Lewis, adapted them so sensitively and mounted them with such fitting splendour. If the Third Programme had done nothing else, this would have justified its existence."

Unlike so many other historic broadcasts, which have been pointlessly and wantonly destroyed, it is reassuring to know that *The Human Age* at least is preserved in the BBC archives in its entirety. And if ever this country gets round to building up a sadly needed National Archive of Recordings (I suspect that posterity will violently denounce us for being so slow to do so effectively) then one may hope that the recording will ultimately be made available to all who are interested. One thing remains fairly certain: with rising production costs and a shrinking budget, it is most unlikely that such an ambitious radio production will ever be mounted again.

★ A pseudonym for Walter Allen.

In view of what I have said about the Third Programme having made experimental broadcasting possible in a way that the other services would never have dreamt of doing, it might be worth recalling how I was prevented from mounting an even more historic broadcast than *The Human Age*. In 1939, with the publication of the full text of *Finnegan's Wake*, it occurred to me that as much as possible of the work should certainly be recorded by James Joyce in his own voice. He had, in fact, recorded only one short passage (from *Anna Livia Plurabelle*) and the technical quality of that was poor, however superb his reading had been. One of my first published reviews for Orage, as far back as 1932, had been a consideration of *Tales of Shaun and Shem*, in which I had pointed out how much easier it was to appreciate the work when listening to it read aloud. I had sent the review on to Joyce in Paris, and had heard from Sylvia Beach that he had brought it round to show her and seemed very happy about it. When *Finnegan's Wake* appeared, therefore, I wrote to him again, and said how keen I was that he might agree to record for the BBC a really considerable selection of readings from the finished work. I pointed out that such readings might go a long way to make the work more understandable to many baffled readers. Despite the difficulties that would arise from his own near-total blindness, Joyce agreed in principle that the recordings should be attempted.

As I happened to know, the BBC had one of its few recording vans over in France at the time. In view of Joyce's promised co-operation, I applied for the use of the van after we had allowed him time to prepare and rehearse the first of the readings with me. I was peremptorily told that the van was not available for any such peacetime projects; it was far too busy recording quizzes and parlour games with the troops of the BEF.

I remember that one such frolic dear to the planners of 1939 was a guessing game played around the catch-phrase, *My Aunt is in Town again buying something beginning with*—*A* or *B* or *C* or whatever. My reaction to this piece of philistine obtuseness was to utter loudly something beginning with B . . . Unluckily, from

14. Hugh MacDiarmid
(Dr C. M. Grieve) and
D. G. Bridson at Biggar

15. Cover of the BBC
Third Programme
Quarterly Plan
announcing
The Negro in America

BBC THIRD PROGRAMME

BBC

THIRD PROGRAMME

America since the Bomb

TWENTY PROGRAMMES UNDER
THE EDITORSHIP OF D. G. BRIDSON

OCT. 8—DEC. 10 1966

FOR TIMES
OF BROADCASTS
PLEASE SEE
'RADIO TIMES'

1 **INTRODUCTORY TALK**
by D. G. BRIDSON

2 **THE AGE OF ANXIETY**
by W. H. AUDEN

3 **KOREA TO VIETNAM** by D. G. BRIDSON
  1 **BOMB DIPLOMACY**

4 **THE SPY SCARE**
by ALISTAIR COOKE

5 **THE SENATOR FROM WISCONSIN**
by EMILE DE ANTONIO

6 **THE INVESTIGATOR**
by REUBEN SHIP

7 **THE FOLK SONG ARMY**
by ALAN LOMAX

8 **THE BEAT GENERATION**
by KENNETH REXROTH

9 **BEAT POETRY**
AN ANTHOLOGY

10 **THE NEW JAZZ**
by NAT HENTOFF

11 **KOREA TO VIETNAM** by D. G. BRIDSON
  2 **BRINKMANSHIP**

12 **THE BIRTH OF POP**
by RALPH GLEASON

13 **BLACKLISTING ON TRIAL**
by JOHN HENRY FAULK

14 **ZOO STORY**
by EDWARD ALBEE

15 **SICK HUMOUR AND SATIRE**
by D. G. BRIDSON

16 **WHITE INTEGRATIONISM**
by COLIN EDWARDS

17 **KOREA TO VIETNAM** by D. G. BRIDSON
  3 **THE MOON OR SOUTH-EAST ASIA?**

18 **SONGS OF PROTEST**
by GUY CARAWAN

19 **REVOLT ON THE CAMPUS**
by RALPH GLEASON

20 **THE SUBCULTURE OF SECESSION**
by KENNETH REXROTH

16. Third Programme leaflet advertising
America since the Bomb

my eyrie in the North, I was too junior to carry any weight in the counsels of the war-torn metropolis: I was certainly unable to get my recording van. It continued to accompany its Aunt, perpetuating something beginning with D—the answer being a great deal of drivel. But who among the programme planners had ever heard of James Joyce? I doubt whether even Basil Nicolls had much time for *Finnegan's Wake*.

My disappointment was made absolute by the Fall of France, Joyce's departure to Switzerland and his death shortly after. Looking back on the incident, I can only regard it as a tragedy. It seems inconceivable that a task of such unique literary importance could even have been prevented by the Blitz, let alone by the humdrum non-event that we think of as the Phoney War. I was still regretting my failure twelve years later when Grisewood expressed to the Programme Board his utter astonishment that 'nobody while he was alive had thought of recording Joyce in his own readings from *Finnegan's Wake*.' I left the Board in no doubt that somebody *had* thought of it, however little support he could get from the programme planners at the time. Unfortunately, planners are rarely as wise as Harman Grisewood.

I was much more fortunate in the case of Ezra Pound. In 1956, rumours were persistent that his health was beginning to deteriorate. A normally vigorous man, he had been in confinement at St. Elizabeth's Hospital for nearly eleven years—to say nothing of the internment camp at Pisa—and it would really have been surprising if the claustrophobic atmosphere of the place had not begun to weigh him down.

I had heard at Harvard the only recording that he had ever made of his work, some lyrics recorded there in 1939, again technically poor in quality. If he had died without leaving any more in voice to remember him by, the legacy would have been even more pitiful than Joyce's. I therefore wrote off again to my well-placed Washington contact, Huntingdon Cairns, drawing attention to the fact. If he could secure the agreement of the authorities, I said that I should much like to come over and make a set of recordings with Pound which would at least do better by posterity. The matter was referred to higher places, and permission was forthcoming. The only stipulation was that the Director of the Hospital, Dr. Winfred Overholser, would bring no pressure to bear on Pound: the decision to record or not was entirely his to make. Counting upon Pound's friendly good will, I took the chance of being refused, and duly arrived at Washington with my own portable tape recorder.

Pound needed little persuasion: the novelty of the exercise would at least be a relief from his usual daily boredom. A room was placed at our disposal by the Hospital (he still did not have a room of his own) and we got down to the task over a weekend. Apart from the recordings of his poetry (which will be discussed in the following chapter), he had something else in mind. He was anxious to have me record a testament for posterity on his own account. As he had virtually given up all hope of ever being released back into normal life, he made me promise him solemnly that the recording would never be broadcast or heard by anyone until after his death. I was then at liberty to do with it what I thought best. To this, of course, I agreed; and assured him that it would be safely locked away in the BBC archives meanwhile.

The piece that he recorded, which he called *Four Steps*, was spoken extempore and without notes: it had obviously been in his mind for some considerable time. It traced the course of his growing exasperation with the encroachments of American bureaucracy upon the life of the private citizen; and to that growth he attributed his own eventual revolt against what he still regarded as the abuse of constitutional power. The four incidents quoted stretched in time from Wilson to Roosevelt. "And that is why," he concluded, "after two years of wangling, when I got hold of a microphone in Rome, I used it."

In due course, I returned to London with my recordings—some couple of hours in all—and waited upon events. I was hopeful that after a tactful interval, the poetry readings at least would be freed by the American authorities for putting onto the air. Before that agreement had been given, however, news was pub-

lished that Pound's release had finally been decided upon, thanks
to the special pleading of Robert Frost. His impending release, of
course, would leave all matters of broadcasting rights at Pound's
sole discretion. I had no doubts about the readings, but would he
regard the broadcasting of *Four Steps* during his lifetime as being
in his own interest or not? As the date of his release was within
the next twenty-four hours, I had no means of consulting him
meanwhile without alerting the authorities. All I could do was to
ring his London representative, A. V. Moore, and tell him of my
problem: should I or should I not be justified in going back on
my promise without Pound's express permission? I was quite sure
in my own mind that to broadcast the *apologia* would be very
much in Pound's interest, but was that sufficient justification for
doing so on my own initiative? And would the American authorities be embarrassed by my having been granted an opportunity
to make it with him in the first place? Moore agreed that I was
probably best advised to rely on my own judgment, but he could
go no further than that: the responsibility for anything I decided
to broadcast was mine alone.

The evening of the day that Pound was finally set free, all
charges against him having been dropped, *Four Steps* was broadcast immediately after the nine o'clock news, in which it had been
carefully trailed. Within half an hour, my phone was jammed
with enquiries from all the main news agencies, both British and
American. The evening papers had been full of the story of his
release, complete with pictures, but Pound had refused to make a
statement of any kind. He had been driven away immediately to a
secret destination: how had the BBC in London been able to
scoop the press of the world? When had the recording been
made, and by whom? Had it been before his arrest, thirteen years
before? If so, why had it not been used at the time? Pound himself was not even contactable to confirm or deny the recording's
authenticity.

Knowing the answers to all these questions, the BBC wisely
refused to say anything at all; I myself gave whatever guarded
answers I thought advisable. I cabled Pound at his wife's private

address in Washington, and explained that—rightly or wrongly—
I had done what I had thought would prove to be for his own
good. The broadcast had certainly been well received. Indeed
many listeners went so far as to say that if he was merely guilty
of have defied bureaucracy, a better plan would have been to
lock up the bureaucrats in his place!

Nevertheless, I was much relieved to have Pound's endorse-
ment of my action a few days later: "O.K. for the 4 Steps/and
better that it was done without my specific permission to use it at
the given date. Thanks for good judgement, yrs and AVM's in
the timing." *Four Steps* was subsequently repeated as a special
item on Third Programme, and used as a trailer for the three
remarkable programmes of Pound's poetry reading recorded at
the same time. Despite its unique historical interest, I am still not
sure whether the piece has ever appeared in print. So far as I can
remember, Hugh Kenner was the only critic ever to ask me to let
him hear it as a playback.

I had already mounted a production of Pound's translation of
Sophocles, *The Women of Trachis*, which had given rise to some
genial correspondence. In turning the work into idiomatic
English, Pound had come up with a truly remarkable slang of his
own, which involved the intermixing of Brooklynese, Cockney,
Cowardese and many other exotics unknown to me. Most of it I
found racy and speakable, but when I found it lapsing back into
twenties jargon, I felt that it might be updated here and there. As
for the Queen enquiring of one of her retainers, "You get this
from some local bloke or a foreigner?" I felt impelled to point out
that no woman ever called a man a bloke unless she was an Aussie
sheila, probably from Wooloomooloo.* I wondered whether he
could settle upon something a bit more Runyonese, but apparently
not! His comments are worth quoting as an example of his
epistolary style:

Dear Brid.

I have NO idea what the SPOKEN language NOW is in yr. isle.

* Oddly enough, the word is now back in fashion among the birds.

I trust you as producer and the Goach* to eschew any words usable by Gilb Murray.

if you sent me a list of synonyms, it might guide me. BUT decline to accept ANY *responsibility* for alterations.

I have no more objection to the varnacular of 1920 than to that of 1590 or 1621.

I am not enamoured of Damon Runyon who is I believe no palace favourite—I mean his vocabulary, nor can the language of any period be brought up to date in another as Dryden's Shxpr etc.

Will *Backfish* do for flapper?? buffer is an *elderly* bloke—inapplicable.

I see no advantage in "doll" "guy" "bum" skoit, tomato—this may be hyper als best as on my part.

I suppose Mussato's gang were orribly shocked by Dant Alighieri.

thazz zall the yole man can excog. this evenink.

yrs

Ez P

what IS a spiv? No one will ever tell me.

no author can control wot gaos on on the styge? or can he?

Herakles' age? ?55 to 60? for comparative date of his vocab.??

So chaps and flapper, bloke and slugger, dicky-bird, screwball and one heck of a messenger it was, which Beatrix Lehmann transmuted into moving and quite compelling dialogue.

There were many other stimulating productions for Third Programme which kept me busy during the fifties, though I still continued to contribute regularly to the Home Service and found my way less regularly onto the Light Programme. In 1952, Sir William Haley resigned as Director-General of the BBC to

---

* Denis Goacher, who supervised publication of *The Women of Trachis* and took a leading part in the Production, had worked with Pound at St. Elizabeth's Hospital in a secretarial capacity.

become the Editor of *The Times*. At the end of the year, he was succeeded by Sir Ian Jacob, who had previously been Controller of the Overseas Service. At about the same time, Harman Grisewood was promoted to be Director of the Spoken Word and George Barnes went on to become Director of Television. Grisewood was followed in the controllership of the Third Programme by John Morris, a pleasantly myopic man who had spent part of his life in Japan and more time prowling around the Himalayas. With Morris again I found it happy and easy to work. He was a man who was rather unsure of his own judgment, and sometimes tended to rely on the advice of people with less. He may have encouraged the idea that his programme was in the nature of an exclusive club, and that certain writers were "not quite right for Third", a tendency to which I could never subscribe. But I found myself readily accepted for membership, or perhaps I went along with the fixtures and fittings.

Over at Harvard, I had met up with Archibald MacLeish, whose *Conquistador* I adapted for Third. Special music for the production was composed by Roberto Gerhard, whose work I had long admired, and whom I rapidly came to admire no less as a person. As he liked my adaptation, McLeish sent me the script of a play he had written for television, *This music crept by me upon the waters*. I gave it its première on Third, where it was received rapturously by all the critics. I was prevented from mounting the première of his Broadway success, *J.B.*, by my departure into the outer darkness of television on a short orbit. By the time I returned, Elia Kazan had already made theatrical history with it in New York. At least I like to remember that *J.B.* was finished in my office, while MacLeish was passing through London.

Another Harvard hangover was an amusing fantasy by I. A. Richards, *A Leak in the Universe*, which I also gave its first production. In a rather more macabre vein was Robert Penn Warren's long poem *Brother to Dragons*, which I adapted for radio: the original is a work which deserves to be far better known. Thanks to excellent performances by Sam Wanamaker, Peggy Hassard, James Dyrenforth and others, it provided some of the most spine-chilling listening I remember. Nearer home, there was my own dramatic poem, *The Last Hellene*, and my dramatic praphrase, *The Quest of Gilgamesh*, which I still like the best of anything that I wrote for radio. It was a BBC entry for the Italia Prize in 1956, which I gather from Gilliam (who was out in Rimini at the time) that it missed by the odd vote. My feelings were mixed, later that year, when I met the American juror, who told me how she had cast her vote against it. "We couldn't have the *British* winning!" she explained to me, not knowing who I was. At least I had won the battle of Bunker Hill in Regent's Park a few years earlier . . .

I also much enjoyed putting Joseph Bard's classic short story, *The Tale of a Child*, onto the air. Since it was published by Orage in 1932, this has always seemed to me to be one of the most enchanting monologues ever written, and it was played no less enchantingly by Patricia Hayes. A true Magyar flavour was given to the occasion by the music of Matyas Seiber; and the programme was probably the earliest example of that style of dramatic monologue which has since been so successful in H. B. Fortuin's Third Programme productions of Gogol's *Diary of a Madman* and Kafka's *Investigations of a Dog*.

Finally, there were two more adaptations that I did with Wyndham Lewis. *Tarr* made quite coruscating radio, with a wittily nostalgic score by Walter Goehr, whose music had contributed largely to the success of *The Human Age*. Roberto Gerhard did equally well by *The Revenge for Love*, his fluency in the Spanish idiom having been a delight of mine since his memorable *Don Quixote* score during the war. I was happy to know how much pleasure these adaptations of his work gave to Lewis, and the last time that we spoke together was over the phone after a repeat performance of *Tarr*. He rang up to enquire once more whether Grizelda Hervey had not been as tight as a tick when she played her scene as the tipsy Anastasya. I assured him that she would not have played it nearly so convincingly if she had been. His final hoot of laughter was a cheerful thing by which to remember him.

For the record, it might be well to recall the last words that

Lewis ever spoke, though I was not present to hear them. Desperately sick, he was finally taken away by ambulance from his beloved flat in Notting Hill Gate, while workmen were actually tearing the building down for a road-widening scheme. His wife Anne went along with him, for he could not abide being tended or touched by anyone else. He deeply resented having to be moved at all, and was only the more exasperated by all the care and attention that was lavished upon him at the hospital. The final insult, so far as he was concerned, was administered by a well-meaning Matron. After all other tests and checks had been carried out, she leaned over him and enquired, "Mr. Lewis, when were your bowels last moved?" Glaring up at her with his sightless eyes, The Enemy spoke for the last time: "Mind your own business!" he roared, and lapsed into the final coma. There could have been no better injunction to the modern world than this last utterance of a true genius of his time.

As this book is a personal story rather than a history, I do not propose to chronicle all the excellent work by other producers that was heard on Third Programme during the fifties. Hearing it on the air was one of the pleasures of life at the time, and sitting in on other producers' rehearsals was one of the easiest ways of improving one's own craftsmanship. A careful study of Douglas Cleverdon's productions would itself go a long way to establishing the canon of the best creative work written for radio during the decade. Dylan Thomas's incomparable *Under Milk Wood*, David Jones's *In Parenthesis*, the satirical *A Very Great Man Indeed* sequence of Henry Reed, his *Streets of Pompeii*, and his strangely neglected *Vincenzo*, J. Bronowski's *The Face of Violence*, George Barker's verse plays, and Ted Hughes's *The Wound* were only a few of Cleverdon's more memorable productions. Louis MacNeice's *Prisoner's Progress*, his *The Mad Islands* and other plays and fantasies, Laurie Lee's *Voyage of Magellan*, produced by Rayner Heppenstall, and Terence Tiller's *The Tower of Hunger* were also outstanding. In the documentary field there were the reminiscent symposia of W. R. Rodgers and Maurice Brown, most notably the composite portrait of James Joyce. There were the experiments in fantasy and ballad opera by H. A. L. Craig and Francis Dillon. And there were a whole host of remarkable adaptations— of Joyce by David Thomson and Peter Duval Smith, of Ivy Compton-Burnett by Christopher Sykes, and of Proust by Pamela Hansford Johnson and Rayner Heppenstall. All these fine productions made radio of an order that we shall be lucky to hear for much longer. Those of us who remember them on the air will recall them gratefully, and have many echoes in our minds by which to quicken appreciation of all that creative writing for radio can be.

9

Poets and Folk-singers

I AM GLAD to be on record among the first who firmly denied that poetry should be seen and not heard. To me, poetry has always implied performance. My own earliest poems were all written for speaking aloud, including *The Northern Dance of the Seven Deadly Sins* and *Second Hymn for the People of England*, which were both belted out among friends before ever I thought of radio as a means to getting them heard more widely. Indeed, I remember one of my performances severely jolting a meeting of the moribund Manchester Poetry Society, the only one I was asked to attend.

It was not merely my strong belief that poetry gains by being heard: I knew that poetry loses immeasurably by *not* being heard. Indeed, if poets could only imagine the droning noise that the average reader makes of their work in his average mind's ear, they would be far more anxious to have it read aloud to him— and adequately. The fact that many poets are lamentably bad readers themselves remains beside the point. Not many composers are *virtuosi* and few lieder writers can sing, but that is hardly an argument against the performance of music.

Once I had become interested in the possibilities of poetry on the radio, I naturally began to consider what forms of poetry could be broadcast most effectively. Obviously enough, the most immediately effective were those that were most direct in what they were saying, and most direct and forceful in their manner of saying it. This was hardly a new thought: narrative poetry has always made for easy and compulsive listening. "Certainly I must confesse mine owne barbarousnesse," said the elegant Sir Philip Sidney, "I never heard the old song of *Percy* and *Duglas*, that I founde not my heart moved more than with a Trumpet; and yet is it sung but by some blinde Crowder, with no rougher voyce, then rude stile: which being so evill apparelled in the dust and Cobwebbes of that uncivill age, what would it worke, trimmed in the gorgious eloquence of *Pindare?*" The answer being: probably farre lesse—until about the tenth hearing. Nor is it likely that Sidney's heart was ever so moved by hearing the poetry of his friend Fulke Greville declaimed, wrapped in abstruse eloquence though it was. For Greville's poetry, like Sidney's own, was not intended primarily to be heard. *Chevy Chase* undoubtedly had been.

The fact was that even in Sidney's time it was still possible to hear the last dying notes of a poetry which had been written expressly for performance. By the end of the sixteenth century, in England at least, the tradition was virtually dead: the bard had been replaced by the man of letters. Admittedly, poetry was still read aloud on occasion. But the poet's attitude to his art had changed: he was no longer concerned with emotional response so much as with intellectual stimulation. And that was generally a matter for careful study of the printed page.

In an essay on *Spoken and Written Poetry*, first published in 1950 in the *Poetry Quarterly*, I pointed out how the invention of printing had changed the style of poetic composition in this country. I also pointed out how the increasing habit of listening to poetry on the radio must change the style again, and this is now a matter of history likewise. Yet it is only in the last fifteen years that the tradition of writing poetry expressly for performance has been revived. In the nineteen-thirties, the idea of booking the Albert Hall or the Festival Hall for a recital of spoken poetry would have been dismissed as ludicrous. Until the present revival, poetry had ceased to be a noise in the ear; it had become no more than a noise at the back of the head.

Poetry written primarily for study on the printed page will always tend to be more cerebral and involved than poetry which depends for its effect upon immediate understanding when heard for the first time. Indeed, it would be very surprising if it did not.

Such written poetry may well be more profound and satisfying to the silent reader. When it has been studied, has been fully mastered and has become familiar, it may even give far deeper pleasure when heard properly spoken. This, of course, has been proved by all the classic poetry readings broadcast on Third Programme. But the wide success of the poetry read-ins now being heard all over Britain and America proves that once again there is a large and eager audience for direct poetry which makes its full impact at the first hearing. No printed text of such poetry needs to be studied in advance: the medium of single performance is the message. For the first time since the Middle Ages, the tradition of spoken poetry is again beginning to make its way in the world. Allen Ginsberg has joined the Bards.

The sudden and rapid increase in the demand for poetry in performance—on the air, on disc, or in the hall—might almost make one wonder whether the habit of listening to poetry may not eventually replace the habit of reading it for oneself. This was quite inconceivable to most people twenty years ago, but Marshal McLuhan is not alone in affirming that the day is coming. Electronics have already begun to challenge the book as a teaching machine. As for the book itself, paperback publication has emphasised just how disposable it is. Indeed, its chance of physical survival in a chemical-sodden atmosphere is already proving something of a gamble. The principle of built-in obsolescence is no longer confined to the motor car: books that once were written to survive are now being largely written to be replaced. But replaced by what, eventually? Electronic reproduction is infinitely easier and cheaper than reproduction by printing, as the underdeveloped nations are already discovering. The libraries of the future may well be filled with recordings and casettes rather than with books. This, I happen to think, would be a pity. But I also venture to hope that all three will learn to survive, side by side.

Without looking so far into the future (a future which none of us may survive to enjoy) I am glad that poetry has at least re-found its voice. Insofar as radio and recording have brought this about, I am glad to have played my own part in the rehabilitation.

My own personal preference is for the older spoken poetry tradition, but whatever one thinks of their respective merits, the fact remains that both spoken and written poetry benefit by performance. As I have said, the poem designed for speaking will generally be more effective at the first—and perhaps the only—hearing. But I know of no poetry at all that cannot be broadcast effectively to a literate audience. Fine broadcast performance can add immeasurably to our enjoyment of 'difficult' poetry with which we are familiar already. Fine broadcast performance of 'difficult' poetry with which we are *not* familiar can send us in search of a printed text to study. It can vastly increase the appreciation of poetry, and vastly increase the demand for it. If I had not been firmly convinced of that, I should not have devoted so much time to putting it on the air.

It must be remembered that back in the thirties, very little poetry was heard on the air. And it would be true to say that of that very little, most was traditional in its appeal. The appropriate thing from Palgrave or the *Oxford Book of English Verse* came up regularly enough in 'mosaics' written around the seasons or the English countryside. Works of the Georgians came up also in features like Val Gielgud's *Gallipoli* or *Lepanto*. Occasional Georgians like Humbert Wolfe or Edmund Blunden might even find their way to the microphone and read their works in the late evening. Yeats himself was heard in one unique transmission, bringing a new sound of poetry to those who had never heard him read before. But when I put a sixty-minute selection of younger poets on the air at a peak listening hour in 1938, this was something of an innovation. The selection, called *The Modern Muse*, was made and introduced for me by Michael Roberts, whose anthology, *New Signatures*, had first called wide attention to the poetry of Auden, Day Lewis, Spender and MacNeice six years previously. Six years is a long time, but I think it would be true to say that their work was still no better known in Broadcasting House than it was in the Admiralty or the Office of Works.

I produced *The Modern Muse* in Manchester, hooking up studios in London, Birmingham and Newcastle. Because I was interested in music, the programme also included settings of certain poems by young composers, Benjamin Britten's settings of Auden being notable among them. Whatever the singing was like, the standard of reading—as I remember it—was far from remarkable. I had heard far better performances at the Ammon Wrigley Fellowship up in the Pennines at Saddleworth, where dialect poetry speaking was still a lively art. Even so, I found it of considerable interest to compare the various poets' reading styles; of which, to my then way of thinking, Day Lewis's was far and away the best.

In the studio with me at Manchester, among others, I had both Auden and Dylan Thomas—Wystan reading his *Six Beggared Cripples* in impeccable Oxfordese, as yet untainted with pseudo-American vowels. Dylan I had first met in 1933 with David Archer and Charles Lahr in Red Lion Square. But so far as I know, he had still not been heard on the air. In a voice which knocked the needle across the meter, he came up with *The hand that signed the paper*, my first experience of his booming public voice. To be truthful, I can't say that I appreciated it at the time, any more than I appreciated Bob Dylan's nasal whine the first time I heard him singing in a dingy New York nightspot. Nor did our tastes in poetry coincide very closely: he did not then share my enthusiasm for the work of Hugh MacDiarmid, nor did I then share his enthusiasm for the work of Laura Riding. He stayed with me in Manchester for a couple of days, but did not endear himself to my wife by emptying his morning tea-pot over his eiderdown when breakfasting in bed. He asked my advice about writing for radio, and I put him in touch with Rowland Hughes, the feature producer in Cardiff, himself a considerable poet (in Welsh) and a Crowned Bard at the Eisteddfod. Correspondence ensued, from which Douglas Cleverdon has dated the first germ of the idea which emerged eventually as radio's greatest script, *Under Milk Wood*.

But though we were never particularly close, over the twenty years I knew him,* I have no doubt at all that far more was done by Dylan Thomas to revive interest in poetry speaking than by anyone else of his time. He was himself, after all, completely convinced in his concept of poetry as performance. It was no accident that he happened to be a Welshman, and followed the old bardic tradition. As I soon came to acknowledge, once I'd got used to the style, in reading his own poetry he was incomparable. His deep sincerity infused new depths of meaning into it: in that incredible voice, his poems glowed and flared like sparks in oxygen. His reading of Milton or Wordsworth or other people's poetry was hardly so successful: they all began to sound like Dylan Thomas. But whatever he chose to read, the atmosphere in a crowded hall began to crackle with static; and his effect upon a whole generation of young Americans was astounding. Over in the States he found a long tradition of poetry speaking ready-made for his purpose; but he utterly transformed the tradition. Travelling round America in his wake, I heard his praises sung on all sides: nobody could draw an audience like him—or hold it, provided he managed to appear. Even when he failed to appear, it had to be accepted as altogether in character. His readings were recorded and listened to as Holy Writ in colleges and high schools all over the continent. His death became as much a part of American folk-lore as the death of Billy the Kid or Jesse James. Nor is the comparison altogether far-fetched, for Dylan himself was an outlaw, by inclination and by proclivity. But outlaw or whatever he was, if anyone gave back its sound to poetry, that man was Dylan Thomas.

The audience for poetry on the air had increased rapidly during the war; and with the coming of Third Programme in 1946, for

* I ought to make it clear, that although we often met up with each other, Dylan was hardly a friend of mine. Indeed, it was only our last evening together, in September 1953, that I really enjoyed. I found him in the Stag's Head having a drink with Joyce Rowe, who was truly fond of him. As I had a date with her, I went over and joined them. After the fifth pint, conversation was getting a lot more cordial. "You've improved," he said to me: "you used to be an unutterable prig." "You've improved yourself," I conceded: "you used to be an intolerable bum." We both guffawed, and like Brutus and Cassius, solemnly shook hands. The rest of the evening was euphoric, and I looked forward to many more. Shortly afterwards, he left on his last trip to New York, and I never saw him again.

the first time it was possible to meet the demand adequately.* In 1950 I was asked by Harman Grisewood to organise a regular series of poetry readings for Third, which I did in committee with Louis MacNeice, Terence Tiller, W. R. Rodgers, Rayner Heppenstall and R. D. Smith, all then members of Features Department. It was felt that poetry merited some such careful representation upon the air as the repertoire of classical music. In addition, as a patron of the arts itself, Third Programme was anxious to provide an outlet for the work of younger and little known poets, apart from that of the more important among their contemporaries. Air time was accordingly allocated equally among the new and the old, the new being equally divided between the known and the unknown. All this, of course, was quite independent of the production of dramatic works by poets such as MacNeice, George Barker, Laurie Lee, Herbert Read, Lawrence Durrell and others, many commissioned specially for radio production.

My own part of the plan was interrupted by my return to America and various other trips, and after Grisewood's translation to higher spheres, the plan was allowed to lapse. It was only with P. H. Newby's arrival as Third Programme Controller that the Poetry Committee as we know it today was instituted. Under his chairmanship, its work in the cause of contemporary poetry has been considerable.

Even so, in the year during which the organisation of poetry reading devolved mainly upon me, a certain amount was achieved. For the most part, I concerned myself with readings from the earlier poets, leaving the presentation of the younger moderns to Louis, Terence and the others, who were anyway better fitted to handle it. Even so, I was happy to mount the first reading of Pound's *Homage to Sextus Propertius*, and a comprehensive selection of the work of Hugh MacDiarmid—both admirably suited to broadcast hearing, even by those not already familiar with

* Excellent poetry readings had already been organised for the Home Service by Patric Dickinson, but these were personal selections and rather more informal than those required for Third Programme listening.

them. I was also glad to be instrumental in getting a first hearing for W. R. Rodgers's fine poem *Europa and the Bull* and the earlier poems of Basil Bunting, some dozen years before *Briggflatts* brought him the recognition so long overdue. Norman Cameron's translation of Villon I have already noticed.

Among the earlier poetry which I produced were selections of the Border Ballads in which they were both spoken and sung, though neither by a blind Crowder: I still prefer the gaelic harp to the fiddle by way of accompaniment. In *Poems of the Sea* I was able to include Pound's *Seafarer*, as well as the storm scene from Gawain Douglas's *Eneados*, which Pound preferred to the latin 'because Douglas had heard the sea'. For brighter broadcasting, I even included some of the extraordinary sounds uttered by Richard Stanyhurst in a later attempt at the same thing. In a more obvious vein, I added a series of readings from Browning, who had loved to speak his poems himself. Among them was a dazzling reading of *Pacchiarotto* by James McKechnie, one of the most astonishing pieces of virtuosity which even that splendid actor achieved. Beddoes, Darley, the Rowley Poems, various Elizabethan pastorals, Drayton's Odes, Defoe's *True-Born Englishman* and Morris's Arthurian poems were also among my personal pleasures as a producer at the time. As read by some of the finest poetry speakers in radio, they made rewarding listening in a style that Third Programme taught us to take for granted. Alas that we shall hear far less in similar vein from now on!

But it was the series of readings that Ezra Pound recorded for me in Washington which really proved to me just how important such recordings can be, when made by the poet himself. There are, after all, two kinds of poetry reading. There is the straightforward enunciation of the text, which aims at clearly conveying the sense of the poem as it is understood by the reader. Such a reading does not add personal overtones to the poem; and because we are generally more interested in the poem than we are in the casual reader, no mere actor should ever seek to do so. For the actor to get between the sense of what he is reading and the listener is merely to spoil the poem and impair the listener's appreciation of it. That is why—at first—I had been rather bothered by Dylan Thomas's habit of inflating his poems in his reading: it had tended to distract my attention from the poetry itself.

On the other hand, the straightforward reading of any poem is a norm easily come by: we can even provide it for ourselves. To have for comparison with it a personal interpretation of the poem spoken by the poet himself may be a very valuable thing. And in Dylan's case, *every* reading of his own work was a personal interpretation. Often enough, it was an entirely new interpretation, for he could almost be guaranteed never to read any poem the same way twice. Different images were stressed, different contrasts heightened, different shades of meaning explored each time that he rolled the poem off his tongue. Needless to add, all his interpretations were equally valuable for a full appreciation of the work. There is no such thing as a definitive performance of a piece of music. Similarly, there is no such thing as a definitive reading of a poem—least of all, by the poet himself.

But quite apart from questions of interpretation, there is the question of personal self-expression. When a reading voice is cultivated—as by Dylan and Pound it certainly was—performance becomes the assumption of a *persona*. And only by a full study of his various *personae* can any creative artist be finally understood. To have a portrait of Dylan Thomas by Augustus John is a valuable thing in itself, but the portrait tells us more about the artist than about the poet. No matter what he looked like, how could one ever have hoped to understand Dylan himself without having the sound of his reading voice in one's ears, and without the consequent perception of what he was using his voice to create? With a poet as complex—and as articulate—as Dylan, creation is a continuous process: it does not end with the final draft of the poem upon the paper. From that time on, the poem itself becomes a stimulus to his creative urge. What the poet does with his work in voice can sometimes give one an indication of what he has done with the poem's raw material in his imagination. To listen to a recording of his own work by Dylan

Thomas is not only to share an occasion: it is to get a clearer insight into the whole poetic process.

The same is true—in a slightly different way—of Ezra Pound. Before my weekend session with him in 1956, I had already heard the few short Harvard recordings which he had made in 1939, so that his reading style was not a complete surprise to me. Even so, it made a striking contrast with his conversational style. As I have explained, I had first met him in 1951, when he was still vigorous and in good health. Five years later, he was a very different figure. He seemed a great deal older, the energy drained out of him, his face and frame far thinner, his beard more venerable. He was no longer impulsive in his movements, but languid and obviously tired. We chatted for half an hour in the room which had been made available to us, and his wife tactfully withdrew. He agreed to make the recordings on two conditions: the choice of the poems should be left to him, and everything that he recorded should be kept in its entirety, and after his death so broadcast. To this, of course, I at once agreed in turn.

He had his books already marked, and I plugged in my microphone. He preferred to read stretched back in his chair, resting his head on a cushion, and holding the text well up before him. I sat on the arm of his chair and held my microphone the usual eighteen inches away from him. At first, he instinctively tried to grab it and hold it himself, much like an old-fashioned upright telephone. I managed to persuade him to leave that end of the session to me, and after a few preliminary tests for level and acoustic, the recording got under way.

Much to my amusement, he started off with some of the Alfred Venison squibs, which I remembered from the days of the *New English Weekly*. The short satirical verses, read in a jaunty would-be Cockney voice, derided the bankers and all their works, and at least got us away to an air of comical informality. As Pound read them, the jingles certainly sounded a lot more lively than they look on the flat page. And from there, having flexed his voice, he proceeded to the *Cantos*.

It was here that his reading really got down to its true rhythm, the slow and measured delivery of a man who is prepared to utter for most of a long lifetime. The voice had changed, not merely from Alfie Venison, but from Pound as I knew him in conversation. The poetry was slowly and movingly intoned. When he was speaking in character, as in the Benton Cantos, he became the American politician: when he was quoting Confucius, his manner became Confucian—all which one would have expected. But it was in his splendid articulation of the poetry where it spoke for himself that the style was set for the whole. This was not speech as it was ever spoken—least of all by Pound himself— but a charging of language by enunciation no less than by his favourite *logopoeia*, 'the dance of the intellect among words'. This stately *pavane* was the poet fulfilling his role, the poet making and bringing to life. His voice filled the lines as wind filled the bellying sails of Odysseus, and the verse moved as slowly and deliberately as a ship. Every word was savoured upon the tongue, the Rs in particular being rolled with a care that only a Scot would normally devote to them. It was not so much a reading of poetry as an actual experience of poetry. This was above all else an occasion, a re-realisation by Pound of all that had gone into the making of the *Cantos*. It was the poet, locked away from the world, reminding the world of what it should know and what it should strive to achieve. In the process of doing so, it was also the poet powerfully reminding himself.

The allusiveness of the *Cantos* became far clearer in that reading; so did comparisons and qualifications. The poetry became far more dazzling, even in those occasional *longueurs* where it was merely reiterating what had clearly been stated already. So far as Pound was concerned, the reading was itself in the nature of a testament, for neither of us expected him then to come back into the world again. The evils of usury were far more important to him than the mere beauties of poetry: the message of the *Cantos* was far more significant to him than the lyrical mood in which they had first set out to assess the world. As he stressed, it was only as a favour to me that he finally consented to record the magnificent opening of the poem.

One thing emerged clearly enough from the reading: unless the casual reader approaches the *Cantos* in the same spirit of full realisation of the poetry, he will get very little out of his reading. Unless he also learns to adopt the slow deliberate intoning of the verse, he will never begin to understand what the poem meant to the poet. Whether he chooses to savour the verse and roll his Rs in the same way, is perhaps of lesser importance. What is highly significant is the fact that Pound so hears his poetry whenever his eye ranges over it. To the casual reader, the *Cantos* may suggest no more than fragmentary hints of experience. To those who devote themselves to the work, realising it in the reading as Pound has taught us to realise it, the *Cantos* can become experience itself. In the chemistry of the voice, the fragments fuse together into an apprehended whole, as significant detail in a picture coheres within the eye to give new understanding of all that has been depicted.

Some years after that first recording, when Pound had been freed and was back in Italy, I asked him about his reading style. I wondered whether it had derived, perhaps, from the reading style of Yeats as I vaguely remembered it. This Pound firmly denied. "My reading style, I believe," he said, "has altered a little since we used to meet at that horrible place called 'The Tour Eiffel' with Stulich's protruding stomach and bulbous nose to enhance the flavour of the food. I believe that what Ford called my 'Northumbrian' was more emotional at that period. I suppose one is more emotional at twenty-whatever-it-was. And Yeats' reading . . . well, in the first place he had Florence Farr who really *could* read . . . and then Yeats, his means of getting, or *seeing* his rhythm, was pulling out the vowels: 'Made a great peeeacock in the priiiide of his eyyyye'—that kind of thing. I think *my* reading now shows more interest in the meaning of what I've got on the page."

What Ford called his 'Northumbrian' suggests to me that neither of them, at that time, had heard Northumbrian at all! Even Basil Bunting has lost the Northumbrian burred R which he uses in conversation, and adopts for his reading voice the rolled

R of the Scots. But at least I began to see why Pound had been so excited by Gawain Douglas's Virgil: whether he had heard the sea in the verse or not, Pound had certainly heard the consonants. As I have said, the Speaker of Poetry is clearly a *persona* which Pound likes to adopt. I happen to believe that only by way of that *persona* can we come to a full understanding of Pound the *maker* of poetry.

It was by an odd coincidence that after making my Pound recordings at Washington, I went on up to Boston and recorded a further selection of readings by Robert Frost, thanks to whose efforts Pound was later to be released. No two men could have been more different, nor could two styles of poetry, nor two styles of speaking it. Where Pound had built on his poetry in performance, Frost quite simply *was* his poetry. He added nothing to what he had written: he merely gave voice to the quality that was in it already. His poems were spoken as they were conceived, the timbre and rhythms of ordinary speech being in them from the first. Indeed, when he had ended a reading, one could never quite tell whether his next words were the start of another poem or merely an introduction to it: pitch was the same either way, and only rhythm decided it. To get the full flavour out of it, Frost's poetry needs to be spoken by a New England voice. New England speech is as much a part of it as Scots is a part of the poetry of Burns. Its dry sense of humour and countryman's irony mean very much less in London English: Frost was American and his poetry is American. Both grew out of the same soil and both drew strength from it.

Though I only met Frost on three occasions, I felt the warmest affection for him. He in his turn was friendly to anyone coming from England, the country that had been first to recognise his talents. Though his attitude to Pound and his poetry was highly sceptical, he succeeded in shaming the American government into releasing him where closer friends like Hemingway had sadly failed to do so. In his last days, he became something of an Elder Statesman, honoured by President Kennedy and sent overseas as an ambassador for American culture and goodwill. His quotations from *Mending Wall* were not lost upon Khrushchev, though they failed to tear a hole in the wall at Berlin. In London he was received almost as a *guru*, and much enjoyed the role: the funny side of it struck him almost as much as the silliness of *guru*dom itself.

I was much amused by a story that I heard of him during his visit. He was staying at the Connaught Hotel, beloved of rich Americans and less rich duchesses. At breakfast one morning he joined his friend Archibald MacLeish, who was quietly buttering lonely toast. The silence of an English breakfast was only faintly disturbed by occasional rustlings of *The Times*. In a suitably subdued voice, MacLeish asked him whether he had read the latest batch of the *Cantos*. "No," said Frost loudly, as the hard of hearing are apt to do: "I get very tired of shit, shit, shit all the time." Newspapers fluttered on every side as horrified faces were turned upon him, he remaining blissfully unaware of the general consternation. "Is there something wrong with the breakfast, sir?" asked an agonised head waiter. "No . . .?" said Frost in surprise, and could not understand why MacLeish continued to laugh all day.

If his opinion of Pound was critical, Frost's opinion of E. E. Cummings was far more so. He told me of their first meeting, in a New York restaurant. Cummings and a party of friends were eating at a nearby table, and one of them recognising him, Frost was asked across to join the party. This he grudgingly did, feeling, as he explained, that Cummings might rather more fittingly have come across to join him. No further notice was taken of him, though much notice was taken of Cummings. "You realise," said a disciple, "that we think very highly of him. We rate his works only second to the Bible." "I rate them higher than that," said Frost: "I should like to see his works *incorporated* in the Bible . . . Preferably between the Old and the New Testaments, where they used to print the Apocrypha." "Or perhaps," he chuckled at me, "you'll now be filling the space with the Dead Sea Scrolls."

In a similar mood, he wondered why MacLeish had bothered to write his play *J.B.* "Everyone knows," he pointed out, "that I myself said the last word about Job long since." The Christmas poems which he sent his friends each year were ever welcome reminders of Frost's genial good nature. The last I received from him arrived on the morning that I read of his death in the newspaper. Sad as it was to me, I think he would have appreciated the irony of that.

Remembering Frost's anecdote, I was happily surprised to find how charming and unassuming E. E. Cummings actually was. I had heard him read at the New York Y—the YM-YWHA, to give it the full title—and had made a date with him to record a similar selection of his poems at his home in Patchin Place. Despite the cloistral calm of the house, we were much interrupted by the passage of air-liners overhead and the sudden clangour of two tons of coke being shovelled down a coal-hole across the way—"noises both terrestrial and celestial" as he called them—but a fascinating recording emerged despite these *obbligati*. The eccentricity of Cummings's typography is a gimmick, which can be appreciated precisely for what it is—a gimmick. The meticulous precision, the wit and the fastidiousness of his reading, reduced the visual intricacies to limpid clarity: his poems became the simplest statement of so many happily simple facts and ideas. Indeed, without the shock value of their erratic disassembly upon the page, many of the poems might well have failed to make their mark in a world where ingenuity tends to be more esteemed than all else. But in his exquisite reading, in a pleasantly mid-Atlantic voice, the poems acquired surprising charm and intimacy. Once again, to meet them only upon the printed page would be to miss their quality entirely. Cummings could emphasise their quality: his printed editions tended to disguise it. In some ways, perhaps, their very idiosyncrasies were a satirical comment upon the tyranny of the printed page. After all, what is a poem? Is it a sound in the ear, or is it a pattern before the eye? For those who have come to think of it as a pattern, Cummings provided a pattern more complex and wittily ingenious than any that had been known before. But the quality of a poem consists in the poetry itself, and that emerged in his reading as a proposition in Euclid emerges from a jumble of symbols.

The four poets I have remembered were all poets whose work gained by their own performance of it. There are many other such that I could have remembered, most of them again being Americans. The only English poet whose reading style deserves to be mentioned along with them is Basil Bunting. Influenced as he was by Pound—both as a poet and as a speaker of poetry—the quality of his achievement as both is still utterly unPoundian. His early lyrics *Gin the Goodwife stint* and *The Morpethshire Farmer* had delighted me back in the early thirties by their mastery of the spoken poetry style in which they were composed. *Brigg flatts* and the later work derive their strength and character from a full appreciation of what that spoken tradition had been. They are poems that need to be studied, but they are never so clear—or so impressive—as in Bunting's fine reading of them. Once again, his reading voice bears no relation to everyday speech: it is a form of creativity in itself. It is certainly not the sound that the casual reader will imagine as he looks at the printed text. But equally certainly it is the sound that Bunting himself heard as the poems shaped in his mind. As such, to my way of thinking, the sound is almost as valuable as the printed text itself.

As a man who spent much of his time producing other readers remarkably well, I was always rather puzzled by Louis Mac-Neice's failure to do equal justice to his own work. Most of it was written in full appreciation of what the voice could do for it, and as broadcast by other readers, his poetry made outstandingly good listening. No doubt he was persuaded that other readers could serve him better, and never bothered to acquire what he was perfectly able to teach. As with Auden, of course, his militantly Oxford drawl was a drawback to begin with, and he must have found it difficult to lose. What he called his 'burglar's lip' gave him a sardonic look at the best of times, as though he could never quite reconcile himself to life as he found it. The same sounded true of his voice, which came from the top of a nose that he always appeared to be looking down. (In actual fact, nobody could have been more amiable.) His reading was as controlled as his writing, and somehow managed to suggest a faint distaste even for his own work. In one sense, this was appropriate: nothing could better convey the detached manner in which he observed his world. On the other hand, nothing could give a falser impression of the man himself. He was a compulsive mixer, who yet contrived to appear to be everywhere by accident. At the centre of innumerable parties, he conveyed the impression of being somewhere on the perimeter, quietly watching himself enjoy them. It was only occasionally one saw beneath the mask to the shyness of the man who probably wore it in self-defence. Perhaps he had cause to fear his own impulsiveness, and no doubt it had sometimes led him into situations that he came to regret. But in his own impervious way, he had an inveterate knack of enjoying the company he kept, and none kept company more varied. Louis was a unique poet: he was also a unique person. No doubt he would have been much embarrassed by the number of friends who mourned him, after his last broadcast had killed him off in such a tragically unnecessary way.*

As for the poets I have known whose work actually lost in their own reading, the number is large enough. It was always something of a surprise to me that Hugh MacDiarmid should happen to be one of them. Brilliant talker as he is, there is little that he can add to the enjoyment of his poems as we find them in his books. His poems in Lallans, admittedly, gain much by his speaking of them, but they can hardly be enjoyed at all *before* they are spoken by somebody. The far more important poetry of his maturity—from *Stony Limits* to *The Kind of Poetry I want*—is a poetry quite beyond his own power to speak adequately: it calls for the virtuosity of a James McKechnie or a Duncan McIntyre, in whose fine readings one knows it for what it is: among the greatest

* While up in Yorkshire recording special potholing sound effects for his play *Persons from Porlock*, he got drenched to the skin in a sudden downpour. Not bothering to change into dry clothes, he caught a bad chill which turned eventually to the pneumonia from which he died four days after the broadcast went on the air.

poetry of our time. Robert Graves, whose poems derive so strongly from the spoken poetry tradition, is even more dependent on the reading ability of others: he is probably the worst reader I ever tried to produce—at least, of poetry so sensitive. W. H. Auden is better, but rather apt to produce a comical parody of himself. As for some of the others, perhaps I had better not express any further opinions . . .

Whatever importance one attaches to the recording of poetry in the poet's own voice—and in certain instances I attach the very highest importance to it—the fact remains that the practice is rapidly finding favour. After a lamentably slow start, the BBC has at last begun to take its own recorded archives rather more seriously. However much they still insist on destroying, a certain amount at least gets kept; and when a National Archive of Recordings is finally established, the BBC Recorded Programmes Library will form a valuable nucleus for it. In America, under Archibald MacLeish and others, a start was made during the last war, and recordings are to be found in the Library of Congress which include most of the leading American poets of the last half century. In the Poetry Room at Harvard, a similar collection has been built up under the guidance of Jack Sweeney; and a large private collection was formed by Lee Anderson, which will doubtless end up in one or other of the American universities. In the commercial field, excellent work has been done by Caedmon, Folkways Records and others in America, and by the Argo Record Co. in Britain. The British Council has itself sponsored much valuable work.

But the achievement of the Third Programme, in recording and broadcasting poetry as a regular feature of its output, was far and away the most important, and likely to have the most lasting results. However it is read—by the poet himself or by the actor—poetry is now recognised as an art which has the right to be heard. And the final effect which this will have on the manner of *writing* poetry cannot be overstressed. Since Allen Ginsberg let out his first *Howl*, a revolution has been in progress. Kenneth

Rexroth, Lawrence Ferlinghetti, Gary Snyder and others in America, Christopher Logue, Adrian Mitchell and their followers over here have made a new impact with work which would have been utterly disregarded some twenty years ago. By the end of the present century, I expect a completely new concept of the poet's place in the modern world, and a completely new style in the poetry that he will be writing. As the novel finally decays, we may even find narrative poetry coming back into popular favour.

As I see it, the current revival of interest in the sound of poetry is merely a hesitant beginning: it will soon lead on to something far more important, the re-marriage of poetry and music. I for one happen to believe that the long divorce between them has not been a lucky one for poetry. I am not referring to the setting of poems by composers, which has always been an accepted part of musical creativity. I am thinking rather of the poet who comes to think of music as a necessary part of his own creativity. The troubadours and trouvères, the minnesingers and meistersingers all conceived their poems predominantly in *terms* of music. The same was true of every writer of heroic poetry from Homer to the *Kalevala*, the *Marko Kraljević* cycle and the rest. In a far more sophisticated way it was true of Campion and the lutenists, whose poems were merely the vehicles for the airs to which they were set. Very few poets today are competent to set their own poems, though many have worked in collaboration with composers. But a new school of folk-poets has lately arisen which is perfectly competent to write, set and perform their songs as a natural function of their art.

Quite apart from songs and singing, of course, there have been many recent experiments in combining music with spoken poetry. This has been done symphonically by Sir Arthur Bliss and others; it has been done with great success electronically by Roberto Gerhard. But by far the most popular of such experiments have been made in the field of poetry and jazz.

Having heard many examples of the poetry and jazz amalgam,

220

I am not by any means convinced of their success. There have been experiments of the sort on Third Programme, *Red Bird Dancing on Ivory* being one of the earliest. In that case, poems by Pablo Neruda (translated by Christopher Logue) were matched with jazz from the Tony Kinsey Quintet, the production being by D. S. Carne-Ross. Insofar as the jazz was carefully scored, it may have seemed wrong to certain purists to describe it as jazz at all, though Jelly Roll Morton, with his insistence on 'playing the notes as he wrote them on the sheet' would hardly have supported the view. I myself broadcast a recording of Jack Kerouac's *Poetry for the Beat Generation*, in which a piano accompaniment was effectively extemporised by Steve Allen without so much as a single rehearsal. If this was not jazz in the strict sense either, it was pleasant musical doodling in the jazz idiom, such as one used to hear in any New York nightspot between the acts.

I have heard many comparatively successful examples of jazz and poetry in San Francisco, where the idea of marrying them first originated. Rexroth, Ferlinghetti and the others have been well served there by musicians of the progressive jazz school. But by far the most effective recording of the kind that I know is *The Weary Blues* by Langston Hughes, with its brilliant jazz accompaniment by the Horace Parlan Quintet and a group led by Red Allen. On this recording, poet and musician are for once talking the same language, and both using the same Negro idiom. Similar music had been in Langston's ears when he wrote the poems, so the marriage was completely legitimate. In most other examples that I have heard, it has been only too obvious that there has been no marriage at all. In most of them, the poet and the musician were talking entirely different languages: each was following his own bent, and mostly they were not even going in the same direction.

Even so, all such bringing together of poetry and music is potentially interesting in itself. When properly worked out, it may ultimately lead to far more effective performance of poetry, and may well heighten its whole impact. But it is in no sense getting back to the tradition where poetry and music were virtually two ingredients of a single indivisible art. Only the folk-singers of our time are successfully doing that.

When I first heard modern American folk-singing during the war, I realised how truly it stemmed from the sung poetry of the past. Not merely was it reviving the proper performance of the ballads collected by Child, but it was producing its own songs and ballads in exactly the same tradition. To hear Leadbelly singing *John Henry* or Josh White singing *Hard Time Blues* was to hear virtually what Sidney had heard when *Chevy Chase* was sung by his blind fiddler. It was to hear poetry which had been conceived of as song in the moment of composition. To read either lyric on the page was to experience something infinitely less, as it is to experience painting or sculpture merely in monochrome reproduction.

The men who were actually writing and singing such songs in my time—Woody Guthrie, John Jacob Niles, Pete Seeger, Ewan MacColl, Bob Dylan and the rest—have given back to poetry something it should never have lost. They have re-created for us what I believe will prove to be the poetry of the future. Poems like Bob Dylan's *Farewell Angelina*, *A hard rain's a-gonna fall* or *I'm alright, Ma*, have better claim to a place in the anthologies of contemporary poetry than most of the pieces that recur there so monotonously. I suspect that Auden, who has consistently included sung poetry in the anthologies he has edited, would be one of the few poets who might agree with me. Admittedly, much is lost when such poems are merely printed, for which they were never written in the first place. But in the best of them, much also remains: their imagery is superb.

I am not alone in thinking that Bob Dylan's work is no less deserving of notice than Dylan Thomas's, and that one of these days work in both traditions will be equally regarded. Speaking the poems of their time—still more, singing the songs—the poets of the future may again begin to wield more influence than the men who make the laws. What we have seen in the last twenty years is no more than the tip of the iceberg. The seas will be seen to thrash around when the hidden bulk rears up and reveals itself for all that now lies hidden. For poetry then will indeed have become performance again, as generations of listeners once knew it throughout the world. I am happy to think that when that day arrives, radio will be known to have played its vital part in the quiet revolution.

IO

Radio in the doldrums

THE LAST TWO chapters have been concerned exclusively with
the work I was doing during the fifties for the Third Programme.
But it must be remembered that this was only a part of my work
for radio as a whole. As Assistant Head of Features Department,
no less than as a writer and producer, I was equally concerned with
maintaining a steady supply of programmes for the Home Service, the Light Programme and the Overseas Service.

I have said that the fifties were a significant period in BBC
history, insofar as they saw the complete swing-over of the mass
audience from radio to television. At the end of the war, it had not
been unusual for Home Service features to attract an audience of
ten million listeners or more: a decade later, the average feature
audience on the Home Service had shrunk to something less than
a single million. Audiences on the Light Programme continued
to be larger, but only a very few features were carried there. As
for the audience for Third Programme—though it was never
larger than minimal, as I have explained—at least it stayed comparatively constant, and compared favourably with the audience
of the entire West End theatre or the circulation of the leading
weekly reviews.

The appointment of Major-General Sir Ian Jacob as Director-
General of the BBC in 1952 had also been significant. He had
previously been in charge of the Overseas Service, though latterly
on secondment to the Ministry of Defence. From the first, his
concern was far more with radio than with television, perhaps
because radio was a medium that he knew. By nature he was conservative, and by birth he was a pillar of what was soon to be
known as the Establishment. He distrusted intellectuals no less

than trouble-makers, and carefully shunned controversy. When he was controversial himself, it was mostly by accident, as when he once complained that the BBC was 'hag-ridden', which was hardly the way to endear himself to his senior female staff! He was a firm believer in the *status quo*, as was rapidly made clear by his various staff appointments. Whenever I met him, he was friendly and appreciative, but I could not think of him as a truly inspiring leader for radio in difficult times. Perhaps that was because he was the only Director-General who regularly arrived at Broadcasting House in a bowler hat. No doubt he had acquired the habit in Downing Street, where he had been Assistant Military Secretary to Churchill's War Cabinet.

I often think that Sir Ian's role with the BBC was to form square in the old manner, and make a firm last stand against the circling hordes of showmanship, commercialism, controversy and wogs. In this he was ably supported by Basil Nicolls, whose final days with the BBC were a steady insistence on peace and quiet and decorum at all costs. Only by keeping out of radio every hint of a desire for change could his own image be kept unsullied, and that way knighthood lay. Indeed, it was a common joke among programme people at the time that once the knighthood had been earned and Nicolls had retired, all of us could relax and get back to writing and mounting rather more lively programmes. Alas! in the event, one knighthood was to follow another. Perhaps that was why radio remained so unadventurous for the rest of the decade. What would it have become if peerages had been involved?

Wellington was a genial man of whom, socially, I was fond. I had worked with him happily in New York and he had always been well disposed to what I was trying to do, provided it was politically and every other way innocuous. I had worked for him ever since he had been appointed Controller and was running— or should I say walking?—the Home Service. Cordial as he was, we nevertheless had a few brushes, and on one deplorable occasion I had actually been warned away from his weekly meetings for expressing myself too freely as to what I thought was wrong with the programmes that he was asking Features Department to write. All was forgiven in due course when I had learnt to keep my opinions to myself.

The trouble was that I wanted a more challenging role for my kind of radio, especially when the rise of television seemed to make it so necessary. I much resented the slur of the 'steam radio' label; if steam were supposed to drive it, at least let the steam gather head and provide a few salutary explosions. It seemed to me that there was little point in doing hesitantly what television was already beginning to do boldly and controversially. Radio was easier and cheaper to mount: it was therefore easier to mount vigorously and effectively. As I saw it, radio offered far more opportunities to the writer: he should be encouraged to use it for making people think and argue and use their imagination. This, however, was still regarded as a highly dangerous doctrine.

I was also critical of radio's unwillingness to promote and build up its own market by elementary showmanship. I firmly believed that it should be moving heaven and earth to improve its wilting image. I felt that it should be loudly calling attention to itself, and putting its programmes across with all the vigour and salesmanship of a concern that really believed in the quality of its product. The *Radio Times* should be turned into something far more lively; announcers should be glamourised, artists, writers, producers and the rest given a new star quality. They represented, after all, so many capital assets: even if they had to be paid more, their value as audience builders would be enhanced. All this was regarded as brash and vulgar, if not as positively unBritish. It was clearly conveyed to me that the BBC was not run by a bunch of hucksters: radio was a business conducted by gentlemen. Personally, the only time I even used the word was when I was looking for a public loo . . .

Wellington's earlier duties as Controller of the Home Service were taken over by Andrew Stewart, a very proper Scot who was even more soberly cautious than Wellington himself. I had known him in Glasgow when he was still Scottish Programme Director: on one occasion he had acted as host and guide to me in my following up on the track of the Young Pretender. In the country of his forefathers, he was altogether in character, and endeared himself to me for the wry pride that he took in being directly descended from (I think) the eighteenth illegitimate son of the Wolf of Badenoch. That was well enough, but in a lively post-war London he seemed remarkably out of place. For him, the scrip of Sir John Reith was still the only legal tender. He even complained, quite seriously, that the commentator chosen to cover some royal occasion had actually been divorced! Only innate respect for the hierarchy could reconcile him to the fact that BBC Directors might now find themselves in the same position.

In an age that was already beginning to blow its top, Andrew Stewart's code of behaviour was presbyterian, to say the most. When I once suggested changing the name and image of the Home Service, he gazed at me in astonishment as though I had suggested changing the shape of the British Isles. Home, I pointed out, was what all bright boys and girls were eager to get away from: the label was middle-aged and losing us a generation of up-and-coming listeners. And was it *really* necessary to deaden every programme gap with the dulcet pealing of Bow Bells? His Grace the Archbishop of Canterbury, he solemnly assured me, would be deeply disturbed if we didn't! Where the young listener was learning to look back only in anger, the BBC Home Service insisted on looking back in complacency. The age-group that it catered for exclusively in the fifties was also in its fifties.

The Light Programme was rather less toffee-nosed under its Controller Kenneth Adam, who still maintained his contacts with life outside the BBC. He was even to be seen taking drinks in the bars with writers and producers; due to the fact, no doubt, that he happened to have trained as a journalist. His successor, Rooney Pelletier, was a French Canadian of equally modern tastes. He even commissioned me to write a satire on some of the mild stupidities which the Light Programme was largely in business to encourage. The play was called *Wilfred Pilgrim's Progress*, and starred Wilfred Pickles in all its fourteen male parts, a lively piece of virtuosity which new tape-editing techniques made thoroughly convincing. I was glad to be paid for the work, but was sorry to find that even the Light Programme audience for Pickles as an actor had shrunk since I scripted *Ex-Corporal Wilf* for him shortly after the war. At least, *Have a Go* was still pulling in the listeners, whatever that tended to prove . . .

Trivial as all such programmes might be, I still felt it was important to keep in touch with the more popular side of radio, especially during this period of diminishing returns. The fact was, I still remembered radio as a medium of mass communication. And much as I personally enjoyed the intellectual temperature of the Third Programme, I was still unwilling to turn my back on all that might be left of the larger audience. In short, I did not wish to preach exclusively to the converted: I was interested in trying to create new audiences, rather than merely writing for the already well disposed. Radio's decline, in an age of television, was obviously inevitable; but I did not believe that the decline need be quite so drastic as timid planning was making it. I felt that radio should be making a fight to keep its proper place in the world. Like many another producer to whom radio was still exciting, I hated to let its challenge go by default.

In 1954, following the start of commercial television, I was summoned to a meeting of senior programme staff called by Lindsay Wellington as Director of Sound Broadcasting. The coming of ITV had proved something of a shock to the BBC directorate, and was viewed with some resentment. To begin with, it was the love-child of the Conservative Party, which the BBC had done so much to conciliate over the years. It posed a serious threat to BBC television, which was growing fast but was still rather amateur in its standards. Furthermore, by a vigorous use of publicity to sell its product, commercial television was doing exactly what I had pleaded that the BBC should be doing in the days of its monopoly. In the course of the next few years, it was to beat the BBC quite startlingly at its own game by winning two-thirds of the television audience. Whatever one thought of it, commercial television had opened a new era in British broadcasting, and for better or worse the role of the BBC had been changed overnight. Where before it had been able to take itself for granted, the BBC now had to prove itself in competition, and prove itself exclusively by the nature and quality of its programmes.

All this was clear enough to those at Wellington's meeting, which had been called to discuss how radio might best adapt itself to the new order of things. Various tentative suggestions were made, none of which seemed to me to be anyway radical enough. I pointed out that the coming of commercial competition had completely changed the function not only of BBC television, but of BBC programmes as a whole. From now on, there was no alternative to competing, other than withering away. The factory, I suggested, would have to be re-jigged. If our programmes had been right before the coming of commercialism, they could not possibly be right still. If they were right now, then they must have been wrong before. Yet the start of the new era had not been reflected by radio in a single way. Surely, the advent of a new threat to broadcasting should be comparable, in its way, to the impact of the nuclear bomb on naval planning. What was called for in both was a faster, more mobile striking force, one which could cope with a new threat in an utterly different way. Even the Admiralty knew that the capital ship had now become as obsolete as the galleon: they at least had realised that their basic strategy would have to be rethought.

With a sadly affectionate smile for my revolutionary ardour, Wellington assured us that he had no intention of scrapping or retiring his battle fleet. Tactics might have to be adjusted, but his capital ships would continue at sea. H.M.S. *Vanguard* might be written off as obsolete, but the nature and character of radio would remain substantially as it had been. With a sadly affectionate smile of my own, I felt quite sure that it would.

In point of fact, radio stayed substantially as it was for the next three years. To judge from the *Radio Times* or from what came out of the loudspeaker, no such thing as commercialism existed in the land. Bow Bells continued to peal, and radio audiences continued to shrink. Even BBC television continued on much the same course, finding its audience rapidly dwindling in turn. Whatever else it lost, the BBC was determined to preserve its dignity: black ties continued to be worn by its television announcers. Perhaps we were lucky that they were not white ties, and if announcers had been in camera at full length, no doubt they would have been.* A new order of living might be coming to birth in the King's Road, but change was as little reflected in the BBC as it was in the Athenaeum.

I do not mean to suggest that there was anything radically wrong with the radio programmes that were heard: most of them continued to be as competent and professional as ever. Third Programme in particular continued to be intelligent, imaginative and forward-looking: the critical notices and the Italia Prizes which it won were certain proof of that. But Third Programme was heard by only a very few people, and what was sadly lacking was a hard core of equally lively listening for what was left of the major audience. Light music was there for the masses, and rock had come to join it, in a rather tentative way that the pirate stations were later to replace with pop far more attractively packaged. But so far as serious listening went—which was meant to provide the backbone of the Home Service output—cosiness was the watchword, where the real need was for trenchancy. In popular terms, radio stayed on the defensive—it never went over to the attack.

Having explored Europe, America and most parts of the Commonwealth, I myself was anxious to take a cool hard look at the Soviet Union. Like a number of listeners, I was interested to find out exactly how good the Russians were at running their own sixth of the world. I was sadly assured that I should never be allowed to see things for myself: all would be window-dressed in propaganda. Let me take a cool hard look, then, at the best that

* I remember the astonishment of the Director of Television when I pointed out to him that so far as most of his viewers' experience went, black ties were only worn elsewhere by waiters or dance bands.

they could show me: in terms of the Cold War, we should surely not underestimate what we were up against. If I could not see how bad they were, at least let me make sure just how good they were. That might be misleading, I was told: a soft warm look at NATO would be far more advisable. I refrained from taking it.

I was anxious to mount an attack on the creeping paralysis of McCarthyism, before the witch-hunt spread to Britain. But it was left to Ed Murrow to defy the Senator and all his works on American television. I wondered about the Integration Struggle in the Deep South, with its obvious relevance to the growing influx of immigrants into Britain. That was not our affair either, it seemed. Most compulsive subject of all, the Bomb was held to be *highly* dangerous—I had almost said explosive. And as for Peace itself, thanks to Communist propaganda, that had become a very dirty word.

Admittedly, most of this attitude stemmed from Whitehall, but that was hardly the point. The BBC should have been saying things, and daring Whitehall to interfere. Producers and writers were still far too restricted in what they were allowed to tackle. Planners still fought shy of anything that might give offence or get itself talked about or give rise to a question in the House of Commons. Subjects were still avoided on which a number of people would have welcomed guidance, or which they were getting used to discussing among themselves. In terms of popular listening, the fifties were unadventurous: they never affirmed anything, they merely balanced points of view until all finally cancelled out. To most of her listeners, the BBC became Auntie, and like the Queen of Spain, she had no legs—least of all, to stand upon. No wonder the younger listeners found coffee-house conversation a great deal more stimulating.

There comes a time in most questions when economic factors begin to weigh in the balance. And when sliding audience figures are coupled with a rise in production costs, the time cannot be staved off indefinitely, even in radio. In America, the swing-over from radio to television had come already, and was absolute. Television meant larger profits, and profits were what the networks

were solely in business to produce. When the balance sheet
suggested it, radio in the States had been written off overnight: it
became no more than a babble of news with disc-slinging patter-
men providing an endless barrage of recorded music in between.
At best, it came up with non-stop marathons like NBC's much-
vaunted *Monitor*, in which news and music were further inter-
spersed with mini-capsule flashes of 'local interest' from hither
and yon. American friends of mine, who came over to help start
up commercial television in Britain, assured me that the same
thing was bound to happen here as well. But critical as I was of
radio's lack of drive, I never believed for a moment in any such
catastrophe. Nor, I am glad to say, is there still any real sign of it
coming to pass, private doubts about the pattern of radio in the
seventies notwithstanding. As a Public Corporation, operating by
Royal Charter and with responsibilities to the listener no less
than to the viewer, the BBC has kept radio comparatively undiminished for a long time. All that it failed to do in the fifties
was to make radio exciting, and liven its own image in response
to rapidly changing times.

By 1957, however, economic factors had begun to suggest that
certain changes in radio were necessary. Unfortunately, so far as I
was concerned, the changes decided upon were all for the worse.
Most unfortunate of all was the first serious curtailment of Third
Programme output. Its five-and-a-half-hour weekday transmission period was cut to three or three and a half, the two-hour
evening space thus cleared being given over to what was known
as 'Network Three'. This emerged as specialist listening for every
kind of minority interest from Buchmanism to bee-keeping: it
soon became known as the Fretwork Network, and attracted even
fewer listeners than Third Programme itself.* Even so, talks were
obviously less costly than concerts or plays or whatever was lost
to serious listening. Sir Ian Jacob, himself no advocate of what he
regarded as long-hair listening, was generally blamed for the
decision. An immediate outcry was raised in the more responsible

---

* Luckily, this soon made way for the rather more useful *Study on 3* as we know it
today.

press, and a *Save the Third Programme* campaign was started up to try and get the cut restored. A deputation led by T. S. Eliot and Ralph Vaughan Williams arrived at Broadcasting House to register a formal protest, but with no noticeable result: the cut was made exactly as planned. At least the Governors promised that no further cuts would be made in Third Programme output, and that later economies would be made elsewhere. (The cuts made in 1970 proved the sincerity of that sober assurance!)

But apart from the cut in Third Programme, fundamental changes were made in programme emphasis on the Home Service and the Light Programme at the same time. News and current affairs coverage was increased, and the output of drama, features and other more ambitious programmes was cut back accordingly. But so far as programme organisation went, the 1957 changes were to prove more unfortunate still: further administrative posts were created at the top which tended seriously to lessen control of output by the programme departmental heads. And whether the changes were for the worse or not, the fact that they had been decided upon without any reference to the programme departments concerned was deeply resented by all programme staff. Faced with a flat *diktat*, feeling among the programme department heads ran high; and the curt insistence from above that all such policy decisions were beyond their competence to discuss was hardly acceptable to most of them. Even Val Gielgud, normally the most amiable of men, was moved to rise in open protest. At a meeting called by him of senior production staff, I found myself for once warmly supporting him. Much to my surprise, however, Gilliam chose to dissociate himself from the protest. Perhaps he felt it was merely a waste of time; and such as it was, it admittedly achieved nothing. A few conciliatory noises were made by the Director of Sound Broadcasting, who now had an assistant to act as his hatchet-man. But the programme changes were confirmed, and the programme staff were left to make the best of them that they could.*

---

* A similarly, dictatorial attitude was at work in 1969. The highly controversial reorganisation of radio outlined in *Broadcasting in the Seventies* was again decided upon without

Few members of the programme staff were really convinced that retrenchment of the kind adopted was either necessary or advisable. Changes in programme emphasis were certainly overdue. But these did not call for a cutting down of the very ingredients which should have been giving radio its quality. The administrative reshuffle, furthermore, ensured that future decisions regarding programme matters would be still further removed from programme personnel, a fact which was later to prove fatal to Gilliam himself. As for the savings effected, such as they were they could have been made at far less cost to the radio service as a whole. Cutting back on non-productive administrative staff would have helped to begin with. And many of us could have suggested substantial economies that could have been made in overall production costs without any lowering of production standards, if any of us had been consulted.

As a result of the 1957 reorganisation—and the changes that had *not* been made in programme policy—I was beginning to feel that the omens were not very favourable for the kind of radio in which I was interested. What had been done showed clearly enough which way thinking at the top was tending; and I even began to hear dark hints from on high that the ultimate role of radio was to be much the same as the 'news and music' formula which had killed it in America. In the event, the rumours proved to be groundless; but I could not help being conscious that radio as a cultural medium was being gradually subordinated to radio as information.

It had always seemed to me that Features Department in particular should maintain a careful balance between the two kinds of

---

any reference to the programme staff, who were peremptorily told to get on with putting it into force. On that occasion, however, the programme staff threatened to rise in open revolt against the *diktat*, and 134 members of the London programme and planning staff signed a protest letter in *The Times*. Regional staff immediately supported the protest and there was a certain amount of lobbying among Members of Parliament. The serious press, on this occasion, drew attention to the almost total lack of communication between the BBC management and its programme staff, and an open rupture between them was narrowly averted.

programme. I had trained myself from the first to write and produce either creative radio or documentary, and took equal pleasure in doing both, provided the documentary had something significant to say. But I was beginning to be disturbed by the fact that creative radio writing was now virtually confined to the Third Programme, and that the standards of documentary on Home Service and Light Programme were getting steadily drearier and more derivative. The creative feature, as written by such excellent outside writers as J. Bronowski, Dylan Thomas, Henry Reed and H. A. L. Craig, or by staff writers like Louis MacNeice, Charles Parker, Rayner Heppenstall, Francis Dillon and Nesta Pain had proved its ability to win Italia Prizes in open competition with the best radio writing in Europe.* Indeed, such writing had established the BBC feature programme as probably the finest radio writing in the world, for BBC Transcription Service had given it a world audience. But departmentally, no less than in the BBC as a whole, the drift was beginning to run away from creativity. Clearly enough, the drift was increasingly towards the everyday bread-and-butter informative documentary which seemed to meet the demands of the Home Service planners. Gilliam's interests were journalistic where mine were either creative or literary, and the fact was being reflected more and more in Features Department output. The sort of radio called for by the recent reorganisation seemed likely to emphasise the fact still further. No doubt that was partly why Gilliam had accepted the new order so placidly.

During the fifties he had been away on his world travels no less than I had. We arranged never to be away at the same time, as the running of Features Department must always devolve upon one or other of us. Over the last few years, however, it had tended to devolve increasingly upon myself. But the planning and decisions regarding features policy were strictly Gilliam's affair: I was there merely to implement them, whether I happened to

* The Italia Prizes were created in 1948, at the instance of Radio Italiana, for the best creative, documentary and music programmes written or composed specially for broadcast performance. They are competed for annually by all the European broadcasting organisations and a few non-European.

agree with them or not. And as time went by, I found I was
agreeing with them less and less.

For one thing, I was bothered about the uneconomic manner
in which our departmental resources were being used. I was also
bothered by the shrinkage in the demand for our product. Most
of all, I was acutely aware of the low state of morale in the department which had been growing over the last few years. In his
book, *Portrait of the Artist as a Professional Man*, Rayner Heppenstall has given an engaging picture of how the average feature
producer was apt to spend his day at the time. If any such ever read
the book, it must have sorely puzzled the average listener, to say
nothing of the average reader who has to earn his daily bread the
hard way. Interminable sessions at the Stag's Head, the Dover
Castle, the Glue Pot and the M. L. Club made drinking a round-
the-clock occupation for many of his ex-colleagues. Plenty of
work was done by many of them, but far less work was being
done by some. The general *malaise* of radio in the fifties had given
rise to a similar *malaise* among many of those who were able—if
put upon their mettle—to write it back into healthy and meaningful activity. As it was, there was an increasing disillusion among
many producers at the way that radio was being allowed to die
on its feet. Sinking his beer among the others, this may not have
been clear to Rayner Heppenstall. But sinking my gin and bitters
on the side, it was clear enough to me.

In 1957, Andrew Stewart returned to Glasgow as the BBC's
Controller in Scotland. His place as Controller of the Home
Service had been given to Ronald Lewin, under the new title,
Head of Planning, Home Service, a demotion of the post that was
itself significant. Lewin was a pipe-smoking modern historian
from Oxford, who had done his best work as a reasonably academic talks producer. Conscientious as he was, he seemed to me
to be short on both imagination and showmanship. His personal
interest seemed to veer towards the flood of war memoirs, would-
be contemporary history, political testaments, strategical and
tactical reappraisals that were currently being published—as indeed, when were they not? And I was depressed to find that these

were becoming increasingly the subjects for documentary treatment. To me, the vast bulk of them were boring in the extreme, and if they had to be reflected in radio at all, they could have been covered quite adequately in short cheap talks, the shorter the better. Instead, the tendency became to blow them up into documentary radio features, in which an expensive army of actors tried in vain to sound like international figures. The result was expensive radio, and painfully dull radio. Or so I was persuaded.

What helped to persuade me still further was a careful analysis of listeners' tastes prepared by the BBC's own Audience Research Department. From this it was only too clear that while radio drama was still popular, documentary radio was sinking to its lowest ebb in public appreciation. When one remembers that the best radio features in the past had been purely dramatic in form —had been classified as drama and appreciated as such—the inference became clear enough.* So far as the listener was concerned, creative and imaginative radio was still in strong demand, even on the Home Service: informational documentary—at least the kind that had been broadcast latterly—was in very small demand indeed. If documentary were to survive, it would have to be documentary of a far more original kind—and with a far more pungent flavour.

As I have explained, now that I was being regularly called upon to arrange for documentary output of a very *un*pungent kind, I found myself in something of an anomalous position. As Head of Features Department, Gilliam had been unmatchable in a steadily rising market: indeed, during the war and immediately after it, his leadership had been superb. His answer to increasing demand had always been bigger and more ambitious programmes, and that way success had always attended him. But the rise of television and the rapid decline of the radio audience had brought

---

* For instance, Louis MacNeice's *The Dark Tower*, Eric Linklater's *Socrates Asks Why?*, Edward Sackville-West's *The Rescue* and my own *March of the '45* had all been included in the Festival of Radio Drama in 1956. The other works were all straight plays by Tyrone Guthrie, Richard Hughes, Philip Wade and Peter Hirche. At least three of the first four were imaginative features, and the other was written by a member of Features Department.

a different state of affairs. Only the audience to the Third Programme remained substantially what it had always been, and even on Third Programme, transmission time had been drastically cut. Faced with a suddenly falling market, Gilliam was not so sure of himself; and when in doubt he tended to react in the old way. More people were brought in on the act and more engaged on contract. The cost of the product rose as demand for it was diminishing.

My own reflexes were entirely different. Having grown up in a slump and being used to shrinking markets, I was highly suspicious of all waste. I believed in a small caucus of extremely adaptable writer-producers whose business it was to keep costs down. If something could be done effectively for fifty pounds, I could see no virtue in doing it more elaborately for five hundred. I believed in the feature programme as a programme that *deserved* to be featured, when something special had to be done. I did not regard it as something to be used for plugging holes in the schedule. I could see very little future for Features Department in regular coverage of the humdrum; such material could be considered far more cheaply in talks and discussion programmes. It seemed to me that by concentrating too heavily on current affairs material, we ran the risk of pricing ourselves out of the business. Occasional treatment of such material—exhaustively and in proper depth—could be far more effective and far more rewarding in terms of departmental prestige. But such ambitious and costly documentaries could only be occasional, and must always be justified by enthusiastic listener response. For the rest, I felt that we should be concentrating on the more imaginative radio that was still popular at all levels. Most important of all, we should be exploring cheaper and more original methods of building up an audience for controversial programmes. We should not be merely repeating our failures and forcing up our costs. If we continued to do so, I felt, we might soon be out of business altogether.

My thinking as to the future of radio features was finally

brought to a head by an offer from the BBC television service. I had been invited more than once to take a training course in television production, but this had never proved feasible: either I had been busy on projects of my own, or Gilliam's absence abroad had left me keeping his seat warm. But in 1957 it was finally agreed that I should be released the following year for a six-month training course and attachment to television Drama Department, with a possible further attachment to television Talks. At which point, it seemed to me, I had to make up my mind as to what future I wanted not only for radio features, but also for myself.

If I took the training course, I had to sign an undertaking that I would not resign from the BBC for at least eighteen months after it ended. This was understandable: why should the BBC be put to the expense of training me, if I were promptly to cross the road and join up with ITV for a larger salary? On the other hand, there was no guarantee that a place could be found for me with the BBC television service; and with twenty-two years of seniority in radio, only the assistant headship of another department would have made a television appointment economically acceptable. In other words, I had to remember that even after taking the course, I was quite likely to find myself returning to radio again, and tied for a further eighteen months to a job I no longer enjoyed filling. I therefore decided to ask the BBC to relieve me of my duties as Assistant Head of Features Department.

In a detailed memorandum, I set out some of my reasons for making the request. To begin with, I emphasised my comparative lack of status and independence after a long career in radio. I reiterated my complete disagreement with the features policy I was being asked to implement. I suggested that the present swing to supposedly topical but demonstrably unpopular documentaries was operating against the kind of radio I had joined the BBC to write. Features Department had itself separated from Drama Department, so that both could pursue their different ways to the best advantage. Perhaps it was now time to carry separation a stage further. If journalistic documentaries were not entirely to

overshadow them, I felt that creative and literary features should
be given independent parity with them.* This could best be done
by creating a separate department to promote and encourage
imaginative radio. Such a department would be responsible for all
original radio writing, apart from radio drama, including creative
radio adaptations. It could also be given the task of organising all
poetry broadcasts and developing the use of folk-song in radio
programmes.

Not surprisingly, Gilliam was strongly opposed to the idea;
nor had I supposed for a moment that he would agree to it. His
own interest lay elsewhere, but creative and literary features had
won considerable prestige for his department, and there seemed
to him no reason why he should relinquish control of them. This
I could understand, and therefore expressed my willingness to
work for the BBC in any other capacity which gave me fuller
freedom to follow my own judgment.

Discussions were opened with our Controller, Michael Standing, and the Assistant Director of Sound Broadcasting, Richard
Marriott. Standing had been appointed to his controllership by
Wellington, in preference to either Gielgud or Gilliam, at the
time of Howgill's retirement in 1952. Though it was still far
from being free and unconfined, his title had been changed from
Controller of 'Entertainment' to the less ridiculous Controller of
Programme Organisation. He was a genial and friendly man who
had grown up in programmes during the thirties and had since
been Head of both Outside Broadcasts and Light Entertainment
Departments.† He had also served as a War Correspondent during
my own spell with *War Report*. We had known each other for

* One of the many causes which finally convinced me that something would have to
be done was Gilliam's unwillingness to release Francis Dillon for writing more of his
highly successful radio fantasies. His *Rumpelstiltskin* had won the BBC its first Italia
award, and I thought it silly to employ him exclusively on hack work, when there were
many far less able people around to do it.

† For the record, it might be as well to correct the impression created by Heppenstall
in his book already referred to. Michael Standing had played a very different part in the
termination of Heppenstall's contract from that which the book implies: but for his personal intervention, it might have been terminated somewhat sooner. Heppenstall's
comical account of his interviews with Standing is accurate as to the chair-borne acro-
batics, but very unfair as to Machiavellian intent.

some time, and he seemed reasonably well disposed to my plea for greater independence. Marriott seemed equally so, though as Wellington's assistant, like Standing himself he was under direct orders. To begin with, the discussions were friendly and sympathetic. In view of my long record as a staff writer and producer, it was suggested that I might be willing to work outside Features Department direct to Marriott himself, as a sort of roving commission free-lance writer upon the staff. After thinking the offer over, I agreed to accept it, only to find that the offer had been withdrawn, presumably by higher authority. Meanwhile, the question of my television attachment had to be considered. As I declined to begin the course unless the eighteen-month undertaking could be waived, this was obligingly agreed.

With my future still undecided, in February 1958 I began my course of television production training. Unluckily, within the week I went down with a bad attack of hepatitis. As the course was virtually over before I had recovered, I was offered one three months later. This I gladly accepted.

There followed a further couple of months of radio production, enlivened by skirmishing over my future status. But by now I found that discussion was rather less cordial. One thing everyone was agreed upon: I was no longer expected to act as Assistant Head of Features, nor had I any intention of doing so. It was suggested to me, however, that since I was dissatisfied with the job, my plain course was to resign. I replied that as I had devoted half my life to the BBC—without benefit of accumulating royalties—I really could not afford to do anything so quixotic.* I said that I was perfectly willing to accept a cash settlement in respect of disappointed expectations, a course that was usual practice in Fleet Street and elsewhere. I was told that the BBC were not in the habit of giving golden handshakes.

* Resignation from the BBC carried no compensation with it: termination of contract by mutual consent did. Best of all, financially, was summary dismissal.

I had all this explained to me by a friendly administrator, who had better be nameless. "For God's sake don't resign," he begged me. "If you really want to leave, my advice to you is this: wait in the Entrance Hall of Broadcasting House one evening, and as the Director-General leaves—help him through the door with your boot. You'll get yourself the sack—and be X thousand pounds better off for it!"

I was finally invited to suggest various other capacities in which I should be prepared to continue working for radio. Of seven new positions that I felt competent to fill, none was deemed to be necessary, though five were created subsequently and filled by other people. It was clear that my future with the BBC would have to be decided in the light of subsequent events, and the matter was left at that.

Meanwhile, I had other things to think about; and in April 1958, along with Louis MacNeice and others, I finally got down to my television training course. In June, again along with Louis, I found myself attached to the television Drama Department.

II

Television Interlude

LIKE ALL THE best love affairs, my liaison with television was a
matter of gratifying my curiosity without becoming involved in
a lasting attachment. Off and on, the relationship lasted for three
or four years, but did not interrupt the regular broadcasting of
my work on radio.

When I moved over to Shepherd's Bush, Television Centre was
still not completed, and my office work had mostly to be done in
a caravan on a vacant lot or bedrooms of converted dwelling-
houses in Lime Grove. I had plenty of friends in the television
service, though some of them were by then so exalted that I saw
very little of them. Gerald Beadle (later Sir Gerald) had taken over
from Sir George Barnes as Director of Television in 1956, and
had been well disposed to me since I used to lecture on feature
programme writing to the Staff Training College of which he
had been head before the war. Cecil McGivern, his Assistant
Director, I had worked with in the North or in Features Department for many years, though we had not seen much of each
other latterly. Controller of Television Programmes was Kenneth
Adam, whom I had known since our early days in Manchester.
With such a trinity at the top, I hardly expected television to
prove so frustrating as in fact it did.

I realised, of course, that I must be very much of a new boy,
and that my standing in radio would not cut much ice in a new
medium. Indeed, it didn't. Though many of the younger recruits
—Humphrey Burton, David Jones, Alasdair Milne and others—
had grown up on my radio work since the war, many of the older
guard were far less friendly and helpful. So far as they were concerned, any recruit from radio represented a potential threat to

243

their own promotion. And they were bitterly resentful of the fact that a number of senior television appointments had recently been filled by radio personnel. To them, radio represented the enemy, against which they tended to protect themselves by encouraging the theory that the two media were irreconcilable. Training in radio, they held, was an automatic bar towards any understanding of camera work. Complete separation of the two services was something for which they worked and prayed, and their distrust of the BBC itself was almost more pronounced than their distrust of the ITV. Many a radio man before me had been faced by this hostility, and more than a few had found it operating against them. For one reason or another, Val Gielgud had already returned to radio with some relief after trying to bestride the worlds and run drama for both services. Gilliam, as I have said, had singularly failed to find a television niche for himself. Leonard Cottrell, one of our most talented feature producers, having been seduced away from radio with specious promises, was then in process of being frozen off the television staff. He had, admittedly, made the dreadful mistake of winning the highest appreciation index to date with his first television documentary—a most unpopular proceeding among television's older guard. But neither Louis MacNeice, Douglas Cleverdon nor I was to find a very warm welcome when we went over to join him in television Drama Department. Meanwhile, of course, we had to grapple with a totally new technique as television producers-elect.

The television production training course was admirably conducted so far as it went. A great deal of technical information was dispensed, and full opportunity given for studying all the studio gear in operation. Here again, of course, the television mystique was carefully inculcated; and so far as television scripting went, everything was done to impress one with the necessity of starting afresh. Pictures, it was insisted, were more important than mere words, and the key dramatic points could best be made visually. This I was perfectly willing to accept, and saw no reason why I should find the idea inhibiting. Having spent most of my spare time for the last twenty years looking at pictures all over the world, my visual sense was reasonably well developed. It should not prove too difficult, I fancied, to think with my eyes no less than with my ears. At the same time, judging by the badness of most television scripting then, it seemed to me that the ears were being sadly neglected in most television production.

As an exercise during the course, each was asked to mount his own television production, adapting a script, casting it and directing the camera crews in a closed-circuit studio tele-recording. I found it amusing to write my own script, which emerged as a fifteen-minute mini-thriller called *The Bullet*. I enjoyed painting my own stills and caption cards, and persuaded two of my actor friends—Charles Leno and Anthony Jacobs—to play the leading roles. I worked out my camera moves and sequences with no great difficulty, and mounted the whole show without any mishap.

The Bullet was seen by Kenneth Adam and others, and when I offered to extend it into a thirty-minute play, it was promptly accepted for transmission. The course once over, I was given production facilities, and got down to the business of losing my television virginity. The process proved painless and even rather enjoyable, though I found it something of a strain carrying full responsibility onto the air with a live transmission. As it was, when the play went out, I had little enough experience to go on, since it was only four months since I had moved over from radio. Even so, the play was watched by a larger audience than I had enjoyed in radio for quite some time, and was enthusiastically reviewed by the critics. Even the old maestro Rudolf Cartier was appreciative and complimentary. All of which, I felt, was a reasonably good beginning.

Along with Louis MacNeice, I had now become attached to television Drama Department, of which Gerald Barry was then head. I had first met him in early post-war television days at Alexandra Palace, where I had sat in on one of his productions. Although he was always perfectly courteous, I never found him particularly friendly; and the idea of having me on the books as one more television producer seemed to appeal to him no more than it did to me. As both MacNeice and I were regarded as established radio writers, however, he obviously felt that something ought to be done to get work out of us while we happened to be around. Thrillers were well enough, but they were also ten a penny; and programmes rather more original seemed to be called for from both of us. Barry therefore invited us to a meeting where discussion was opened as to what we could write for television by way of verse drama. This rather amused me, for Gielgud's earlier mounting of *The Lady's not for Burning* had proved quite unacceptable to the cauliflower-eyed audience, and apart from Shakespeare, verse drama had been virtually out on television ever since. Rather to my surprise, it was suggested to us that half a dozen poets might be commissioned to write their own treatments of the *Everyman* theme. I was not unduly intrigued by this idea, as my *Aaron's Field* had followed the pattern as nearly as I wanted to do, and that was already on offer. Louis must have been more interested in the idea than he seemed, for he sat down promptly and wrote *One for the Grave*. Whether he ever submitted it, I have no idea, but nothing more was heard of the scheme by either of us.

Thanks to the enthusiasm of Eric Crozier, however, I was invited by Religious Broadcasting Department to do my own adaptation of *The Christmas Child* for them.* Poor as Mary and Joseph were, it did not seem to alarm them unduly, and a place was found for it in the schedule the following December.

This time, the production was far more complicated. It involved a transformation scene, and as the show was again being put onto the air live, split-second changes of costume from Oldham 1958 to Bethlehem 4 B.C. The show was also a musical, and carols in elaborate settings by Matyas Seiber had to be sung by

---

* I had always found Religious Broadcasting Department very friendly, and old agnostic though I am, always tried not to let my private opinions obtrude in any dealings with them. When asked to assist them, I had always gone out of my way to advise them on writers or lend them producers. I found them refreshingly modern in their thinking, and far more go-ahead than some of their lay brethren. Even so, I was rather surprised when one of their eager padres asked my help in "taking Christianity—and knocking it about a bit on the air." Tempting as the offer was, I decided it might be wiser not to accept it!

principals and chorus. All this music had to be pre-recorded to save production costs, which necessitated studio miming. The George Mitchell Choir made the recordings for me, with Isla Cameron as Mary and Edric Connor as one of the Magi. The part of Joe was again played by Wilfred Pickles. As no studio space was available in London, the whole production had to be taken up to the North and mounted in Manchester. All in all, I found the operation remarkably intricate and something of an anxiety. That way, it seemed to me, lay dyspepsia and stomach ulcers.

All went off exactly as planned and without a hitch, but this time the result was not so well received by television Drama Department: apparently they liked their fantasies to be more ethereal, whereas my production was firmly down to Oldham—as the verse itself had been.* The *Guardian* and the *Sunday Times* were pleasantly appreciative, but Philip Purser in the *News Chronicle* was honestly abusive. I was quite willing to believe he was right in all he said, but even so, the Audience Research Report was surprisingly favourable. Such criticism as there was from viewers confined itself to religious scruple; as for the production itself, it seemed to have been well liked by most of the four million who watched it. At least I seemed to have broken down the popular dislike of spoken verse on television.

I was under some pressure, by now, to try my hand at a television documentary, but this I had no intention of doing. Those that were being produced at the time seemed to me no less dull and unimaginative than the ones that were being done on radio, and I wanted no part in them. The only ones that appealed to me were the finely observed documentary studies of Northern life being written and directed by Denis Mitchell. But as these were generally frowned on by his colleagues as being 'more radio than television', there seemed no point in ploughing a similar furrow.

---

* The verse of *The Christmas Child*, of course, was as earthy as that of the *Secunda Pastorum* play, and aspired no higher. Finding virtue in that fact, Maurice Wiggin in the *Sunday Times* amused me highly by his comment: "Mr. Bridson is an authentic minor poet just as surely as Mr. Betjeman: of about the same candlepower, though they use their light to illuminate very different worlds in much the same sort of sentimental glow." I hope that Mr. Betjeman enjoyed the comparison as much as I did.

Indeed, I had convinced myself by now that television directing was not a pastime that I really enjoyed. Having tried it twice, I was quite content to let things go at that, and concentrate in the future merely upon writing for the medium. This I did from then on, much to the benefit of my digestion.

With the end of the year, my attachment to Drama Department ended, and in 1959 I moved over to television Talks. There I found the atmosphere rather more congenial. Leonard Miall, the head of the department, I had known in Washington, where he had been our news correspondent for some years after the war: then he had returned to London and had even considered joining up with us in Features Department. His Assistant Head, Grace Wyndham Goldie, as already mentioned, had been radio critic for *The Listener* before the war, in which capacity she had been a staunch champion of my earlier radio productions.

Grace was quite one of the most lively minds and personalities in television. Her drive and imagination had raised television coverage of current affairs to a pitch unknown elsewhere in the BBC. Indeed, if she had been allowed to do as much for radio while she was still in Broadcasting House, I should have found the Home Service a great deal more stimulating to work for. As it was, her work at Lime Grove had done more to beat commercial television at its own game than anything else being done by the BBC at the time. She had an unerring knack for picking bright recruits from the universities, training them and then giving them their heads. Donald Baverstock, Michael Peacock, David Attenborough, Humphrey Burton and many others were indebted to her for a chance to prove themselves; and if all her nominees were withdrawn from television today, there would be a surprising number of absentees from the ranks of both BBC and ITV.

After I had been given a chance to move around and find out all that Talks Department were doing, I was attached to *Monitor*. This, the first successful arts magazine programme on television, was under the editorship of another of Grace's protégés, Huw Wheldon. I had known this ebullient Welshman—who rather reminded me of the Bailiff in *The Childermass*—while he was still in Publicity Department. I found him a highly amusing man to talk to, and a quite infuriating man to try and reason with. The vehemence with which he expressed his opinions on art and literature was only equalled by their eccentricity. And his claim to represent the taste and knowledgeability of the average viewer was probably the only matter on which I agreed with him.* Until I actually tried it, I had much looked forward to working with him. Unfortunately, when he was around there never seemed any work for me to do. Apart from my good offices in getting people like Joan Littlewood and Paul Robeson onto the programme—where Wheldon, of course, conducted the interviews—there seemed precisely nothing that I could contribute to it. Indeed, if the poor man had not gone down with hepatitis himself, I doubt whether I should have been allowed to write a single word for the show.

As it was, during his absence on sick leave, *Monitor* was run by Peter Newington, who had apparently been contracted to run it in the first place. Newington was an excellent director and producer, with whom I got along extremely well. I immediately sold him on the idea of my writing a television profile of Ezra Pound, which he agreed to direct.

Following his release by the American authorities, Pound had returned to Italy. After living for a while with his daughter and son-in-law at their castle above Merano, he had moved back with his wife to his beloved Rapallo. To oblige me, he agreed to return to the castle for the shooting of the film, the location being one of the most dramatic and unlikely one could imagine. Meeting him at Rapallo, I drove him up to Merano, where Newington duly repaired with his sound and camera crew. I also took along with me my own portable recording-machine, having separate plans in mind for the Third Programme.

If ever I had doubted that Pound was a natural born actor,

---

* What Wheldon thought that *I* represented, he never explained to me. In view of my association with Third Programme radio, perhaps I represented a threat to the normalcy of teleculture. If so, my bomb was firmly, if somewhat gingerly, defused.

watching him before the cameras would certainly have convinced me that he was. For four days we shot and recorded a variety of sequences with him and his family, in which he took direction as to the manner born. Silhouetted upon the battlements, confronting Gaudier's bust of him that dominated the garden, pacing the stone corridors and climbing the spiral staircases, fingering at his harpsichord or moving silently round his study, writing Chinese ideograms with a brush to prove his points, facing the viewer like Nemesis and lecturing him like an Old Testament prophet, reading his blistering indictment of Usura to the world or reading *Brer Rabbit* to his grandchildren, nobody else could have come up with such a mesmeric performance. Knowing Pound as I did, I had dissuaded Newington from trying to get him into the usual camera interview: he was never a man to answer questions, he had far too many of his own to propound. I sketched out a sequence for the action, listed the points which ought to be made, and wrote the commentary which I later dubbed in London. Otherwise, Pound himself was the sole protagonist, with a Disneyesque Brunnenburg Castle and the snow-capped mountains above the Stelvio as a suitably improbable backdrop.

Profile of a Poet, as the film was called, emerged as a quite remarkable study in self-expression. As *The Listener* critic put it, "His impact as a personality was one of those television surprises. His recitation of his anathema on 'Usura' still rings in my ears." Thanks to the camera work of Charles de Jaeger and the sensitive direction of Peter Newington, the film subsequently won an award at the Bergamo Festival as an outstanding documentary. But while it had been in the making, I had also had the chance to record three programmes of conversation with Pound which gave him an even more valuable chance to express himself. These I shall be saying more about in the next chapter.

There was a rather comical sequel to *Profile of a Poet*, which nonetheless might have proved acutely embarrassing to me. When reading over the text of my commentary to the film, Huw Wheldon had insisted that it needed more of a challenging overture. "Nobody knows who Ezra Pound *is*," he explained to me.

"We need a better selling line—'Some say that he is a genius, some say that he is a Fascist, some say that he is mad'—that sort of thing." Needless to say, that sort of thing in reference to the greatest living poet left me distinctly sick to my stomach. After the usual argument, I reluctantly accepted some such formula, provided that Pound was then allowed to say everything in the film that he had wanted to say. That included a number of good hard knocks at the monetary system, the influence of the bankers and the system of taxation, all of which were duly hammered without further interference. Much embarrassed by the way I had been induced to open my commentary, however, I wrote to Pound and explained that by conniving at a stupid introduction I had at least got him onto the air without censorship and *in toto*.

I was astounded, a month later, to receive from some anonymous source in America a duplicated photostat copy of my own letter. Obviously, many others had been sent around to all interested parties, and who in hell *they* might be I had no means of knowing. Needless to say, I was rather alarmed at the prospect of my letter falling into the wrong hands. Taken out of their context, excerpts from the letter might well have made it appear that I had been guilty of loading the dice (as Lindsay Wellington would have called it) in favour of political pleading. And naturally, as a BBC producer, that could have been serious for me. Also, I had no knowledge of where the letter was circulating; and knowing some of the gang of political no-gooders who had used Pound's name in America to give an appearance of respectability to their own fascist and racialist activities, I had visions of being quoted in very unsavoury places. I wrote off to Ezra in some indignation, pointing out the harm that he might have done me by such an indiscretion.

Obviously enough, this aspect of the matter had never even occurred to him: he had merely been passing on to a friend—for the information of other friends—news of his television appearance. But once alerted to the possible consequences, he set about putting matters to rights with quite surprising thoroughness. Cables, letters and post-cards began to fly to and fro—I myself received an almost daily bulletin—ordering the recall, suppression and destruction of the photostats wherever they might have been distributed. I soon began to wonder whether such insistent orders might not be even more unfortunate: they certainly implied that there was something compromising to hide!

I was not much reassured by a further letter from Ezra which seemed likely to make matters even worse:

Cher B

Sending formal note to the B.B.C. office, in hope it will put you rectus in curia, and leave the official files as impersonal as even the Listener cd/ desire.

I SHOULD have had the energy to copy the news from yr/ earlier letter and not implicate you.

que tous les hommes nont pas bon sens assis

E.P.

this to explain the ton sec of the note to TV office.

Wherever the 'note to TV office' ended up, I have no idea. It must sorely have baffled some administrator, and if not lodged in my staff file at the BBC, it was probably referred to M.I.5! I was utterly charmed, however, by a suggestion in Ezra's next letter: "it occurs to me you cd/ defend, by saying: 'the man is a certified lunatic, or if not, OBviously eccentric, it is necessary to HANDLE him.'" I can think of nobody else whose sense of humour could have thought up that one, or whose anxiety on someone else's behalf would have caused him to pass it on as a valid idea! But as he said in the same letter, "Gawd knows, my Hawkwood, I did not have designs on yr/ livelihood." Over thirty years, nobody had done more to promote it.

Profile of a Poet was to be my only contribution to *Monitor*. After being encouraged to make approaches to contacts in the National Gallery, the Royal Academy and the Slade, two further items that I had been lining up were finally turned down, again to my embarrassment. Far more unfortunately, so was a filmed profile of Hugh MacDiarmid—projected as a follow-up to the profile of Pound—which had wasted a whole week of his time in the making. On this occasion, Peter Newington had had to hand over direction of the film to Paul Johnston: Karl Miller, then on the *New Statesman*, was brought in as interviewer and the usual shooting circus descended on Biggar in a body. Resplendent in his kilt McDiarmid paced the fields, leaned on gates and drank with the locals at his hostelry. He read Marx by lamplight while Valda his wife cooked supper for him over a hot oil-stove. Lengthy sequences were shot up and down the countryside to illustrate everything from *The Watergaw* to *A Drunk Man looks at the Thistle*. All in all, we came back to London with some quite interesting footage.

Once again, so far as Wheldon was concerned the question was: who is Hugh MacDiarmid? To me, it seemed rather late in the day to be asking such a question at all, but I went along with it. Wasn't he a Communist? Undoubtedly! Wasn't he also a Scottish Nationalist or something? Right again! And he also happened to be the greatest poet living in the British Isles. That was all very well, it seemed, but who among the *Monitor* audience had *heard* of him as a poet? At this point, I blew my top. If the *Monitor* audience was as ignorant as all that, why put *Monitor* on the air at all? A good question, maybe, but the Editor's decision was final. Despite protests from all concerned, the whole film was scrapped, and once again I had to make my apologies.

It was lucky that MacDiarmid—or Christopher Grieve, as I knew him—happened to be another old friend of mine. Otherwise, he might have been a lot more angry than he was. Luckily, I had again spent each evening recording conversation with him, and as Third Programme audience at least knew him for what he was, some good resulted from the otherwise wasted journey. Eight years later, I was suitably sarcastic when television finally got around to hearing about him. They put out a rather belated tribute in honour of his seventy-fifth birthday . . .

Not surprisingly, perhaps, I was rather glad to see the end of my attachment to the television service. As no permanent job was available to me at my grade, I packed up my papers and returned to radio, where my work seemed to be in rather more demand. Indeed, while I had been working ostensibly for television, my shows had been going out regularly on Third Programme. I still attended meetings of Third Programme Committee, and since control of the service had now passed to P. H. Newby, I found as ready a market there for my work as I had before.

Once again, negotiations were opened as to my future status, and after some discussion a formula was finally worked out by Michael Standing, which established peace with honour. My duties as Assistant Head of Features were taken over by Christopher Holme, whose position as Chief Assistant to the Third Programme had been axed by the recent cuts in output. It was agreed that from now on I should be regarded as an independent writer-producer, domiciled for administrative purposes in Features Department, but free to write anything that I wanted for any service which happened to be interested. I had direct access to all the service heads in radio, and could be lent to television whenever they might need me. And as television direction had made it clear that they were still anxious to have me work for them on special projects every so often, I was now free to enjoy myself more than I had been doing for some time. Relations with Laurence Gilliam were restored to their old cordiality, and my new independence was achieved with no loss of salary or prestige. Indeed, I found I had emerged from the negotiations as the highest paid staff writer in radio.

One of my first pleasures in my new capacity was to write and produce for the Home Service in 1959 a ballad opera called *My People and Your People*. This told the story of a group of West Indian immigrants in London, and the love affair between one of them and a young Scots skiffler. The girl was played by Nadia Cattouse and the Scot by Ewan MacColl, the other leading parts being taken by Cy Grant and Edric Connor. The action of the story moved from the warmth and gaiety of the Caribbean to the squalor and wretchedness of life in Rachmann's London, rising to its inevitable climax in the Notting Hill race riots. I have the deepest affection for my West Indian friends, and perhaps no show that I wrote for radio in the fifties gave me more pleasure to mount or seemed to me more worthwhile. The music, arranged for me by Ewan MacColl and Peggy Seeger, was lively and magnificent, the contrast between its Scots and West Indian rhythms being no less intriguing than the contrast between the two idioms and accents. The authenticity of the latter, I might add, was notably helped by the collaboration of Andrew Salkey, whose ear for the richness of West Indian speech is far more accurate than mine.

My People and Your People was very well received by the radio critics. As Ian Rodger chose to put it in *The Listener*, "It is rare to hear a work which is aesthetically satisfying, technically interesting and sociologically important." *The Times* remarked that the production "roars with the vitality, simplicity and gaiety of the West Indians" and admired its colour and pace. Hugh Ottaway in *Musical Opinion* said much the same thing, adding that "the production had an authenticity that lifted it right out of the studio". He also went on to comment:

"There are few things so stimulating as a new work in which some urgent contemporary theme has been honestly and successfully grappled with. Our cultural climate being what it is, such works are few. Apart from a 'committed' handful, established artists are disinclined to involve themselves—for a variety of reasons, no doubt—and most of the 'angries' are sadly off target. As for the B.B.C., it has not exactly a reputation for encouraging controversy, even in the guise of art. All the more credit, then, to those who gave us *My People and Your People* (Home) at a popular hour one Wednesday evening; for in its treatment of London's 'colour troubles' this West Indian Ballad Opera seemed to me both honest *and* successful."

Tom Driberg in the *New Statesman* was equally appreciative, referred to the opera as "one of radio's most notable recent productions" and looked forward to the television production of the work which had been projected. Perhaps rather naïvely, so did I . . .

The producer assigned to the show was Christian Simpson, one of the first to win a reputation for himself in television. His record with Music Productions had been outstanding, and I had again been much impressed by his recent direction of *Amahl and the Night Visitors*. He also had the distinction of being one of the most likeable and unassuming personalities in television.

My idea had always been that the opera should be filmed on location in the Notting Hill area, as I was anxious that the setting should be absolutely authentic. But it soon became clear that this would be out of the question. The budget allotted to the production was about half of what Simpson knew to be necessary: indeed, for such an elaborate musical, it was utterly ludicrous. Any idea we had of filming had to be abandoned, and the adaptation amended for the very simplest form of studio production. Even then, it was apparent that the budget would not allow for adequate sets, and Simpson was forced to settle for a sort of constructivist mock-up which was quite unsuitable for such a realistic treatment.

Luckily, the show was to be pre-recorded: indeed, I for one would have had the gravest misgivings at trying to put it on the air live. Various visual exotics like limbo dancers and a steel band had had to be paid for by cutting rehearsal time well into the bare bone. And long before Simpson got the show before the cameras, it was clear to me that the final result was going to be very far from what I had hoped. If it had not been for his tireless enthusiasm, I should have been only too happy to wash my hands of the whole thing.

We should both have been well advised to do so. The show was pre-recorded somehow, but despite Simpson's efforts it emerged as something of a shambles. It certainly lacked all trace of the polish that he would have given it, granted a fair chance. More important to me, it lacked all trace of the sometimes frightening authenticity which I had been able to give it on radio. I was not surprised when the production was finally written off and scrapped: I was merely relieved. But I was irritated that so much effort had again been used up to no purpose: I was also conscious of the quite considerable sum of money that had been poured down the drain. However inadequate it had been in terms of television, I realised how much I could have done with it in terms of lively radio. My old dislike of waste was beginning to make me wonder again whether working for television was really worth the time and trouble.

While Christian Simpson had been battling with *his* people, I had still been working for *my* people. I had had a series of notable successes on Third Programme, and was shortly preparing to go over to America for them. At this point, Cecil McGivern suddenly rang me to ask whether I was free to take an urgent television assignment in New York. I told him that I was going there shortly for radio, but he explained that the job he had in mind for me would need my whole attention for some time.

It seemed that the BBC had contracted to carry a series of television documentaries based on Winston Churchill's memoirs, *The Second World War*. Rights in the book had been bought by the American producer Jack Le Vien, and a series of twenty-six programmes was in process of being made by the American Broadcasting Company. From the first, the BBC had been in some doubt as to whether the Americans could make a series of programmes about Winston Churchill which would prove acceptable to the British audience. But with such a series being made, the BBC could hardly run the risk of its proving a wild success on ITV. They had accordingly signed a contract to buy the first six shows, with the right to opt out of the rest of the series if those proved disappointing. The first six scripts had now arrived, and McGivern was profoundly unhappy about them. Up to a hundred thousand pounds was involved in the whole deal, and he was desperately anxious that the series should prove a success. One of the terms of the contract had given the BBC the right to have its own adviser attached to the operation, his job being to answer for the accuracy of the British material and the authenticity of the local scenes. McGivern wanted to know whether I was prepared to take the job on: if so, I should have to leave for New York the following week, probably for at least six months.

It so happened I had recently got married again, and even by BBC standards I had not got off to a very good start as a husband. As Gilliam was acting as my best man, I had gone to collect him personally, to be sure of getting him to the registry office on time. He then needed a drink to steady his nerves, and by the time I had screwed his courage away from the sticking place in a nearby hostel, the bride-elect was setting out for home. We persuaded her to stay for the ceremony, after which it was suitably celebrated. Unfortunately, I had to leave almost immediately to spend what should have been our honeymoon recording Robert Graves in Mallorca. Luckily, as a member of the BBC herself, Joyce Rowe of Publicity Department—now Joyce Bridson in her spare time—was used to such eventualities. She cheerfully agreed that six months in New York were something I ought not to miss. Helping me pack my bags, she came to see me off at the airport.

Over in New York, I found that the ABC were no less unhappy about their series than Cecil McGivern had been. They had taken the unusual step of changing their producer in mid-stream, and my own arrival on the scene coincided with that of Robert D. Graff, who had been moved in nearly at the eleventh hour to take charge of a tottering operation. We were introduced to the all-American production team at the same time, a fact which made my rather delicate task a great deal easier. When Graff asked me rather guardedly what my precise function was, he seemed to enjoy my reassurance that I was only the spy from the BBC.

Of the various things that I did for television, one time or another, I can truly say that working along with Bob Graff and his colleagues on the making of *The Valiant Years* was far and away the most enjoyable, and the most rewarding. Like Graff himself, the members of his team had all been contracted specially for the job—they were not staff members of the ABC. A suite of offices had been hired for them in Times Square; recording, viewing, editing, dubbing and special filming facilities were booked by them as needed up and down the city. Anything less like a BBC operation could hardly have been imagined at the time.

Although my own part in the operation was purely advisory, I found it remarkably worth-while; and the insight it gave me into American television production methods proved highly interesting.* During preparation and revision of the earlier scripts, of course, I reported back to McGivern in detail on the whole operation: the apparently hand-to-mouth manner in which it was being tackled had left him highly alarmed. ABC had never tried its hand at any such prestige venture before, and in terms of their own studio resources were quite unfit to succeed at it. Indeed, my first business was to size up the whole exercise and advise him at once if I felt he should cut his losses and opt out of it forthwith. But within a couple of weeks I was able to set his mind at rest: from what I already knew of American production methods, I was confident the series could be made successfully, however alien to BBC thinking such piecemeal assembly up and down the town might appear. As I expected, the first six shows— as rescripted and doctored—proved well up to BBC standards, the contract was fully ratified and the remaining twenty programmes bought. It was sad news to me, however, that before the series even went on the air, McGivern's career with the BBC had been terminated. But that, as I was beginning to realise, was life in television . . .

Although I had worked for a year in New York during the war, this was the first time that I had worked almost exclusively with Americans: there had been far too many English in Rocke- feller Centre. Racially, the little army gathered to pay homage to Churchill was almost a cross-section of America itself, speaking six or eight languages between them and able to curse in many

* Unfortunately, the BBC never thought fit to put it to much use, but at least my services as a watchdog were rewarded by a handsome bonus.

more.* As in every other branch of the New York entertainment industry, most of them were Jews, and shared that hilariously Jewish humour which ranges from Zero Mostel to Philip Roth. To my astonishment, nearly all of them were under analysis, which seemed to be quite obligatory for anyone in American television. Never in my life had I come across so many people paying so much money to their psychiatrists, with so little reason for doing so. Whatever they fancied their private problems to be, they remained the most uncomplicated and easy people to work along with. And before *The Valiant Years* were finally disposed of, I had struck up some of the most valued friendships that I enjoyed even in New York.

The business of vetting and working over the scripts proved to be far less troublesome than I feared: Graff was always prepared to meet my suggestions, provided I could convince him that they were advisable. As for advice in the selection of shots from the vast body of newsreel material available, here again I could often be of some help. After all, I had acted editorially on BBC's own *War Report* and had mounted innumerable war documentaries in collaboration with all the Allied services. On matters concerning life in wartime England—evacuation, the Home Guard, the Blitz, the buzz-bombs and other irritations—I could speak from personal experience. I was also able to use my good offices in getting recorded sound out of the BBC Effects Library in London.

For the voice of Churchill himself, Richard Burton had already been contracted, and came in regularly to record from the cloud-cuckooland of *Camelot* just round the corner. I was happy to work with him again, if only because we shared the distinction of neither speaking BBC English. His gift for conveying Churchill's manner—purely by phrasing, pitch and intonation—proved to be quite uncanny. Where he might have been tempted to parody, he avoided every hint of it: nobody could

* On my departure, my own set of the Churchill volumes was inscribed for me in Hebrew, Persian and Japanese, as well as the local cursive of German, Italian, French, Polish, Irish and other assorted Americans on the team.

have matched more naturally the wartime speeches and broadcasts which were still so fresh in people's minds. The American narration was spoken by Gary Merrill, whose pace and attack provided an excellent foil for Burton when the action called for it.

Music for the series was specially composed by Richard Rodgers, whose flair for coming up with the instantly popular could hardly have been matched. His challenging signature tune to the programmes was as apt as it was heroic, and the various themes with which he followed and pointed up the changing moods of the story gave to the whole series a striking unity. The many recording sessions at which Rodgers presided were one of the greater pleasures of the whole operation. No less enlightening were the sessions in the cutting rooms with some of the Hollywood film-editors, who set their seal upon the finished product with equal effect.

As for the production side of the work, it was stimulating to watch craftsmen carving their way through Churchill's six solid volumes like a task force charged with the reduction of a stubborn garrison. Apart from Bob Graff himself—who had trained at NBC with Davidson Taylor and was then running his own independent film production company—they were a pleasantly professional group. Ben Feiner, ex-Yale, ex-Hollywood, in charge of production; Jack Le Vien, the gay impresario who had talked Churchill into the whole idea, and was soon to do as much for the Duke of Windsor; Victor Wolfson the scriptwriter, ex-Hollywood and Broadway playwright; Len Giovannitti the researcher, whose award-winning novel *The Prisoners of Combine D* was one of the best American war books I remember; John Lord, ex-BBC and recent expatriate directing the filmed interviews; Beatrice Cunningham, ex-model, ex-NBC television, in charge of film research; Marion Magid, soon to be known for her wickedly astringent articles in *Commentary*—they were an enterprising bunch to spend six months among. If I never persuaded them to smoke cigars, I did at least persuade them to eat their lunch in restaurants instead of from containers, and also to drink their wine and brandy like Europeans. Churchill himself, I fancy, would have approved of that.

In the event, *The Valiant Years* scored a remarkable success on television throughout the world, and in Britain attracted vast and enthusiastic audiences. Though criticism might be levelled at details, the viewers were in no doubt that this was the story of *their* war, told by their own war leader, and reminding the world impressively just what their own courage and steadfastness had achieved. That this series should have been made about them by the Americans merely increased the pride that they could take in it. Such was the response, that while the series was still running it was started up again in repeat, thus being on the air continuously during 1961 for forty-five weeks out of the fifty-two. After Churchill's death in 1965, many of the programmes were re-peated again as a further tribute to him.

Before I left New York, I was joined by Kenneth Adam who had just been appointed Director of Television on Sir Gerald Beadle's retirement. He told me that one of his last acts as Con-troller of Programmes had been to accept a series of thirteen shows that I had offered the previous year in collaboration with Edgar Lustgarten. We had written a sample script, and in my absence a pilot production had been mounted which he felt held out promise for a new and original series. Each programme was to be a confrontation in which the modern technique of cross-examination could be brought to bear upon some well-known historical character. As an ex-barrister himself, Lustgarten was admirably fitted to lead for the prosecution, each character being forced to answer for his actions in a way that he had not been called upon to do during his lifetime. George Washington, for example, could be grilled on a charge of High Treason, Karl Marx on a charge of incitement to violence, and so on. The historical research I could undertake myself, the replies of the accused being based upon the facts so far as they could be established; points of law and legal usage could be answered for by Lustgarten. Adam had much liked the idea and assured me that all I had to do on my return to London was to settle down to the scripting. Drama Department had been alerted, and choice of a producer could be settled in consultation with them.

Unfortunately, when I returned to London, I found that this was not exactly the case. Stuart Hood had succeeded to the Controllership and was far less enthusiastic about the series. And while under instruction to mount the programmes, Gerald Barry seemed no more happy about it himself; at least, as a commitment for his department. Having been contracted for it, however, Lustgarten was in no mood to see the project shelved; and his knowledge of the law of contracts being what it was, quite firmly insisted that something should be done. After the usual tiresome negotiations, we finally agreed to settle for a series of six.

The next argument came over how the series should be produced. As the idea for the series had been mine in the first place, I had always made it clear how I thought the shows should be handled. As I saw it, after his first address to the viewer, Lustgarten should step out of camera: he was a brilliant radio performer, and his voice alone could carry the examination from then on. Once it had begun, in fact, I felt that the focus should be hard and fast upon the face of the accused: he should be given no chance to collect himself, no chance to evade or prevaricate without it being immediately apparent to the viewer. This close-up technique had provided some excellent television in the *Face to Face* interviews directed by Hugh Burnett; and with star actors and actresses undergoing intensive interrogation, it seemed to me to offer opportunities for exciting star performances. Unfortunately, this static camera technique was not in favour with drama producers, who preferred to switch around and make their points by cross cutting. Paddy Russell, the producer finally assigned to the series, also preferred a more mobile treatment. As I have always been averse to back-seat driving, I felt it best to refrain from bothering her with my own ideas any further. In the result, she made a very competent job of the series, though not exactly the job I had always hoped would be done.

For me, the programmes still made quite compulsive viewing.

Even when one was reasonably convinced of the guilt of the accused, the relentless battery of questions, the half-truths exposed and the accidental contradictions, all evoked sympathy for the fighter with his back to the wall. Each programme amounted to a bullfight, from which every so often the bull was finally allowed to escape. Basil Sidney as Henry VIII, under examination on a charge of bigamy; André Morrell as Cromwell, charged with genocide at Drogheda; Alexander Knox as Washington, calmly pointing out that successful treason emerges as patriotism; Donald Wolfit's performance as a highly irascible Karl Marx; Maxine Audley's moving self-defence as Mary Queen of Scots; and Rosalie Crutchley's impassioned plea for Mary Shelley's right to devote herself to serving genius—each was a fine television performance. For that reason alone, *Return and Answer* was a rewarding series for anyone to have scripted.

By 1962, however, with the completion of the series, I felt it was just about time to put an end to a love affair that was rapidly growing stale. No doubt the fault lay in me, but going to bed with television seemed to call for a perseverance that I really couldn't be bothered to summon up. I decided to return myself— to my true love, radio—and answer as best I could its far more encouraging demand for work that I found congenial.

As the next seven years were to prove, an exciting amount of new work was still waiting to be done.

12

Conversations and other things

IF THE FIFTIES could be called the great age of the creative feature in radio, the sixties were soon to emerge as the decade of the radio documentary. I have already mentioned the increasing emphasis which was being placed upon current affairs broadcasting by the Home Service planners, but it was only with the gradual easing of the old restrictive policy control that I began to get caught up again in topical documentary writing myself. When that occurred, it was to be documentary writing of the trenchant order I had always hoped would be possible.

At first, the thaw did not affect me in any way, as I was heavily committed to literary and creative productions, mainly for Third Programme. As I have said, while I was with the *Monitor* unit at Merano, I had taken advantage of the evenings to record three programmes of *Readings and Recollections* with Ezra Pound. When the day's filming was over, we retired to his study, where he stretched out on his bed and unwound. The topics we talked about ranged over his whole career as a poet since he had arrived in London before the First World War. He remembered his friendship with the sculptor Gaudier-Brzeska: "the most absolute case of genius," he said, that he had ever run into. He remembered evenings with T. E. Hulme, Wyndham Lewis, Eliot, Yeats, the publication of *Ulysses*, for which he had been largely responsible . . . Then it was Paris in the twenties with Hemingway, Picabia, Picasso, and Jean Cocteau "playing a drum in a jazz band, and not with any African fervour, but as if it were a veeery difficult mathematical operation that had to be thought out . . ." From them the talk went on to the *Cantos*, Fenollosa's theories on written Chinese, Confucianism, the One Commandment of

Christianity ("Thou shalt attend to thy neighbour's business before thou attendest to thine own"), bimetallism in the Roman Empire, the donation of Constantine and the question of taxation in the modern world . . .

Pound had scored a notable success with his appearance on television; but the broadcasting of *Readings and Recollections* on Third Programme had a far more lasting effect. Since their publication, the conversational parts of the programmes have frequently been quoted in critical estimates of Pound's poetry.* But quite apart from what he said, it was Pound's manner of saying it which gave one such a vivid glimpse of the man's personality. I for one had never heard anyone talk more provocatively or brilliantly on the air, and to judge by their reaction, neither had most of his listeners. As Robert Robinson declared in the *Sunday Times*: "He was a great man talking. He was the thing itself."

There was much talk at Merano, unfortunately, which did not get onto the tape at all. A great deal more was said on the subject of monetary reform, to which Pound had devoted more time and study than some of his friends might have wished. He repeatedly urged me to take up the subject on the air; but much as I shared many of his basic ideas, I had to point out that the time was not particularly propitious. He seemed surprised when I told him that since most people in Britain at last found themselves with something to spend, they were hardly interested in revaluing the currency. To quote Macmillan, they were of the opinion that they had never had it so good . . . Like many other facts of life in the post-war world, this was something he found it almost impossible to accept: his thinking had still to adjust itself to modern life as he found it. After all, having been quite cut off from the outside world for thirteen years, it was not surprising if he stayed with a few earlier obsessions. "What is bothering me far more than the control of credit at the moment," I pointed out, "is who has the Bomb, and where they're going to drop it." Pound waved the

* They appeared in the miscellany, *New Directions 17*, edited by James Laughlin and published by New Directions—or Nude Erections, as Pound preferred to call them—in New York, 1961.

subject aside: "My dear Brid," he announced, "it's no use expecting me to concern myself with side-issues at *my* time of life." If it hadn't seemed strangely sad, I should have found the remark as funny as it sounded . . .

The success of the Pound *Conversations* created a demand which I found it very enjoyable to meet for the next couple of years. In due course, as mentioned, I followed up with a couple of programmes recorded in Scotland by Hugh MacDiarmid. If the setting at Merano had been palatial, that at Biggar was precisely the opposite. Only the Scots—or to share the blame, the British—would cheerfully leave their greatest living poet to write his finest work in a two-room cottage—then without benefit of either lighting or plumbing. By comparison with MacDiarmid's home, the Burns cottage was like a manor house and Dove Cottage at Grasmere a Roman villa. Out on its cart track through the fields, it found itself in winter drifted up to the eaves with snow; and on one occasion, after a Burns Supper, MacDiarmid was heard by his wife stumbling about on the roof vainly looking for his front door!* Even so, his tiny living-room was lined with books, and MacDiarmid seemed to find it quite suitable for his needs. (Valda his wife may have had other ideas, while she still had to fetch all water from a tap in the cabbage-patch.) At least, it was always a cottage where good talk abounded, and the days that I spent with them there were certainly stimulating enough.

Where Pound had spoken completely at random, MacDiarmid spoke more ruminatively, following out his ideas in perfectly turned prose. Once again, the subjects that we discussed ranged over a wide field: the theory behind his invention of Lallans, Gawain Douglas and the makars, Burns as a poet as opposed to Burns the image, the shortcomings of the English language—and the shortcomings of the English . . . He discussed the function of nationalism in the Communist world, and explained how, having been expelled from the Communist Party during the Spanish Civil War, he had rejoined it again after the rising at Budapest. I

* Half asleep in her bed, his wife Valda heard the scrabbling overhead, and thinking it was a sheep, turned over and dozed off again.

was interested to find that he agreed with me over the necessity of getting back to the spoken tradition as exemplified in folk poetry: "I question in the long run whether our development of great artistic poetry is going to prove a good thing," he admitted, "or is going to prove an adequate compensation for the loss of that touch with the common people, which was felt all over Europe in the intertraffic of the ballad traditions and the folk-song traditions of the various countries."

It was a fact that just as he "outgrew the small lyric", Mac-Diarmid had largely outgrown the use of Lallans. His longest and greatest poems had all been written in plain English, even *The Kind of Poetry I Want*. He admitted that Lallans wasn't sufficiently malleable for coping with the whole clanjamfrie of scientific and aesthetic ideas with which his later poetry was concerned, but denied that this implied any withdrawal from the militantly anglophobe position he had always maintained. "Instead of writing a different kind of poetry from the English in a different language," he explained, he was now "attacking English from the inside." I much appreciated the distinction, and wondered when I should be forced to abandon it to him . . .

I have always appreciated MacDiarmid's company, but never more than on one occasion a few years later. During the General Election of 1964, the BBC had been loudly assailed by the Communist Party for failing to give them time on the air to state their political programme. MacDiarmid, who was opposing Sir Alec Douglas-Home in his own constituency, wrote to me to say that he was coming to London that weekend, and would like to have a drink with me. His letter only reached me the evening that he was due to arrive, so I rang the telephone number at which he said that his movements would be known. It proved to be that of the Communist Party, who promptly put me through to John Gollan. Gollan told me he would be seeing MacDiarmid in the morning, and would ring me back with news of where I could find him the following evening. As I had to be out of town the next day, I asked him to leave a message for me with the Duty Officer at Broadcasting House, where I worked. At this, Gollan loudly erupted, until I pointed out that his argument was with my Director-General and not with me.

The following evening, I returned from my trip and rang the BBC Duty Room for a message: I was told that MacDiarmid was waiting to see me over at the Lamb and Flag. We spent an uproarious evening together in which he gave me the story of his campaign. "I told them candidly," he said, "that Sir Alec Douglas-Home is a Prrrrime Ministerrrr who will be rrrrememberrred for absolutely nothing—unless I choose to immorrrrtalise him in a couple of lines of verrrrse." He invited me to hear him continue the attack the next day (a Sunday) in Hyde Park. I regretted that I should be busy scripting, wished him well at closing time, and sped him on his way to another parrrty.

The following evening, switching on my television set for the news, I was astounded to see MacDiarmid, surrounded with red banners, marching at the head of a large demonstration. It was advancing on Broadcasting House to present a complaint to the Director-General against non-representation of the Communist Party during the election campaign. And who was there to receive the complaint? The same Duty Officer who had put me in touch with MacDiarmid the previous evening! Whatever part he presumed I had played in organising the demonstration, he tactfully kept quiet about it. But it was typical of MacDiarmid's own tact that he had carefully refrained from mentioning what he was up to, in case it would have embarrassed me. He told me later that he couldn't bear the thought of my loyalties being divided; still less, of my feeling bound to warn the BBC in advance.

Robert Graves, who accidentally happened to defer my nuptials, took me rather further afield. I flew out to meet him in Mallorca, where I spent a pleasant week getting him down on tape, or as he might have preferred to call it, putting him through the mangle. Striding in from his garden, dressed like a *peon* and wearing what appeared to be a donkey-hat, I was again conscious of the size of the man, and when he took his ridiculous hat off, his striking resemblance to Michelangelo's Brutus. He fidgeted around while we got through the preliminaries, and I set my tape-recorder on the table beside me. After suggesting a starting-point for discussion, I switched it on and led off with an opening gambit. Graves switched on his own ignition, stuttered and coughed like a cold engine, teetered and finally stalled completely, his eyes goggling at my machine in horror. I switched it off and asked him what was wrong. "That damn thing going round," he blurted. "It keeps going round and I can't think what I'm saying." I tactfully put the machine on the floor out of sight, and we started again.

This time it was going in for a swim: he skirted around it gingerly, tested the pool with his toe, and finally jumped. Splashing around more confidently, he very rapidly warmed up, striking out vigorously in all directions. I had been ready for the energy he would bring to everything that he did; but I was slightly taken aback by the spluttering way in which his thoughts emerged in fits and starts, the agonising pauses, followed by accelerating bursts of qualification and self-correction. After the first half hour, however, he became a great deal more coherent, and once fairly into his stride began to talk quite racily. Everything that he said was highly Gravesian, quirkily eccentric and studded with pet enthusiasms. Things got better and better as the work proceeded over the next three days, and by the time we had worked around to folk-song, he was reciting, singing, laughing and almost dancing in illustration of his points. All this, added to his strong sense of humour, made him one of the most engaging people I have ever recorded.

I was particularly delighted by the oddities which kept cropping up in unlikely contexts: "I was making a bed one day in the war, and I was just tucking in the sheets, and suddenly it occurred to me, Milton was a trichomaniac . . ." Herrick? "One very endearing thing about him was that he had a tame pig that he used to feed with ale from a silver tankard. He wasn't a *characteristic* clergyman . . ." "Swinburne was a sort of childish nightmare of mine—a funny little gnome rushing up and down patting babies on the head . . ." "If a knock came to the door and somebody said 'This is Virgil calling—would you like to see him?' I'd say

'Throw him out!' If a knock came and someone said 'Homer wants to see you,' I'd jump up, knock down everything on the table in front of me, and rush to greet him . . ." (That I could well imagine: things are frequently knocked off the table when Graves is around.) Starting a poem? "It's just like a feeling that you get that something is brooding in you: it must be very much how cats feel before they have kittens for the first time . . ." We both laughed at his recent television *riposte*, when someone had taxed him with writing potboilers to subsidise his poetry. "Me write potboilers?" Graves had answered indignantly: "Name me six!"

It was when he was talking about the poetic process, of course, that he was most in his element. And from questions of the nature of inspiration, he was quick to get round to the existence, or otherwise, of the White Goddess. His book about her, he insisted, had been a case of compulsive writing which verged on the automatic. ("I began to suspect my own sanity, and I even had to set myself tests for sanity to make sure that I wasn't going off the deep end . . . I didn't really like it.") Into that particular grove of trees, I was not quite able to follow him; but when he got back to the beneficial influence of folk-song on his work, I could hardly have agreed with him more. He was quite firm in his contention that a knowledge of English and American folk-song was "one of the best possible trainings a poet can have for his rhythmic sense".

In view of his interest in folk-songs—of which he claimed to know three or four hundred—and as he was shortly going over to New York, I gave him the telephone number of my old friend Alan Lomax. Graves had a great admiration for Lomax's work in the field, and the meeting between them should have been something of an occasion. He rang up soon after he arrived, and was asked along for an evening's session in Alan's flat in Greenwich Village. He announced his arrival at the bottom of the stairs by bursting into an Irish song himself, though he may have been shorter of breath by the time he had climbed to the top of the four flights. Unluckily, Alan had damaged his hand in a fight the day before, and he had to apologise for not being able to play his guitar. Urged on to sing without it, he felt himself so handicapped that he began to forget the words of the songs, no doubt because he was writing a book about something else at the time. He was even more embarrassed to find that the drink was running out as well, and in desperation suggested that he take Graves on to a party round the corner to which he had been invited. When he had been corrected after introducing Graves as "The English poet—Robert Bridges," he decided that it simply wasn't his night. So apparently did Graves, whose dislike of Bridges' poetry was intense, apart from the fact that he had been dead for thirty years. I never heard whether he looked in on Alan again, the next time he was in New York . . .

At least Graves was gratified by the reception of the programmes we recorded. He told me with some pride that his friends told him they had never known him to speak so clearly and forcefully before. Remembering the seven hundred odd editing cuts that I had made in the tape, and the ums, ers, gaps and spoonerisms that I had neatly eliminated, I wasn't entirely surprised. For once at least it was good to hear him speak as crisply as he writes, and the process of polishing up his speech was only what he had always been at pains to do for his prose. I know few people whose conversation would not be much improved by tidying up in the same way; but in Graves's case, it was a labour of love.

My sessions with Lawrence Durrell were equally rewarding. We got on extremely well together, and I couldn't have wished for a better host. After Graves, he seemed remarkably compact, and under his Provençal grizzle, his grin had the same sprightliness as the leprechaun that he sketched for me on the tablecloth of the local bistro. His farm was pleasantly tucked away against the Mistral about half an hour's drive out of Nîmes, where I found the cooking of the exquisite Claude worthy of Dodin-Bouffant himself.

Comically enough, our first attempt at recording was completely wrecked by the aerobatics of the French Mystères which zoomed and cavorted, rocketed and machine-gunned away in a mock invasion practice nearby.* Our only recourse was to the *pastis*, but luckily the battle petered out on the second day. The *pastis* held out splendidly.

Considering the quantity of it that we consumed over the next few days, our conversations were remarkably lucid and un-blurred. Durrell was a natural born talker, and thoroughly enjoyed reminiscing about his early days in Paris with Henry Miller, his days in Alexandria during the war, and the various Mediterranean islands that he had virtually made his own. On the subject of Cyprus, he had many interesting things to say, additional to what he had foretold of the troubles there in *Bitter Lemons*. But it was what he had to say about *The Alexandria Quartet* which really gave substance to the recordings. Starting from his discovery of *Time and Western Man*, he went on to explain his whole concept of time and the novel, tracing out the different approaches of Proust, Joyce and Virginia Woolf. Then he went on to discuss his preoccupations with relativity, with particular reference to the position of the observer in a given field, a theory to which the *Quartet* owed the striking originality of its form. "The meaning shifts with the position of your observer," he pointed out, "and the observer can't observe a field without disturbing it. So I mean, in a sense, relativity is a notion of resignation, because you can never observe a field in its normal state. The act of observation disturbs your field." The changing field as observed by Darley and the others made that point clearly enough. As for the different approach to the time factor in the typical *roman fleuve* and the *Quartet*, he illustrated it—by analogy —as the difference between a camera panning shot and a back-track: where one is merely a succession of experiences, the other is a widening of the field of experience.

---

* As a local reporter put it in the *Midi Libre*:

"D. G. Bridson qui, pourtant se séparait moins volontiers de sa flegme insulaire que de sa barbe faunesque, était consterné: 'Si je passe "ça" sur les antennes de la B.B.C. on va croire qu'il y à a la guerre civile en France et j'aurai une protestation de l'attaché touristique de l'ambassade . . .!'"

To hear him talking about the philosophical concepts behind his writing, Durrell would persuade one that the work was merely incidental to the theory. Nothing, of course, could be less true. The practical working out of the construction of the *Quartet* is infinitely more ingenious than his explanation of it. But the explanation, obviously, was all part of the fun. And I was delighted to find how ready he was to be led into deeper and deeper abstruseness in following up his ideas. As we had both been up the night before on a monumental bender, his long disquisition on the philosophical implications of the continuum struck me as quite a splendid performance. It may not have impressed the scientist—which I am not—and it may, as he puts it elsewhere, have made Einstein turn in his grave; but as an example of gymnastic post-rationalisation it was superb! Indeed, it was his engaging readiness to commit himself which made his conversation so lively, whether one felt that he had proved his points or not.

When the shows went on the air, P. H. Newby—the rival Alexandrian—had been sardonically amused by the way he felt that I had managed to make Durrell commit himself. There was, however, no question of 'making' him do anything: it merely amused him to play games. When the ball came over the net, he took pleasure in returning it with a suitable flourish. Or, as he chose to put it himself, like all Micks he had the gift of the Blarney. I much admired him for it.

It so happened that both Durrell and Henry Miller attended the novelists' jamboree at the Edinburgh Festival, later the same year. I was thus able to get them together in a three-handed session—or rather, to act as catalyst to a duologue between them. Perhaps this was an even more enlightening performance, for each had an equal aptitude for sparking off the other. I was much intrigued to find the sage of Big Sur in a mood to consider his work candidly. He was quite right, of course, in refusing to regard himself as a novelist at all. "When you invent characters and dialogue and creatures whom you've never met, no matter whom you have as models in the background, these are naturally fictive characters." And fictive characters were something he couldn't swallow. He had always been at pains to portray people he really knew; primarily himself, and then the friends with whom he had shared experience. As for the current habit of treating his works as Holy Writ—particularly in France and America, where certain clergy were reported to be reading *Sexus* from the pulpit—this amused him no less than it did me. "I think that is how it should be," he confessed, stroking his shiny skull, "though I didn't write it with such people in mind, exactly . . ." I enjoyed the chuckle which completed the thought.

The most illuminating remarks came when I asked Durrell why, having written so much about love, he had never written explicitly about sex. "I'm rather *pudique* about it," he admitted. I pointed out that Miller, on the other hand, had written plenty about sex, but hardly a single word about love. "Love!" he protested, "Oh no—I should feel *pudeur* . . ." Their identical explanations appeared to me to throw a great deal of light upon both of them. Perhaps this also explained their friendship and the sincerity of their mutal admiration.

After my six months on *The Valiant Years*, I had stayed on two months longer in America to line up further *Conversations* with some of the poets over there. Conrad Aiken had been a close friend of mine for twenty years, and it was this fact, probably, which persuaded him to submit himself for treatment. I put it that way, because he obviously found it an almost psychiatric experience. Being a very shy man, the sight of a recording machine affected him in the same way that it had affected Robert Graves, and I had to be careful to keep it out of sight, much as a dentist does his forceps. We met up each Monday morning for a month or so in his New York apartment and talked for a couple of hours, by which time Conrad was mopping his brow and calling desperately for the martinis. Mary Hooper, his wife, dispensed them in the regulation silver goblets—fresh from the teapot in the ice-box—after which we looked at her latest paintings, then all repaired round the corner to chew clams. It was only when I had finished the sessions that he admitted having literally had nightmares about them. He said he had dreamt that his entrails were being wound out of him onto a drum . . .

As one can understand from reading his autobiography *Ushant*, which manages to conceal almost as much as it states, he had always been rather diffident. There had been tragedies in his life about which he was loath to speak, and his poetry itself was invariably oblique in its personal references. But once I had got him talking easily, his reminiscences of the early days at Harvard with Eliot and the days in London with Pound and others had been frank and unusually interesting. (It had been he who had brought the manuscript of *Prufrock* to London and put Pound and Eliot in touch with each other.)

The complexities of his poetry, however, called for a far more analytical approach, to which he submitted it as meticulously as he could. It was the problem of consciousness itself with which he had mostly been concerned, so that even the poetry was analytical to begin with. He was particularly concerned with the fragmentation of consciousness, and was much interested in Freudian symbolism. He told me that he had decided against putting himself into analysis with Freud, being fearful, as a writer, that "he might explode the unconscious in the wrong way and run the train off the tracks". As for the part played by the unconscious in the writing of poetry, he was in no two minds about the matter: "It is the *stuff* of poetry, and no amount of taking thought could possibly produce any substitute for it."

By a process of boiling down, referring back, cross-cutting and footnoting, *Conversations with Conrad Aiken* emerged as probably the best approach to his work that Aiken had ever achieved. Yet the fun in the man was always there at the back of it—the softly chuckling asides, the kindliness, even the occasional asperities—and the overall self-portrait was as good a likeness as voice and manner could make it. Painful as the process had been, even he admitted—once it was over—that he had found it therapeutic.

The last time I saw Conrad Aiken was in 1968, when I went down to visit him at Savannah and record his reading of *Thee*. At his suggestion, Mary drove us out to the cemetery at Bonaventure, where his parents are buried. The terrible circumstances of their deaths had been hinted at in *Ushant* and elsewhere, but had never been fully told. As we sat and talked under the trees, the Spanish Moss trailing down like gossamer from their branches, he admitted again how deeply the tragedy had upset him. I suggested that he might like to record his own remembrance of it, in view of the strong bearing that it had on so much of his creative work. This he finally agreed to do, provided that the recording should never be heard during his lifetime; and in his own hesitant words, the story proved to be even more moving than I had supposed. As a quite unique example of what recording can do for posterity, that particular tape is one of my most valued legacies to the BBC.

In view of the success I had had with Pound and Aiken, I was naturally anxious to have Eliot make a similar recording with me. After all, his name had cropped up in their reminiscences like a recurring theme. Talks or poetry readings he had occasionally been willing to undertake, but unscripted discussion was something from which he shied away. In his character of the Old Possum, he had a natural distrust of exposing himself in any such way: as he once explained, if he appeared on television, for instance, people might recognise him in the Tube! I pointed out that recorded talk could hardly be so hazardous, but that failed to sway him. "I want people to know me through my works," he insisted. "I know that is a vain wish nowadays, but still, the tortoise can pull in its head." The last letter I had from him was evasive in the old way, but at least held out fair hope that I might talk him into it one day. Unhappily for all of us, he died before I had my final chance.

Looking back on them, perhaps the series of nine *Conversations* that I recorded from 1959 to 1962 were among the most important things that I did for radio.* (I certainly wish that somebody had been able to do such things with earlier poets—Byron, Shelley and Keats, Browning and William Morris or Hardy and Yeats, to

---

* The other three were with Langston Hughes, Robert Penn Warren and Kenneth Rexroth.

look no further back.) For I should stress that the *Conversations* were in no sense mere interviews; they rather set out to provide examples of conversational style. By reducing my own part in them to a mere abstract, I was able to focus attention exclusively upon the subjects themselves. In their whole conception, the programmes amounted to studies in manner and character. In this, they were notably different in intent from the interviews with various writers published in the *Paris Review*, though those too were based upon tape recordings.

I like to think that it is now possible to hand on to future times a far more accurate idea of writers and personalities than could ever be gained from their written words alone. The spoken word need no longer be lost with the speaker: henceforth it can be recalled as uttered, and heard as it flies abroad perennially.

Apart from the *Conversations*, there were many other things which kept me busy during the first years of my newly won independence. I went over to see Auden at Kirchstetten, where he recorded for me three excellent appreciations of the poetry of Graves; and in due course he was to do two more for me in New York on the Shakespeare sonnets, for which Marius Goring supplied some splendid readings. I also recorded a fascinating piece by Leslie Hotson at Yale on the story behind his discovery of the true facts in the murder of Christopher Marlowe.

In 1962, I went over to Washington to cover the National Poetry Festival which was staged to celebrate the fiftieth anniversary of Chicago's magazine *Poetry*, to which I had contributed back in the thirties. There I met up again with Robert Frost, who received a standing ovation from the audience in the Library of Congress theatre—and kept it on its aching feet for twenty minutes while he thought up a few more anecdotes. I also met there various of the younger American poets: Randall Jarrell, Howard Nemerov, W. D. Snodgrass and John Berryman among them, all of whom I was happy to record in readings of their work. I spent a couple of rollicking nights with Kenneth Rexroth, after he had recorded a highly amusing think-piece for me, stretched out on my hotel bed while his wife slowly filled him with whisky. I was equally entertained to get myself drawn into a violent argument between Berryman and Oscar Williams as to which of them had rated the higher in Dylan Thomas's affection. Dylan would have much enjoyed being fought over like the body of Patroclus . . .

My first night in Washington, that trip, was a highly alarming one. News had reached us at the Library that the President was to address the world that evening on television. Switching on the set in my hotel bedroom, he suddenly confronted me with an account of the firm measures he had taken over the Russian rockets in Cuba. The broadcast must have been alarming enough even in London: but it was infinitely more so to watch in America. As the rockets were obviously aimed at Washington, furthermore, and as I was no more than a couple of blocks away from the White House where Kennedy was actually speaking, I could only feel that I was well and truly in the eye of the cyclone. There seemed something rather ridiculous about setting forth again, still dazed by the threat of imminent annihilation, and returning to the Library of Congress for Randall Jarrell's lecture on the last fifty years of American poetry. One rather wondered what he meant by "the last" . . .

Less alarming times had taken me back to Turkey, a few months previously, for another look at what one American friend of mine had described as "the Wild West of the Near East". The sacrifice of a jackal on the Plains of Troy, a dancing bear near Izmir and dancing dervishes at Konya, the ruins of Pergamum and Ephesos, the rock-churches of Cappadocia and the great Roman theatre at Aspendos were only a few of the pleasures to be described. The following year it was Iceland again, where I gave myself the nostalgia of following up the traces and recollections of Morris in the saga country. The charred rafters of Njál's old steading at Bergthórsvál seemed as unlikely to come upon as the cakes burnt by King Alfred, yet there they were to examine. Two years later, along with Professor Gwyn Jones, I was to fly from Iceland to Greenland in search of the story behind the recent discovery of the settlement of Eirik the Red at Brattahlid, from which Leif Eiriksson had sailed away to discover Vinland the Good. The laying bare of their skeletons after nearly a thousand years, tucked away under the Greenland ice-cap, was one of the most romantic pieces of archaeology that I ever recorded. As with the story of the Dead Sea Scrolls, I was gratified to find the shows so well received by the listeners.

Such excursions into the past were far more to my liking than excursions into the current. But the main emphasis of my work was still upon creative radio—my own or other people's. In 1959 I had written what proved to be the last of my creative documentaries for the Home Service. This was *Hazard at Quebec*, in which I was able to reflect the latest historical estimate of Wolfe's near-disaster on the St. Lawrence. My knowledge of the Canadian scene, a love of Canadian wild-life which I shared with Audubon, the colourful presence of the Algonquins, and the ebb and flow of the action itself gave me a chance to write verse narration once more for Stephen Murray. Ewan MacColl was again on hand to sing the songs that the campaign had given to history, and John Hotchkiss provided a suitably evocative score, which followed the fighting to its triumphant close. All in all, *Hazard at Quebec* was the sort of show that I had enjoyed writing for something like twenty-five years, and I was glad to find that the romantic formula still worked. 'Hand of the Master', ran Paul Ferris's headline in *The Observer*, and reading his appreciative review,* I began to wonder whether it wasn't perhaps time that I tried my hand at something new.

---

* As he has given me worse notices since, I hope I may be forgiven for quoting from it, for it well describes the difference between what I would call imaginative documentary and the sort which I found boring:

"As Grierson is to film, Bridson is to radio," he handsomely affirmed. "Some of his earlier documentaries are models of their kind, and he has never done a really bad one. In *Hazard at Quebec* the hand of the master was there all the time, playing the same simple tricks with the same bland assurance.

There are several essentials. Narration must not be a hollow heavenly voice or a series of benzedrined chirps. Facts must emerge as a form of energy, not items on a shopping list. Detail must be massive, but there must never be a sense of phoney finality: the ideal documentary is a bit humble as well as highly polished. All this

Three years later, I was commissioned by the BBC to write another verse play as part of the celebrations for their fortieth anniversary. In America, researching for my documentary *The Bomb* (of which more later) I had come across a television discussion on the subject of fallout shelters. They were then being manufactured and sold all over the United States—no doubt the Cuba Crisis had increased the demand for them—and were very much in the news as yet another status symbol. The possession and use of one's own fallout shelter had become a privilege of American citizenship—no less than the right to bear arms. In the course of the discussion programme, the question had come up as to the right of every American to guard the sanctity of his shelter in the event of a national panic. One of the disputants was a priest who solemnly affirmed—with or without the authority of the Church—that an owner was fully justified in shooting all and sundry who tried to force their way into his shelter during an emergency! This statement seemed to me so preposterous that it gave me the idea for a counterpart to my wartime morality play *Aaron's Field*. As the hero of *Aaron's Field* had not survived its climax, perhaps I should have called the sequel *Son of Aaron*, but as radio memories are short, I imagined the poor man reincarnated, and called it *Aaron's Fallout Shelter*. This time, and rather against his inclination, the hero is persuaded to build a shelter in his garden, as a place of possible refuge for his neighbours. At first, needless to say, he is merely reviled by them, and remembers wistfully the foxgloves and other flowers that have vanished under the hideous concrete. Only when a war scare develops do his neighbours come flocking round, blessing him as their preserver. When the shelter is nearly full, a self-appointed Warden—backed up by the local vicar—decides it is quite full

Bridson managed to achieve without once sounding clever.

The technique, in fact, is simply that of spade and archaeologist. Blade cuts through the soil and brings up a load of material—Wolfe, the carping brigadiers, the Indians, the general misery, all stuck in a nice hard lump of topography.

Stephen Murray, the narrator, stands well back, ironic and well informed, and gives you his expert but not omnipotent opinions. In the end you've seen a piece of earth and understood a piece of history."

enough: nobody else must be admitted. When Aaron tries to protest, he is warned to quieten down on pain of being shot. This he reluctantly does, till a knock is heard at the door, and a voice pleads for sanctuary. Aaron runs to open the door, and is shot down for his pains by the Warden. So is the figure that enters, miraculously *through* the bolted door. Both end up with more than wounded hands . . .

As *Aaron's Fallout Shelter* also proved to be the last thing of its kind that I was to write for radio, I was pleased to find it so well received.* A friendly note from Val Gielgud admitted enjoying it immensely—and properly, as he said, on the wrong side of his mouth, if he might coin a phrase! Oscar Turnill in the *Sunday Times* appeared to be equally pleased: "The play and its production seemed a shrine of Corporation virtues; it is these and not the label of long-distance runner that justify all the birthday brouhaha. And life, somebody has said, begins at forty."

Turnill's notice served to remind me that I myself was now fifty-two, and had still a number of things that I badly wanted to do. I had no desire to go on repeating myself, however friendly the response: there were far too many interesting things to try for the first time. I had already mounted a stereophonic production of my play *The Bullet*, to familiarise myself with the new technique, but felt there was little in stereophony which really interested me. For one thing, the audience was microscopic, and generally more interested in three-dimensional effects than in what they were being used to drive into the listener's head. I was far more interested in radiophonic sound, which could be used more significantly. A Radiophonic Workshop had just been set up at Maida Vale, and this was doing interesting things for both radio and television.† Electronic music was now being used experimentally by many composers, and both Roberto Gerhard and I were interested in the possibility of using it to reinforce the per-

* The Appreciation Index revealed by the BBC Audience Research Report was unusually high. One enthusiastic listener affirmed that "this should be made compulsory listening for the world's political leaders".

† This had been one of the projects that I had offered to tackle myself. The idea of such a unit had been turned down at the time as unnecessary.

formance of poetry. We had done many programmes together, and Gerhard's interest in radio—apart from his brilliant originality as a composer—made him an ideal collaborator. Lorca's *Llanto por Ignacio Sánchez Mejías* quickly suggested itself as an ideal poem to 'set' electronically. The poem was recorded in Spanish, and then in A. L. Lloyd's excellent translation, *Lament for the Death of a Bullfighter*. To Stephen Murray's reading of the translation, Gerhard worked out a quite remarkable electronic background. As finally assembled in the Radiophonic Workshop, this gave almost a new dimension to the work, providing a commentary in pure sound as pictures might have provided a commentary in vision.

Another interesting experiment of Gerhard's was the symphonic treatment which he wove around selected passages from Camus's *La Peste*, for which I again recorded a reading by Stephen Murray. With Antal Dorati to conduct it, the BBC Symphony Orchestra and Murray himself as soloist gave the work its first performance at the Festival Hall in 1964. I was sorry that Gerhard's immense creativity carried him on to so many purely orchestral works that he never had time to pursue the marriage of music and speech still further. In the sheer inventiveness of his treatment, he might have achieved the perfect consummation.

A project which I had cherished for some time was the mounting of a new production of Pound's Villon opera, *Le Testament*. A copy of the score, as used by Harding in 1931, had been kept by the BBC but was lost shortly after the war. By some chance or other, a microfilm of Pound's original score—as conducted in Paris by George Antheil in 1926—had turned up in the Library of Congress. Working from this, the Canadian composer Murray Schafer had produced a transcript for concert performance. This I promptly offered to Third Programme in a new production, and thanks to the enthusiastic sponsorship of Alexander Goehr the offer was accepted. Headed by John Shirley-Quirk, a team of first-class singers was assembled, an orchestra booked with John Carewe as conductor, and a cast for the spoken dialogue. Pound's friend Agnes Bedford, who had attended the 1931 production, also came in to advise us; and with all this expert assistance, I hoped to record an adequate performance of the work. I can only say that I and the others were much delighted by the result. The setting of the *ballades* was unlike any music I had heard; and as Roberto Gerhard himself assured me, it was years ahead of its time as musical thinking.

Pound had taken a keen interest in the production, which I flew out to discuss with him at Rapallo. Indeed, he even offered to come and play the drum for me—as he had at the Paris première in the Salle Pleyel—but this luxury I could not afford on my budget, apart from what the Musicians' Union might have said! At least I was able to send him a tape recording of the production, which I hoped would give him pleasure to hear.

It was some time before I got over to see him again at Venice, by which time, as I knew by report, he had entirely stopped talking even to his friends. Perhaps after one more misrepresentation of an interview he had given to *Epoca*, which had been viciously garbled in the American press, he had finally decided that trying to communicate with his world was merely a waste of time. Whatever the reason, by 1963, as is well known, he had lapsed into almost complete silence. Naturally enough, my meeting with him was a sad one. Sitting there utterly quiet, listening with apparent interest but saying nothing in return, I only succeeded in coaxing a single remark out of him in the two or three hours we were together. Suddenly remembering the recording I had sent him, I asked him how he had liked my production of *Le Testament*. Giving me a steady look, his lips slowly opened at last. "That," he said with infinite candour, "was a considerable MESS."

Funny as it sounded, I must admit I was somewhat put out by the remark. Nor would he amplify it in any way, so that I was completely baffled as to the grounds of his criticism. It was not until after Menotti's production of the work at Spoleto that I finally solved the mystery as to what had gone wrong. It appears that in sorting out and simplifying Antheil's score, Schafer had misinterpreted—or simply changed—some of the highly individual rhythms which Pound had written into the work. In view of Pound's somewhat eccentric ideas of notation, perhaps this was not surprising.* But the changes, slight as they were, had at once been apparent to Pound when he heard the recording, for he carried every nuance of the original performance in his head. Thanks to his extraordinary memory, when playing the recording over to Menotti, he had been able to demonstrate in which way the rhythms should be corrected. This they apparently were in the Spoleto production.

As I was able to point out, when next I met Pound with Olga Rudge, I could only produce the work in the form in which the score had reached me. This being understood, I was duly exonerated and received back into the bosom of the family. Even so, Pound's conversation remained virtually suspended, as it has ever since, alas! At least there is some of the best of it on record to remember him by.

There were many other productions in those, my last years in creative radio. There was the 1960 production of Nathanael West's acerbic *Miss Lonelyhearts*, in which Sam Wanamaker excelled himself as the suffering hero-heroine, and George Colouris provided a suitably blasphemous Shrike. My fondness for good bawdy led me to do an adaptation of Rabelais, *Panurge would take a Wife*, in which Hans Carvel's ring sparkled on the air for the first and probably only time. Francis de Wolff and Hugh Burden, my Pantagruel and Panurge, also appeared as my Uncle Toby and Corporal Trim in an equally bawdy quintessence of *Tristram Shandy*, in which young Tristram was duly circumcised. There was Michael Ayrton's moving *Testament of Daedalus* and Elisabeth Ayrton's nostalgic *Numancia*; while Charlotte Holland came

---

* Murray Schafer's explanation of the problem is set forth in an article on *Ezra Pound and Music*, which appeared in the Summer 1961 issue of *The Canadian Music Journal*. Among other interesting things, he has this to say: "All the songs are hectic rhythmically and Pound takes further delight in packing his sentences and verses close together, seldom allowing the customary pause for reflection and breath. Some of the songs are terrifying. Villon's mother's prayer, where bars of 27/16, 12/16, 9/16, 22/16, etc., in the vocal line are intended to be synchronized with bars of 4/4, 3/4, 2/4, 4/4, etc., in the accompaniment, is daring become folly."

up with an exquisite performance in *Four Unposted Letters to Catherine*, after I had persuaded a reluctant Laura Riding to let me bring her back briefly to the literary scene. There was also my adaptation of *Ape and Essence*, which went some way to counteract a virulent *New Judgment* on Aldous Huxley by Brigid Brophy.

In the field of poetry reading, I collaborated with Donald Hall to introduce William Carlos Williams's *Paterson* to English listeners. Cummings, Robinson Jeffers, John Hall Wheelock, Robert Penn Warren, Langston Hughes and Norman Corwin were other American poets that I produced, many of them in their own readings. Nearer home, there were readings of Auden, Louis MacNeice, Robert Graves, Norman McCaig and others; while MacDiarmid's translation of the Swedish poet Harry Martinson's space fiction Odyssey *Aniara* was serialised in five parts.

Among traditional poetry I had my fun with Byron's *Childe Harold* and *Beppo*, *Don Juan* having been stolen from me—and admirably serialised—by Terence Tiller. After Dryden and Pope, I mounted three series of *Satire and Invective*, in which I was able to make the air crackle with some salutary bursts of fine scurrility. Finally, I had the special pleasure of producing a series of readings from the *Canterbury Tales*, which were read with modern vowel sounds, but in which I adhered firmly to the original text with all its final Es. One does not adopt a sixteenth-century pronunciation for playing Shakespeare, and I have never understood why a strict adherence to fourteenth-century vowel sounds should come between the average listener and his enjoyment of Chaucer. As heard without it, his poetry is perfectly easy to understand—final Es and all—as listeners and critics were rather surprised to discover. And much as I appreciate the larger audience which Professor Neville Coghill has won for him by the modernisation of his text, I regret the serious loss of flavour which has resulted from it.

All this last medley of radio, needless to say, was produced for the Third Programme. By 1960, the audience for features on Home Service was not very much larger, so that I had grown used to devoting most of my time to the service which gave me the greater freedom of expression. Since 1960, in any case, the emphasis in Home Service had increasingly been placed upon the sort of topical informational documentaries for which I could summon up small interest. Two that I mounted for them, however, were among the most ambitious documentaries that I produced for the BBC—my programmes on *The Bomb* and the exploration of *Space*. But these can best be remembered in a different context, for they were among the last important programmes that I wrote specifically for Features Department, of which the long forboded dissolution was shortly to be decreed. And the story of that disaster, which almost marked the end of radio as I valued it, deserves a chapter to itself.

13

The end of Features Department

THE BBC HAD entered the sixties with a new Director-General, Hugh Carleton Greene, and his leadership was soon to be felt throughout the organisation. Greene had started as a newsman: he had had wide experience as a foreign correspondent in Europe before and after the start of the war. He had joined the BBC in 1940 as Head of the German Service, and had left again in 1946 to organise German radio in the British Zone. I had seen a certain amount of him in the early fifties, when he rejoined the BBC as Assistant Controller of the Overseas Service, and admired the drive and directness which he brought to everything he did. In some ways, he was to prove himself the ablest Director-General since Sir John Reith; and unlike Sir John, he happened to be of my own generation. For the first time, under his leadership, broadcasting seemed to have caught up with the times; on occasion, it even managed to pull slightly ahead of them.

Greene's influence was to be seen most clearly, of course, in television: and he will be best remembered by most people as the sponsor of topical satire and the onlie begetter of *That Was The Week That Was*. He certainly gave new candour and independence to the medium, and under his aegis producers were given a great deal more freedom. Though both sides of most questions continued to be stated in the programmes, they were not necessarily stated at one and the same time; and by virtue of actually *saying* something, BBC television acquired a new vigour. I for one found the change highly salutary.

In radio, Greene's influence was mainly felt at first in a complete reorganisation of news and current affairs broadcasting. To begin with, drama, features, light entertainment and the rest continued to reflect the caution of Lindsay Wellington, though here again horizons were gradually widening. But ever since Hugh Greene had been appointed Director of News and Current Affairs in 1958, the recent emphasis on both had continued to grow rapidly. When he became Director-General two years later, a series of staff changes were put into effect which resulted finally in the appointment of George Camacho, lately in charge of the Light Programme, being appointed Head of Talks and Current Affairs. A new empire was emerging, and stated in the simplest terms, Features Department had been largely squeezed out of the current affairs market. For such current affairs documentaries as they still did, feature producers had now to refer for policy guidance not to the head of their own department, but to another department entirely.

As I was technically only domiciled in Features Department, this did not affect me in any special way: I was used to working with people all over the Corporation. But various unfortunate uproars ensued when feature producers failed to refer controversial political issues to the proper quarter. And it was perfectly obvious that Gilliam's position was being made untenable in the field in which he had chiefly hoped to operate.

I had first met Camacho while he was Head of European Productions in Bush House. He had produced the sixteenth-century Kichua play, *Apu Ollantay*, for the Latin American Service in a Spanish adaptation by Angel Ara. From this he had subsequently prepared an English translation which I was asked to produce for the Third Programme. In the many discussions we had over the script we had grown quite friendly; and when he moved over to Broadcasting House—one of the first of the so-called Bushmen who were soon to invade it in strength—I saw far more of him.

As a loyal administrator, he had won the confidence of the management by his scrupulous attention to detail, his reliability in policy matters, his adroitness as a negotiator, and his wide grasp of all political matters. He was also a born committee man, a compulsive talker, and an inveterate memo-writer. More to my own liking, perhaps, he was a roaring extrovert, lively over

his food and drink, and the proud possessor of a hearty laugh—
which admittedly, after a time, could become a little irksome.
While he was Head of Planning to the Light Programme, I had
worked with him regularly and found him shrewdly well informed. Over *The Bomb*, I was to work with him far more
closely.

The idea for a programme designed to show, dispassionately
and in scientifically accurate terms, exactly what nuclear war
implied was one I had been considering for a long time. During
the fifties, under Sir Ian Jacob, such a programme would never
have been allowed onto the air. The general climate of official
thinking on the Cold War had been such that any completely
honest statement of the consequences of a nuclear attack would
have been regarded as so much Communist propaganda designed
to undermine public morale. The view had come to be accepted,
in fact, that ghastly as nuclear war would be, it could not be much
more ghastly than any other warfare. Seventy thousand people
had died at Hiroshima, but fifty thousand people were reputed to
have been killed by 'conventional' bombs in the R.A.F. attacks
upon Hamburg and Dresden. So what was the essential difference?

Many scientists were much disturbed by this complacency in
official thinking; and the inauguration of a national scheme of Civil
Defence did little to allay their fears. Some of them, like Professor
P. M. S. Blackett and Professor J. Rotblat, had spoken out on the
subject; but like Bertrand Russell and the Aldermaston marchers,
they were generally dismissed as alarmists or sentimental cranks.
A Shelter Programme was being avidly discussed in America,
and the feeling appeared to be growing that given adequate
measures for ensuring the public safety, one could learn to live
with the Bomb without worrying. The fact that no such measures
could ever possibly be adequate was being carefully glossed over.

It seemed to me that the full power of the Bomb, as by then it
had been proved, should be rather more fully understood. The
H-Bomb of the sixties, after all, was several thousand times more
powerful than the Atom Bombs dropped on Hiroshima and
Nagasaki. And its lethal threat to life, thanks to its high fallout

hazard, spread vastly further than most people seemed to realise. With this in mind, and in view of the greater freedom that had come to radio in the sixties, I put forward a carefully worked out scheme for dealing with the threat of the Bomb in a large-scale documentary. It was bound to win wide publicity for Features Department, and might well prove something of a breakthrough in the documentary coverage of current affairs.

After it had been discussed at a suitably high level, my synopsis was accepted, and I was given permission to write and produce the programme, subject to certain safeguards and policy supervision. With a subject so politically dangerous, it was stressed that negotiations with Whitehall would have to be very carefully handled, or the programme could lay the BBC open to a charge of political bias. At this point, the matter passed out of Gilliam's hands, and the nature of the negotiations had to be worked out in collaboration with George Camacho. There was obviously no enthusiasm for such a programme in either the Ministry of Defence or the Home Office—concerned as they were with promoting a Civil Defence programme—but it was necessary that both should co-operate and put up their own spokesmen.

I had had some experience during the war in placating the watchdogs of Whitehall, and conducted my end of the negotiations with some relish. After a few sessions I was able to convince them that the BBC was determined to assume full responsibility for the programme, and intended to retain full editorial control over it. This once firmly established, I had no particular difficulty in getting them to see that co-operation was in their own interest. The process took some time, but with the full backing of the BBC—which Camacho was able to ensure—the programme was given grudging sanction, and the official spokesmen agreed upon.

Plans for the programme could now go confidently ahead. Joe Burroughs, one of the most gifted feature producers, had come forward to help me with the handling of the vast mass of recordings that I needed to collect, and to act as scientific adviser I brought in John Maddox, then Science Correspondent of *The*

Guardian. Tom Margerison, then Science Editor of the *Sunday Times*, and Mary Goldring of *The Economist* were also inducted, and between the four of us a questionnaire was drawn up covering all aspects of the investigation, and a short-list of leading scientists to whom it could be submitted. Sir George Thomson, Professor Otto Frisch, Professor J. Rotblat, Professor Rudolf Peierls and Dr. Peter Alexander all agreed to record their opinions on matters coming within their particular fields.* Five spokesmen for the Ministry of Defence and the Home Office recorded official thinking on the same subjects. I flew over to America to record similar statements from Herman Kahn, the nuclear strategist of the Hudson Institute, and various other authoritative opinions were either recorded specially or collected from the American network archives. James Cameron, who had reported a nuclear explosion at Bikini, and Dr. J. Bronowski, who had studied the effects of one at Hiroshima, completed an impressive muster of expert testimony.

All these recordings, gathered by Maddox, Margerison, Mary Goldring and myself, amounted finally to some five or six hours listening, and organisation of this mass of testimony proved to be one of the most difficult jobs I had attempted. As the programme was designed for popular listening on the Home Service, I was determined that it should be crisply stated, fast moving and easy to follow. The final script dealt in sequence with the power of the H–Bomb, the possible area of destruction, the means by which the Bomb could be delivered to the target area, the number likely to be employed in an all–out strike, possible means of interception, the nature of bomb devastation, the effectiveness of shelter protection, and the effects of radiation on the human body. The gist of all testimony under these heads had then to be tied into a well-shaped whole by Edward Ward's narration, which was designed not only to direct the course of the investigation, but also to summarise the arguments and underline the key points made.

* Professor Blackett at first declined to take part. By the time he had changed his mind, it was too late to include him.

Even when compressed into sixty minutes, the body of evidence assembled was truly terrifying. Six out of New York's eight million people could be killed by a single 20-megaton bomb . . . Herman Kahn's estimate of American casualties in a multiple nuclear attack was anything up to 90 million: in Britain, the number could be from 10–20 million . . . An ICBM could probably be dropped within half a mile of its target at a range of 7,000 miles . . . No means of interception was available in this country, and there would be only a four-minute warning of any attack . . . The American estimate was that an all-out strike could be as high as 263 rockets launched against 224 American cities, with an explosive power nearly a thousand times greater than that of all the bombs dropped on Germany during the Second World War . . .

The sober relation of these hazards by informed scientists and strategic experts in Britain and America added up to sixty minutes of the most shattering listening I have ever heard on the air. And the admission of the defence experts as to the impossibility of affording any protection in the target area, coupled with the pitiful means available for lessening the casualties outside it, did little to reassure the mind. Bronowski's terrifying vision of daily life as the survivors would find it in a devastated country made a fitting close to the recital.

The Bomb was probably the most authoritative feature programme on a controversial subject that had been mounted up to that time.* It was not an expensive programme, costing only twice as much as the normal run of documentaries had become; but its impact, both inside and outside the BBC, was something far greater. It was, in fact, the sort of hard-hitting documentary that I had been wanting to do for the last ten years as a counterbalance to my creative and literary work for Third. And treating

---

* It was also more informative than any programme on the subject of nuclear attack that had been seen up to that time on television. I should like to think that it may have prepared the way for Peter Watkins's brilliant film *The War Game*, which gave visual treatment to many of the hazards which *The Bomb* had discussed. Unfortunately, *The War Game* was felt to be too horrific to be shown on the air, though it was widely seen as a film at certain cinemas.

of a subject of the broadest possible interest, it had been done for the Home Service. I should have liked to see it broadcast on the Light Programme—where it would have found a far larger audience—but that would sadly have disturbed the usual run of narcotic entertainment . . .

It was the policy implications of the programme which interested me the most, however, since it bore witness to a far more courageous and forthright attitude on the part of the BBC direction, for which Hugh Greene was certainly to thank. Broadcast as it was shortly before the publication of the Government White Paper on Defence, it was bound to have some effect on public opinion. It had been billed in the *Radio Times* as "An enquiry into the possible nature of a nuclear attack on Britain", and it had concerned itself equally with the probable results of any such attack. As *The Guardian* was quick to point out, the programme seemed "to have broken new ground in its criticism of Government policy on civil defence". But in fact, no such criticism had been made: the facts had merely been left to speak for themselves. In the weekly forum of *The Critics*, the programme was praised for having stated "a set of truths that ought never to be concealed from anyone", and so with having served "the most important of all purposes". And despite the dismay which it must have engendered among many listeners, the Audience Research Report showed that the programme had been given an Appreciation Index far above the average.

I was amused by the comments of two dissentient voices. The Defence Correspondent of *The Times* (now Lord Chalfont), who was perhaps closer to government thinking than to any other, airily dismissed "the flood of popular science" which had gone into the programme, and complained that "this obsession with the horrors of the nuclear weapon overwhelmed some sensible contributions on the need for a measure of civil defence". Conversely, his opposite number on the *Daily Worker* accused the BBC of being committed to *boosting* the Government's civil defence policy, and claimed that "this programme was undoubtedly designed to do just that". Perhaps the gap was bridged by the

Sunday Times, whose critic stated, "One's sympathy is entirely with the man who states, at the first warning, you should jump into a large paper bag. Where else?"

Laurence Gilliam was particularly enthusiastic about the programme and the way that it had been steered through onto the air. By now he also was conscious that documentary output over the last few years had failed to justify itself in high places, and that a new assertiveness in popular features was urgently necessary. *The Bomb*, he felt, had opened new horizons, and we began to consider what other subjects could be covered in similar ways. But thee months' planning, assembly and editing had gone to the making of the programme, and I was myself too heavily involved with other commitments to cope with anything more on the same scale for the time being. Apart from *The Bomb*, I was to have forty-two other shows on the air in 1962.

By the following year, I was free to work out further documentary plans with him, but by then, as events were to prove, it was already too late: the dissolution of Features Department had been decided upon.

As I have said, the end of Features Department came as no great surprise to me: I merely deplored it as yet another wrong decision at the top, this one more likely than any other to put an end to the kind of radio I valued. The end would possibly have come sooner than it did but for the advocacy of Lindsay Wellington and his personal loyalty to Gilliam. With his retirement in 1963, there was apparently nothing to delay it further.

So far as I was concerned, the doldrums in the late fifties and the recent reorganisation had been as much responsible for the decline in the features market as anything else. The demand on Third Programme remained what it had always been, but Third Programme alone could not support or justify an entire department. Demand elsewhere continued to dwindle, production costs were rising as overall output was going down, and more than one Big Brother was quietly watching from the wings.

Since my return from television, it had become increasingly

clear to me that the latest administrative changes were operating both against Features Department as a whole and against Gilliam personally. Having occupied a highly respected and privileged position in radio for a long time—and with every reason—it was at first hard for him to admit as much. But the in-fighting was going against him, and the Current Affairs side of Talks Department was clearly in the ascendant. It began to be felt in management circles that Features Department—like another Poland—was ripe for dismemberment. And with the appointment of Frank Gillard as Wellington's successor in 1963, plans for such a dismemberment began to be considered in detail.

I had myself been critical of the way that the talent available in the department had been misapplied on occasion; but if too much money was being poured into the wrong kind of effort, that was something which could easily have been corrected. There was certainly no need to cut the cost of housekeeping by demolishing the house, which was the way that the tidy mind of administration reacted to the problem. The best work of Features Department, after all, was still winning most of the critical notices in the press, and it should have proved easy enough to cut the cost and improve the quality of the rest. To suppose that the highest standards could be maintained for long by dividing up Features staff among other departments showed just how little the creative faculty in radio was understood by those who never possessed it. Even so, I knew the pattern of BBC administrative thinking far too well to believe that once it had become set in a wrong direction there was any chance of reversing it. By the Autumn of 1963, rumours of the impending dissolution of Features Department were circulating freely in Broadcasting House. They were even beginning to appear in the press.

The low standard of morale that these rumours induced among the feature producers has been well described by Rayner Heppenstall in the book already mentioned, *Portrait of the Artist as a Professional Man*. That they should have come as any surprise to him, in view of what had been going on—or not going on—over the previous few years was a matter of equal surprise to me. If all his colleagues' indifference to portents had been as bland as his own, it might be a source of surprise that the department had lasted as long as it did. Reading his book, I could only wonder whether he was quite such a professional man as he himself appeared to believe.

The tragic death of Louis MacNeice, coming as it did when the rumours were beginning to gather head, only served to increase the general gloom. To increase it still further, it was soon evident that Gilliam's health also was beginning to break down. He had already had to go into hospital for two serious operations, but had returned to work apparently little the worse for them. The general air of uncertainty in which he soon found himself, however, was hardly conducive to peace of mind. And cheerful as he appeared on the surface, it was clear enough to those who knew him well that he no longer had the drive to fight a tough battle for survival. He had much on his mind to worry him, and while his real ailment remained organic, uncertainty as to his own future must have done much to aggravate it. Meanwhile, the running of his department had to go on: there was still no clear indication as to when its fate was finally to be decided. The suspension of finality, after all, is a well-known instrument of policy: it does much to confuse resistance to unpopular decisions and the downright opposition which sudden action might arouse.

Gilliam and I saw much of each other during this unhappy period, though we avoided all discussion of the nature of the coming changes. Indeed, there was very little to discuss usefully, and rather than go over old ground again we concerned ourselves with programme plans for the immediate future.

I was now freer of major commitments, and we finally decided upon two large-scale documentary projects which were to take up much of my time for the next twelve months. Gilliam had an idea that a series of features could well be mounted for Third Programme (which alone would be ready to give us enough space) on the place of the Negro in modern society. He felt that a study in depth of the emergent sense of Negro identity throughout the world would provide compulsive listening, and Howard

Newby appeared to be keenly interested. I felt that a world canvas would be far too diffuse, as aims and problems varied from country to country. But provided I could confine myself to the rise of the Negro as a political and cultural force in the United States, I was eager to tackle the assignment the following year. This was quickly agreed, and *The Negro in America*, a series of nineteen programmes ranging from plays and documentaries to jazz and gospel song, poetry and open discussion, was drawn up and approved. The series was scheduled for the fourth quarter of 1964, when it would coincide with the presidential election campaign, in which the integration issue was likely to prove important.

Meanwhile, something else on the scale of *The Bomb* was needed for the Home Service. I suggested a full investigation into the economics and motivation behind the American Space Programme. Such a documentary would be a logical sequel to *The Bomb*, as it would call attention to the military implications of space research no less than the more spectacular aspects of the moon project. This idea also was accepted and I got down to planning the programme forthwith.

Space was billed as "An Enquiry into the cost and objectives of Space Travel", and was scheduled for transmission in February 1964. The team recruited was similar to that which I had gathered for *The Bomb*, and the form of the programme was substantially the same. John Maddox again acted as scientific adviser, and the recordings were made by Tom Margerison, Angela Croome, Nicholas Lloyd and myself. The experts whose opinions were canvassed were again the most authoritative available—Sir Bernard Lovell, Sir Edward Bullard, Professor A. D. Baxter, Professor Fred Hoyle, Geoffrey Pardoe and A. V. Cleaver being among them. In a series of recordings made in Washington and New York, I was able to pull in the latest American thinking on the vast undertaking of the National Aeronautics and Space Administration, or NASA, which had been charged with the task of putting men onto the moon before 1970, at an estimated cost of some thirty-five billion dollars.

Many highly critical opinions—both British and American—were represented in the programme. Enquiry ranged from the military implications of space research to the infinitely more costly programme of the American Defence Department, the prospect of manned orbital laboratories, the use of communications satellites, the commercial value of space research spin-off, Britain's part in the European space programme, and the credit side of the balance sheet by which humanity might expect to benefit from the coming of space travel. So far as Maddox was concerned, the American moon project represented "a betrayal of the intellectual heritage of the last five centuries". So far as NASA's director James Webb was concerned, 93 cents out of every dollar his administration spent was contracted out to American industry, and the whole programme managed on a mere 7% of its total appropriation. Perhaps it is no coincidence that the first two moon landings should have been followed by the threat of another American trade recession . . .

Once again, the best part of three months' work went into the making of *Space*. Three days before it went on the air, I was summoned to a special meeting at which plans for the dissolution of Features Department were formally announced by Frank Gillard, the Director of Sound Broadcasting.

Both Gilliam and I had known Gillard from his days as a War Correspondent, his despatches from France and Germany having been one of the mainstays of the BBC *War Report*. As I have mentioned, I had also seen him here and there in South Africa during the Royal Tour of 1947. Before the war he had been a schoolmaster, and had joined the BBC's West Regional staff in 1941. He was a brisk, healthy man, a confirmed bachelor, and one for whom sex appeared to have no charms. He had risen to be West Regional Controller before succeeding Sir Lindsay Wellington as Director of Sound Broadcasting the previous year. He had also worked for a time as Wellington's Chief Assistant shortly before the reorganisation of radio in 1957, and was generally supposed to have been partly responsible for the lines which it had taken. Certainly, his own ideas about radio were very different from mine. They were equally different from Gilliam's, being far more concerned with information than with showmanship, and far more provincial than metropolitan or national. He had already devoted much of his energy to the promotion of local broadcasting, and over the course of his six years in office was to cumber the BBC with a chain of local broadcasting stations. I must admit they seem to me a very parochial substitute for all that national and regional radio has lost in making way for them.

Temperamentally, Gillard was a very different man from his predecessor in office. Wellington had been almost comically averse to any unpleasantness, and had discreetly delegated his hatchet work to others.* Gillard, on the other hand, made a virtue of the brusqueness with which he took such work upon himself: once a course had been decided upon, he could be quite implacable in forcing it through. In every sense of the word, he was an organisation man. On the occasion of his first and only confrontation with Features Department, however, he chose to be diplomatic.

I had been expecting such a confrontation for the last few months. As rumours became ever more persistent that the axing of his department had been decided upon, Gilliam had found himself strangely excluded from the management's deliberations. He had merely a few dark hints to go upon, but all firm details had been carefully kept from him. Meanwhile, even darker hints were beginning to appear in the newspapers, presumably based upon the fears and speculations of his own producers, among

---

* On Lindsay's retirement, I could not resist the temptation to put in the needle for once. As we were saying goodbye, I admitted that in all the years we had worked together, he had played me only the one dirty trick. Alarmed as to which bit of skullduggery I had found out about, he looked deeply distressed. I merely reminded him of an office party in New York, at which some of the secretaries had got happily high on his martinis, and were daring each other to drag him under the mistletoe. Much embarrassed, he had suddenly remembered another engagement, looked at his watch, asked me to lock up the office for him, and left me to get a dozen of his maenads safely off the premises for him!

His look of relief that I had brought up nothing worse gave me a lot of pleasure.

other people. His position was becoming impossible, and the growing sense of isolation was obviously a source of deep distress to him.

My own feelings were divided between sympathy for Laurence personally, and regrets for the mistakes which had laid him open to attack. He had certainly underestimated the forces which had been ranged against him, but that was a poor reason for such a bitter ending to such an achievement as his had been. There had been no question of his failing to promote the highest standards in radio writing and production. All that could be charged against him was slowness to adapt himself to competition in a far more ordinary field, where economy had become a major factor and in which a number of cheaply effective competitors had long been underselling him. If anything could be blamed for the end of Features Department, it had been a wrong deployment of effort: in the event, the unnecessary had operated against the best. With these thoughts in mind, I went along to hear Gillard's announcement.

It was a curious comment on the new division between management and the programme staff, that when he arrived at the meeting, Gillard had to be introduced to the assembled producers by Gilliam himself. To most of them he was merely a name, a shadowy figure somewhere upstairs, with whom their work had never brought them into contact. Glancing round at the sixteen producers present, most of them better known to listeners than he was himself, he quickly got down to the matter in hand.

He began by paying handsome tribute to Gilliam personally and to the work of Features Department as a whole. He agreed that their work had had a profound influence upon radio writing and production, and that it had pioneered many effective styles and techniques which had since been generally adopted throughout the BBC, indeed throughout the world. But pioneering was not an end in itself, and as radio was now evolving, consolidation was far more necessary. The excellent work of feature producers would always be wanted in programmes, but the time was coming when that work could be done more economically in different circumstances. Current affairs were now being dealt with increasingly by other departments, and the inventiveness of documentary producers would be better employed in a cross-fertilisation of ideas with producers in Talks and Current Affairs Department. Similarly with creative writing and production: this would benefit by a closer association with the work of Drama Department, where, of course, it had first been nurtured. One or two producers might even be moved into Light Entertainment Department, where there would be new scope for their ability. In other words, by dividing out the talent available in Features Department among its neighbours, it could be more economically and usefully employed. No precise date had been assigned for the reorganisation (suspended finality was still operative, of course) and it was being announced at this time simply on account of rumours that appeared to be circulating. Indeed, it was quite possible that reorganisation would be deferred until after Gilliam's retirement (as this was not due for another three years, it seemed unlikely) but in any case, work in the meantime would continue as before. All this, he emphasised, was strictly confidential: it must not be discussed with anyone outside Broadcasting House.

Gillard had been accompanied to the meeting by our Controller, Michael Standing, who looked somewhat ill at ease, but actually said nothing throughout the brief proceedings. Having once been Head of Outside Broadcasts Department, with which Features had worked in closely for many years, he may have felt that the management's decision was a sadly misguided one. At the same time, he was better aware than most people of the criticisms which had been levelled at Features Department behind the scenes, and also of the true reasons behind that decision. So far as I am aware, he had had no direct hand in planning the assassination; but as Controller of Programme Operations, he would have to arrange for the interment in due course. Having heard the announcement through, and the dead silence which greeted it, he followed Gillard out of the room.

Long as it had been feared by some of us, this brisk writing-off of a department which had won high esteem for BBC radio over the last eighteen years apparently came as a deep shock to others. In his account of the meeting, and the stunned dismay which followed Gillard's departure, Rayner Heppenstall has wondered why I did not choose to say anything myself. That I was deeply sorry for him personally, both Laurence and our friends already knew. But this was hardly a moment for expressing personal sympathy: all present were equally affected by the sentence. My close friendship with Laurence was something quite apart from our work together, and after serving for sixteen years as his deputy, my stewardship had been ended without that friendship being affected. As for the work itself, we had sometimes agreed to differ. Since my return from television, I had been working closely with him again, but I was only technically a member of his department. My feelings on hearing the end of that department decreed, after my long and close association with it, these again I did not feel that I needed to express. Appropriate words were said by Joe Burroughs, who was working with me at the time, and with those I cordially agreed. I was ready to let it go at that.

As regards my own future, I had less cause for concern; no matter to which department I was attached administratively, I had established my right to work for any other that I might want. Radio or television, plays or documentaries, creative features or literary, I should continue to write and produce what I chose. I had, after all, resigned as Assistant Head of Features Department so that I could be free to do precisely that. I had begun writing feature programmes in the North before Features Department had come into existence: I knew that I should continue to do so still. Even so, of one thing I was absolutely certain: the feature programme itself, the spearhead of creative and controversial writing on radio, would not survive for long once Features Department had been abolished. But that was something I need hardly have said on such a depressing occasion: we were all far too painfully aware of it.

Although the actual date of its demise was still indefinite, the sagging morale of the department slowly began to improve after the management had declared itself. Whatever was due to happen eventually, no immediate upheaval was involved. Work went on as before, and feature followed feature onto the air without any noticeable change. As for Gilliam's own future, that was obviously a matter for personal negotiation when the time came. Whether he had been offered promotion before the blow fell and had refused it—as others have declared—he was certainly offered nothing afterwards. His health was still deteriorating, and he himself presumed that an early retirement would be arranged for him; as everyone hoped, on suitably generous terms. Meanwhile, unwell as he was, he continued to take his old interest in the work remaining to be done.

I myself had still a very full schedule, but once I had got *Space* out of the way, I turned my attention to the coming series on *The Negro in America*. And although the programmes that I projected for it included straight plays and musicals, poetry, jazz and folk-song recitals, discussions and straight talks, no less than documentaries, the series was still recognised as a Features operation. As he was keenly interested, I kept Gilliam closely in touch with my plans at all times, and we discussed them regularly during the evenings he spent with Joyce and me in Highgate. I had arranged for my old friend Langston Hughes—who had been concerned with the integration struggle since its inception—to act as co-editor of the series with me; and at the beginning of April 1960, I went over to work out the final details with him and get down to the necessary research.

As I have already said, I have a warm affection for the Negro people everywhere, and I was happy that at last I should have an opportunity to rally sympathy to their cause. I had seen intolerance and prejudice at work against them in every white society; and I had been filled with admiration for the way they were at last beginning to stand up for their rights in America. Their history there had certainly been a hard and bitter one. The centuries of slavery had given way to something little better; and with a complete denial of civil rights in the South, discrimination against them in the North, and a ghetto existence everywhere, they had little enough to be thankful for in the land of so-called opportunity.

Since the Supreme Court decision of 1954, however, which had declared that racial discrimination in American schools was unconstitutional, they had begun to demand their rightful place in American life. And starting with the Montgomery bus-boycott the following year, the struggle had begun to escalate. Even so, the violence had all been on the other side. Under the leadership of Martin Luther King, the Negroes had adhered firmly to a policy of non-violence which had won them respect throughout the world. They had fought back when attacked, and there had been sporadic outbursts of rioting, but these their leaders had been the first to condemn and to pacify. It was only in the later sixties, when non-violent methods were seen to be making little progress, that a new militancy began to emerge. The murder of Martin Luther King was to spread it far and wide over America.

There were few signs of militancy during the summer of 1964, and my evenings up in Harlem with Langston were as pleasant and amusing as ever. He decided against the Long Island duckling at Franks' on 125th Street—"no one can cook it like Joyce," he asserted—but Brownie McGhee and Sonny Terry were still on Lennox Avenue and Odetta was still around the town. There were also many new people to meet, including Arthur Spingarn, the grand old man of the National Association for the Advancement of Coloured People, its then leader Roy Wilkins, James Farmer who had led the Freedom Riders, and the young white organisers of the Student Non-Violent Co-ordinating Committee. Interviews had to be lined up between Nat Hentoff, jazz critic of the *New Yorker*, and Cannonball Adderley, Charlie Mingus, Red Allen and Dizzy Gillespie. Gwendolyn Brooks, Arna Bontemps, LeRoi Jones and other Negro poets had to be chosen and arrangements made to record them all over America. Gospel singers had to be selected from those I had heard in Harlem at the Apollo and elsewhere. There was an open discussion to

305

arrange between Langston, James Baldwin, LeRoi Jones and Alice Childress on the aims and problems of American Negro writers; and a conversation to record with Langston on the whole question of discrimination in America at the time.

Unluckily, copyright difficulties eventually prevented me opening the series with a recording of *In White America*, the documentary stage show which had been running in Sheridan Square; but the loss was amply made up for me by Langston Hughes's new documentary musical, *Jerico-Jim Crow*, which was still to be seen playing off Broadway. Deeply stirred by its fine singing, and remembering the success he had had in London with his *Black Nativity*, I was in no doubt of the pleasure it would give to English audiences. In due course, I was glad to hear it thundering out over the air three times.

Funnyhouse of a Negro, Adrienne Kennedy's unbearably poignant study of a Negro girl's fantasies in a hostile white environment, I had seen on a previous visit to New York. I had been so moved by it—unradiogenic as it was—that I reassembled the original cast, and recorded it in a special adaptation. Emlyn Williams, who had been equally impressed, supplied a commentary on its frightening visual symbolism and the strangely balletic unfolding of its action. A special score composed for the play later by Roberto Gerhard rounded off an original and highly unusual piece of listening.

Alice Childress's comedy *Trouble in Mind* I brought back with me to record in London, with Elizabeth Welch in the lead. It was a wittily satirical story about a company of Negro actors rehearsing an Uncle Tom play set in the Deep South. The way they entirely rewrote the play in terms of the emerging South they knew reflected the new spirit which the integration struggle had given to the Negro people.

All these programmes, and others that I arranged later on, were to make up the flesh and blood of *The Negro in America*. But the hard backbone of the series was to be supplied by the three major documentaries, *Ten Years of Integration*, which gave shape and a purpose to the whole. *Space* and *The Bomb* had given me a lot of experience in the marshalling and presentation of fact, but in them the fact had been scientific and impersonal. The facts that I needed for *The Negro in America* were of far greater human interest. They were to be facts reported throughout in human terms, facts reported by the men and women who had seen and suffered and lived through the story they had to tell. Like the people I had first brought into radio thirty years before, they were ordinary, simple people whose dignity alone raised them above the circumstances of their lives. They were people of rich character, whose sincerity was in their voices, and the story they were telling was a story that concerned the world. As for the other protagonists in the story—the politicians, the rabble-rousers, the journalists and the commentators—they were no more than so many foils for the Negro people themselves.

My first task was to search through the American sound archives for all the relevant material that had been recorded over the last ten years. The integration struggle had been fully reported both on radio and television, with much actuality material included, and virtually none of this coverage had been heard in Britain. The task of collecting the best of such a wealth of statement proved almost endless. By the time the work was finished, I had gathered no less than two hundred and fifty recorded excerpts. Each of these had to be re-recorded, edited, transcribed, classified and indexed for easy reference. But exhausting as the task was, it proved completely fascinating. Interviews, statements, eye-witness accounts, speeches, running commentaries and vividly exciting sound sequences, each added its own colour and detail to the jigsaw. And as I began to sort the pieces out, they sometimes began to fit together strangely. A network recording of Martin Luther King calming the congregation in a church in Alabama while the mob howled at the doors could be matched with a BBC commentary by Erik de Mauny on the frenzied scene outside. The statement by Medgar Evers, in which he foretold his own murder, could be matched with the terrified account of his neighbour who found him dying in the street. Evers had been shot down by an old bolt-action rifle with a telescopic sight, and President Kennedy's shocked condemnation of the murder was soon to be followed by his own death, shot down in turn by a bolt-action rifle with a telescopic sight . . .

The dramatic incidents which went to make up the integration story were there for all to hear. Gathered together for the first time, they made hypnotic listening: Rosa Parks's retelling of the incident which triggered off the whole campaign at Montgomery, the lunch-counter sit-ins and the jeering of the white mobs, the beating-up of the Freedom Riders, the shameful scenes at Little Rock and the campus riots at the University of Mississippi over the admission of James Meredith, the meetings of the Ku Klux Klan, the dynamiting of schools and Negro homes, the lynching and the floggings and the general racialist brutality, the quiet dignity of the March on Washington, Martin Luther King's great speech, *I have a dream*, the echoing gunfire and smashing windows of the Harlem riots—this was history in the making which emerged as great radio. Introduced each time by the inspired singing of Pete Seeger as he led a packed and ecstatic audience in Carnegie Hall in the rallying song of the whole struggle, *We shall overcome!*, the three documentaries of the Integration story were better received by listeners than almost anything I had brought to the air.

The success of *The Negro in America*, which had owed its genesis to his own idea, was a great pleasure to Gilliam in his last days. It was hailed by the critics as "the most important radio event of the year", and even, by one of them, as "not only the greatest series of the year but possibly the best of all time". Whatever the doldrums of the past may have been, Features Department was at least going out to a good press. Howard Newby had been delighted with the critical response, and the series had certainly won an unusual amount of publicity for the Third Programme. The very variety of the material which had gone to the making of it had established a useful precedent by breaking through so many departmental barriers. And so far as I was concerned, this boded well for the future. Regional training had long ago given me experience in every kind and style of radio production, but for the first time *The Negro in America* had given me a chance to use them all to one and the same end. Nineteen separate shows to put on the air in twelve weeks had undoubtedly proved something of a strain, but at least I had been able to give the series the impress of an individual style.* And intensive as the effort had been, I looked forward to repeating the experiment in the future. I was to have one more opportunity.

Before I returned to America to gather my final recordings after the Presidential Election, I looked in on Laurence, who had had to go back into hospital for further treatment. He was obviously far from well, but seemed remarkably cheerful again. He told me that the terms of his retirement had been agreed with the BBC, and that he was much looking forward to all that he intended to do in the future. As Features Department was now due to be wound up in the New Year, he asked me what my own plans were: he presumed that I would be opting for a base in Drama Department. I told him that in view of the success of the Negro series, I should probably start by taking a spell in Talks and Current Affairs. I was keen to tackle further controversial series in the same way, and that might prove easier from the Current Affairs enclave. After all, I should still be free to do creative writing for other departments as well, that freedom being guaranteed by my special status. I also suggested that if enough feature producers joined me there, the group might well be able to make a certain impact. This idea appealed to him strongly, and he even began to speculate whether a new Features Unit might not be created in that rather hostile territory. He poured out the champagne I had brought him, offered me one of his cigars, and we drank to that happy thought.

I was away in America for little over a week, but when I returned to London I was met by Joyce with news that I could scarcely believe. With tears in her eyes, she told me that Laurence

* When *In White America* had to be cancelled at the last moment, I included John Howard Griffin's recording, *Black like me*, as a substitute. This was edited for me by Rayner Heppenstall: the remaining eighteen shows were all produced by me personally.

had died the previous night. In Lorenzo the Magnificent, we had both lost an old and much loved friend.

In the New Year, as an epilogue to *The Negro in America*, I recorded one more programme that Laurence would have liked to have heard. It was an interview with Malcolm X, who was passing through London at the time. He spoke powerfully and cogently, and I was much impressed by what he had to say. This last statement of his aims proved to be virtually his testament to the Negro people. For even before the interview could be broadcast, he too was dead.

14

Arts, Science and Documentaries

SHORTLY AFTER MY return from New York, and while I was still in process of coping with the Negro series, I was summoned to a conference with Richard Marriott, the Assistant Director of Sound Broadcasting. With him was George Camacho, who was talking about yet another reorganisation of Talks and Current Affairs Department. It was already the largest production department in radio, with something over fifty producers on its staff. These were divided between the two departmental sections of General Talks and Current Affairs, headed respectively by C. F. O. Clarke and Stephen Bonarjee.

Marriott explained that with the expected arrival of some half a dozen ex-feature producers, which would bring production strength up to nearly sixty, it had been decided to divide the department yet again. The third section was to be given control of all arts and science talks on Home Service, all talks whatever on Third Programme and all documentaries on both. With some twenty producers of its own, Marriott pointed out, the section would be slightly larger than Features Department had been. And he ended by hoping that I would agree to run it myself, under the resounding title of Programme Editor, Arts, Science and Documentaries (Sound), to which I could only add [sic]. He admitted that no increment would be involved, as my salary was already more than was on offer, but although under the general overlordship of Camacho, the post would carry the full status of departmental head.

As the post would make me responsible for half the old Features Department output—among many other things—it seemed a reasonably interesting offer. On the other hand, it would make me responsible for the part of Features Department output in which I was least interested. Even so, it seemed likely to give me a chance of developing the sort of combined operation that I had initiated with *The Negro in America*, and that was interesting in itself. If I accepted the post, furthermore, it might be possible for me to carry on the old Features Department tradition elsewhere, as I had suggested to Gilliam. I was also amused to notice that Camacho did not seem over happy about the idea, which had only just been sprung upon him. This in itself rather predisposed me to accept the post and see what I could make of it. In the end, after some discussion, I tentatively agreed to take it, given a chance to discuss the details more fully.

Thinking the matter over that night, however, I realised that such a job would be likely very seriously to interfere with my own continuing work as a radio writer, which I was quite determined not to give up. I felt that I should once more be getting bogged down in administrative chores, and once more saddled with the implementation of much that I heartily disliked. Most important of all, I should be surrendering my own independent status in radio, which I had fought hard to establish. Accordingly, I returned to see Marriott the next morning and asked to be excused for turning the offer down.

Marriott was clearly disappointed by my decision, which I discussed with him for some time. He was a man I liked very much personally, though I felt no more sympathy with his ideas on programme matters than I did with those of Gillard. I pointed out that I had done my best work for the BBC since I had been relieved of administrative duties, and that on current showing I was still on top of my form as a producer—to say nothing of my bent. I was mounting some forty or fifty shows a year, and that seemed to me the best way I could serve the BBC.

Marriott argued in return that programmes would always be produced by somebody. I agreed, but suggested rather testily that they might not be produced by 'somebody' quite so successfully as they were by me. This qualitative argument appeared to him quite irrelevant; obviously, programmes were merely something which filled up a schedule.

The crux of the matter, of course, was that the new post had to be filled quickly. He stressed the point that nobody was available whose knowledge of the arts or science or documentaries was equal to mine, and that the job could not be filled adequately unless I agreed to take it on. This I firmly denied, pointing out that there was always 'somebody' to run a department. He asked me whom I could suggest by way of alternative, but I countered by saying that the problem was his and not mine. Finally, he asked whether I was willing to keep an open mind on the matter until Frank Gillard had had a chance of talking it over with me. To this I reluctantly agreed.

Later that week, I was summoned up to Gillard's office. He repeated all the arguments that Marriott had used, and again emphasised the fact that the management felt there was nobody but myself with all the qualifications that the post required. Of this I refused to be convinced: there must surely be dozens of people, where there were literally hundreds to choose between. He disagreed, and again turned the question on me: whom could I suggest? As I felt it was necessary that the post should go to someone from Features Department, I made a suggestion. It was promptly turned down on the grounds of insufficient seniority and administrative experience.

Shifting my ground, I then queried whether the job could be done effectively by anyone, least of all by myself. I pointed out that talks and documentaries were utterly different products, which called for utterly different approaches. Talks producers had merely to find their material: feature producers had to create it. Feature producers were writers themselves: talks producers were not. It seemed to me unlikely that they would bed down very happily together.

Not surprisingly, I was told that it was far too late to go into all that: the matter had already been decided. Of this I was well aware, but still regretted the decision. The short answer was that behind the decision had been the desire to bring talks production into closer contact with documentary techniques, and that cross-fertilisation of ideas could only be valuable. I refrained from pointing out that cross-fertilisation is best confined to the same species, unless one is looking for a hybrid such as a mule. Clearly enough, they were.

Gillard, I must admit, was very patient with me: the interview lasted for some time. He asked whether I would agree to take the post for a trial period: if I honestly found it impossible to knit the department into a smoothly working unit, I should be free to say so and opt out of the job at my discretion. Everything that I asked for, by way of assistance or facilities, would be given me. And I was free to set a limit to the time that I was willing to try my hand at the job. If at the end of that time I did not wish to work at it further, I should be free to return to my present independent status, with nothing held against me. He knew that writing and production were my real interest in radio; but if I agreed to take the post for a couple of years, I should still have four years left for further writing and production before I was due for retirement.

Remembering the good times I had spent in the BBC as virtually my own master, the pleasant trips which had always been freely agreed for me, and all the other consideration and privileges I had enjoyed, I felt it was wrong of me to refuse to give the job a trial. Two years was not for ever, and I was even free to opt out sooner if I found the task impossible. On these terms, I at last accepted the post against my better judgment. Gillard, after all, had almost fallen over backwards to be accommodating. He told me that he was grateful for what he realised had been a rather unwilling decision.

The reallocation of the feature producers took place later the same month, November 1964. Whether or not any of them knew of my appointment at the time, I cannot say: it was not officially promulgated until after the reallocation was complete. Those who were to join me may or may not have been glad to do so, but at least they knew me as an old colleague, and someone who had enjoyed their own background and training. For the most part, reallocation had been a matter of the management's deciding on past performance whether a producer's work lay more in the creative field or the documentary. Like myself, many of them were used to operating in both, but as finally arranged the deployment was reasonable. Christopher Holme, my old successor as Assistant Head of Features, was appointed joint Assistant Head of Drama Department, his twin being Hallam Tennyson. Dorothy Baker, Joe Burroughs, Douglas Cleverdon, Rayner Heppenstall, Nesta Pain, David Thomson and Terence Tiller went to Drama along with him. Maurice Brown, Alan Burgess, Robert Pocock, Christopher Sykes and David Woodward came over to join me. John Bridges, who had been in charge of *Saturday Night on the Light* for a long spell, went over to join Light Entertainment Department in the Aeolian Hall. I took a belated month's leave in the New Year, and returned to my new duties in February 1965.

To be perfectly candid, my two-year stint as the cultural boss of the BBC (the description is Alan Brien's, so I make no apology for it) were quite the most boring and frustrating that I spent in radio. To begin with, it was tiresome having to play the part of poacher turned gamekeeper, even though I had learnt to play it on occasion before. My early brush with Alan Brien in *The Spectator* was a case in point, when I found myself in duty bound to back up two of my lady producers on *The Critics* who objected to his selecting Norman Mailer's novel *The American Dream* for discussion in that particular programme.* Although I had not yet read the book myself, I had every faith in their judgment; and partial to Mailer as I was, forbade the banns accordingly. I was intrigued to find myself promptly pilloried as another Pastor Manders. But though I have no objection to sodomitical practices myself (among consenting adults) I still think they might have proved unacceptable to the old ladies of Cheltenham if the book had been recommended to them over lunch one Sunday morning. The same goes for the process of strangling your wife, washing off the body and throwing it down into the street. Even so, as Mr. Brien sagely observed: "The really disturbing thing about

* It was already down for discussion on Third Programme.

the BBC is that none of us outside can know how often this process occurs without ever being challenged in public." He was, of course, referring to my banning of his discussion . . .

But far more irksome than programme matters was the wild proliferation of departmental and administrative meetings which had been going on in the BBC since I had last been under the obligation of sitting in on them. Before being readmitted to the hierarchy, I had never in all my years been forced to spend so much time sitting listening. The mania for holding meetings has always been an occupational disease in the BBC, but life in my new job exposed me to a raging epidemic. Until I had opted out of a few, I found myself arriving at eight regular meetings a week—some of them lasting up to three hours—apart from the *ad hoc* getting together which sometimes proved necessary. The passion for contemplating the communal navel is a form of group therapy which has never appealed to me, but administration appears to thrive upon it no less than on Parkinson's Law. After a few months of being bored by it, I began to wonder how programmes ever managed to get onto the air. Certainly, very little of my own writing did.

Most high-powered meeting of all was that presided over each week by Frank Gillard himself. It was here that the decisions of the Board of Management were passed on to the heads of the programme departments and the chiefs of the various services, Home, Light and Third, as they were still called. It was there that I first saw clearly just how wide a gap now existed between the BBC management and its programme and planning staff.

Unwisely as it had seemed to me, the daytime Music Programme had already been inaugurated, but plans were now afoot to start up a programme of pop music designed to counterbalance it. The activities of the pirate stations—Radio London, Radio Caroline and the rest—were held to have created a demand for uninterrupted pop, which, once the pirates had been suppressed, the BBC appeared to feel in duty bound to perpetuate.

The logic of this I utterly failed to see. Radio Luxembourg had been churning out uninterrupted dance music all through the thirties, but Sir John Reith had never felt any need to follow suit. And because a demand for pop had been created illegally and irresponsibly, I could see no reason why the BBC should be forced to pander to it against all better judgment. After all, if a pirate television station had begun to broadcast blue films (no doubt one will any moment now), would the BBC feel it incumbent on them to follow suit?

Naturally enough, I have nothing against pop music, the best of which I enjoy thoroughly, if not uninterruptedly. But if nobody had thought up a diet of continuous classical music—which I happen to enjoy rather more—would such a riot of pop have proved necessary anyway? When the Music Programme came on the air, even dedicated musicians began to complain about musical wallpaper. Blathering D.J. wallpaper seems only appropriate to Bedlam.

Both programmes, needless to say, involved the BBC in vast extra expenditure just at the moment when they were sternly calling for economies. Both programmes were decided upon without any proper discussion between management and programme staff. Many of those present at Gillard's meetings, where the plans for them were first made known, shared my own misgivings as to the wisdom of adopting them. But none of those present, as I was intrigued to observe, ever once raised his voice in protest. Like Lord Cardigan at Balaclava, they accepted orders without demur, and promptly went into action. It may have been magnificent, but to my way of thinking it was hardly the way to make war. It was certainly not the best way to make good use of dwindling resources. I am fairly sure that careful discussion of both programmes at responsible programme level would have thrown up a large body of loudly dissenting opinion; for which reason, no doubt, discussion was not invited.

But whatever my feelings about the opening up of two new daytime music channels—and Radio 1, 2, 3 and 4 were now being thrust upon us—my feelings about the BBC's commitment to Local Broadcasting were far more difficult to contain. There was no popular demand for it; there were no resources to pay for it;

and once committed to the policy, there could be no turning back from it. In the event, it was to disrupt national and regional broadcasting disastrously, yet once the decision to promote it had been taken at the top, the rest of the staff grew dumb. The decision was duly endorsed by the Board of Governors, and the whole future of serious radio was undermined.

If it had only been realised at the time just what would have to be sacrificed before Local Broadcasting could be opened up, something might have been done to challenge the decision. But by the time the sacrifice had become apparent, it was far too late to do anything. The new pattern of *Broadcasting in the Seventies* had been quietly settled in the mid-sixties, without anyone attempting to query it. No doubt I should have queried it myself, but junior member of the hierarchy that I was, I hardly flattered myself that my arguments would have carried any weight. As it was, like Comrade Khrushchev and the others, I kept my mouth shut and survived. It seemed to me at the time that I had problems enough of my own in trying to make my new department function, however trivial the problems seem by comparison in retrospect. But I can't help feeling that those with a closer insight into what was really at stake might well have spoken out at the time. No hopelessly belated Campaign for Better Broadcasting could possibly hope to repair the damage later.

As regards my own problems, I should not have been surprised when the offer of 'all assistance and facilities' failed to materialise: such offers invariably do. But I was irritated to find how much of my own effort had to go into making good the deficiency. As it was, being unwilling to fall back on my escape clause, I had perforce to make the best of a bad situation. I had agreed to try and make the new job work, and no matter what frustration resulted, that I was determined to do; for the couple of years agreed upon, so I did.

The real anomalies which I had inherited quickly made themselves apparent. For one thing, I was exasperated to find that all my talks producers were equally at the beck and call of General

Talks section, to which their loyalties were naturally rather stronger. But that was one of the lesser problems. As it had been officially decreed that there should be no falling-off in documentary output under the new order, I was faced with a serious shortage of documentary producers. For the previous output of all those transferred to Drama Department had now to be made good somewhere else. Worst of all, I had now to make up my *own* previous output, for sitting at a desk or attending meetings left me little time for writing and production. Whatever they made of the job, 'somebody' had to be found to write my own programmes for me.

The five documentary producers available to me were all excellent practitioners, but it was quite impossible for them to double their old output, even if I had asked them to try and do so, which I did not. Luckily, Francis Dillon was regularly available on contract, having retired four years previously as one of the best and oldest feature writers ever. Keith Hindell and others were eventually recruited to help in the mounting of a revived weekly *Focus*, in which controversial issues were now open to treatment. And with more shows drummed up round the Regions, or bought in from America and the Commonwealth, I was able to keep the documentary output undiminished. But as for raising the *prestige* of the documentary, that was too much to be hoped. Much to my irritation, I found myself once more committed to a policy of quantity rather than quality, and I could take little pride in the fact.

As for the vast bulk of talks which were put out by the section, they were organised and produced by those who knew far more about the business than I did myself. But here again, insistent demands for a high output kept matters stretched almost to breaking point, so that it was not surprising that a good deal of time was taken up in trying to keep everybody happy. I had never fancied myself in the role of a Dutch Uncle: I liked it even less when it was suddenly thrust upon me.

Dr. Archie Clow, the science editor, and his science producers, David Edge and Mick Rhodes, looked after their own affairs quite admirably, with no more than my moral support. Leonie Cohn, Jocelyn Ferguson, Philip French, Joseph Hone, Robin Hughes, George MacBeth, Michael Mason, Helen Rapp and Carl Wildman were all well respected in their own particular sectors of the arts front and maintained a steady flow of ideas which Lorna Moore helped me to channel into the programmes. Apart from their individual concerns, they also helped me to start up a weekly programme on *The Lively Arts*, which I looked on as the creative artist's answer to *The Critics*. As for *The Critics* themselves, despite attempts to suppress them from higher up, I was able to keep them on the air for a further two years. In Current Affairs talks for Third Programme, excellent work was done by Anthony Moncrieff and Neil Crichton-Miller. George MacBeth continued to exercise his near monopoly in the presentation of contemporary poetry.

For all this, and the good nature with which the talks producers accepted my presence among them, I was duly grateful. I can take no credit for the many excellent things they did, for they had all been doing similar things before I came on the scene. Only two of them had been personally selected by me at an appointments board, but of those two Michael Mason deserves particular mention by reason of the originality which he injected into talks production. His splendid programme *A Bayeux Tapestry* (co-produced with George MacBeth) and his marathon *Rus* (co-produced with Helen Rapp) were among the most notable achievements during my sojourn with the department. Mason's imaginative use of pure sound, as an adjunct to pure information, harked back to the golden age of radio, while his mastery of stereophonic effect looked well into the future.

One of my main hopes in trying to weld together talks and documentary thinking had lain in the direction of extra-departmental planning. As I have said, *The Negro in America* had broken new ground by combining every form of radio programme for the treatment in depth of a phase of recent history. For the autumn of 1965, therefore, I planned and mounted a similar series on *Britain in the Thirties*, a phase of history that I was old enough to have experienced at first hand. Administrative chores prevented me from tackling the whole series myself—dearly as I should have liked to do so—but there was an abundant choice of talent to recruit for it from three departments.

Once again, the idea behind the series was to relate cultural expression to the social scene and the economic background, each acquiring new significance by reference to the others. So far as the thirties went, the predominant factor had been the economic stagnation—which had given rise to the threat of Fascism, and a far more stimulating burst of intellectual activity on the Left. These three aspects of the decade were given full documentary treatment in scripts written by Constantine Fitzgibbon and produced by Robert Pocock. They included vivid reminiscences of the time, and provided the necessary background to the other programmes in the series.

Neil Crichton-Miller came up with a remarkable curtain-raiser to the whole, *In Defence of Gold*, which examined the evidence given before the Macmillan Committee in 1930 by Sir Montagu Norman. The anti-social implications of this Master Banker's economic orthodoxy went far to justify the vigorous indictment of the *Cantos*. Two plays were included in the series—Auden and Isherwood's brilliant *Dog beneath the Skin* and Eliot's no less influential *Murder in the Cathedral*. Further documentary treatment was given to the scientific discoveries of the thirties by Dr. Archie Clow and Mick Rhodes in *Science and Society*, to *Mass Observation* by Bill Naughton, to *The Novel* by Walter Allen, and to *The Visual Arts* in two programmes by Andrew Forge. There were talks on *Marxism* by Professor J. M. Cameron and *Logical Positivism* by Professor A. J. Ayer, a lively survey of popular tunes of the thirties, *The Music goes round* by the equally lively Charles Chilton, and four programmes of thirties' poetry. Apart from the duties of general editor, my own contributions were confined to producing selections of the poetry of Auden and the *New Verse* group, the latter being chosen and introduced by Geoffrey Grigson.

All in all, the series made remarkably interesting listening, was well received by the critics, and even elicited praise from the Board of Governors—uniquely in my experience! It showed quite clearly, furthermore, just how much was being lost to radio by the watertight departmental planning which I had always done my best to break down. Once again, Third Programme gained the credit for having provided so much space in the one quarter for careful presentation of related work in an interesting field. The programmes would certainly have attracted far less notice if they had merely been mounted piecemeal in the usual way.

One of the outcomes of *Britain in the Thirties* was an application to the High Court by Sir Oswald Mosley for a writ of attachment against the BBC based on references to his activities in Constantine Fitzgibbon's documentary *The Rise of Fascism*. He held that these would prejudice the jury in an action for libel which, for the last two and a half years, he had been threatening to bring against the BBC and Paul Fox—and so amounted to contempt of Court. He had not, in fact, been invited to speak in the programme as I was not of the opinion that he should be given a new platform for his views: what he had said in the thirties was already fully on record. I was rather surprised to hear the Lord Chief Justice express "considerable sympathy" for Sir Oswald. "Here is a vast organisation which has the ear of the whole public," his lordship declared, "and who can, within the law of libel, give free expression to their views, while the subject of those views is wholly incapable of presenting his in the same medium." Nevertheless, the action was dismissed.

I had, of course, taken legal advice on the matter before the programme went on the air; but I was glad to learn that the Director-General gave full backing to my own part in keeping Mosley out of the series in person. As Hugh Greene had declared recently in a speech at Rome: "There are some respects in which the BBC is not neutral, unbiased, or impartial. That is, where there are clashes for and against the basic moral values—truthfulness, justice, freedom, compassion, tolerance." I hoped that my own biased decision had been in conformity with that policy.

With the completion of my first year as Programme Editor, I let it be clearly understood that I had no intention of continuing to function as such for a day longer than the agreed two years. The ear-bashing was leaving me punch-drunk, the callouses on my bottom were beginning to bother me, and I could stand very few further administrative meetings. More to the point, I was increasingly anxious to get back into productive and useful work. As something would have to be done to relieve me sooner or later, George Camacho decided that sooner would be the better. A suitable incumbent was sought for in other places, and for the first time in my life I found myself indebted to the aristocracy, Lord Archie Gordon being appointed as my deputy and successor-elect. His arrival immediately began to make life interesting again. Being no less sympathetic than long-suffering, he was able to relieve me of a great deal of administrative work. The pressure of this being lessened, I was able to phase myself back into programmes, and began to plan one more marathon series for Third.

It had long occurred to me that many of the growing manifestations of restlessness and national self-criticism in America could be traced back to her possession of the Bomb, and the policy of Communist containment which it had underwritten for her over the years. Her whole involvement in the Cold War—so contrary to America's traditional isolationism—had been obviously dictated by the knowledge that her monopoly of nuclear weapons could not last for long, but that it would enable her to hold strategic positions in the world for at least as long as she enjoyed it. These positions, furthermore, represented a needed insurance against the dangers of coming parity with—or even inferiority to—nuclear armament in the Soviet Union. All this was obvious enough, but what effect had possession of the Bomb had upon America's political and social life as a whole?

As Alistair Cooke has pointed out, there is a danger in presuming that because events follow in sequence, one is necessarily the

cause of the other. On the other hand, a sequence of events is
something that can be studied, and from that study cause and
effect can sometimes be established.

With atomic secrets at risk, was it merely coincidence that
America had suddenly erupted into a spy-scare, and would Alger
Hiss have been convicted if no such scare had broken out? If there
had been no Hiss trial, would Senator McCarthy have been able
to regiment fear and intolerance for so long? Without McCarthyism would blacklisting ever have been possible in the entertainment industry? What part in the backlash against both was played
by the protest song, and the new concern with civil rights to
which it gave expression? Without this concern, would white
students have taken upon themselves to organise a voters' regis-
tration campaign in Mississippi? Without the experience gained
in Mississippi, would Berkeley students have set the pattern for
student demonstrations all over America? Without the students'
lead, would demonstrations against the war in Vietnam have
become as vocal as they did?

Similarly with what one can only describe as the American-
born anti-social *malaise*: was revulsion against the American way
of life *solely* responsible for the emergence of the Beat generation?
Or was some form of bomb-neurosis also behind it? To what
extent was the same neurosis traceable in the work of the Beat
poets, and the new American dramatists? Was anything to be
deduced from a study of new trends in jazz, the craze for rock
music and the birth of pop? If so, did acceptance of life in an
age of Bomb-rattling have anything to do with the sense of
guilt? Had it given rise to what Auden had dubbed the Age of
Anxiety?

It was naturally out of the question to *prove* a chain of cause and
effect in any such sequence, but the sequence itself was so much
historical fact, and afforded food for speculation. It was with this
in mind that I planned what was to be my last major project for
the BBC, *America since the Bomb*. Twenty programmes went to
the making of the series, which kept me busy for every minute I
could spare away from my desk during the summer of 1966.

Three further trips had to be made to New York, where I had almost come to regard the Algonquin as my second home.

Once more, I relied on the formula that had served me well before: a series of varied programmes grouped around three major documentaries, *Korea to Vietnam*. In these, the story of America's growing preoccupation with the Cold War was traced through the phases of *Bomb Diplomacy* and *Brinkmanship* to the point where national aspiration seemed to pose a choice between *The Moon or South-East Asia?*, a strange choice for the children of the American Revolution to be faced with having to make!

The same laborious combing through American sound archives produced a still more daunting wealth of material, from which some four hundred recorded extracts were finally selected. The mounting outcry in America against the escalation in Vietnam provided a highly topical close to the trio of documentaries, and for that the material available was dramatic in the extreme. But the whole evolving story was fascinating for the light that it threw upon the Vietnam commitment, and the almost inevitable steps by which it had come about. To me, it was merely a clarification of events as I remembered them, but a whole generation had grown up since the Truman Doctrine had been proclaimed, and for them the story proved something of a revelation. As one of my younger producers remarked, it was fascinating for her to learn just what had been happening in her lifetime.

Writing *Korea to Vietnam* was stimulating enough in itself, but it was the ancillary programmes in the series that gave me the greatest pleasure to assemble and produce. Emile de Antonio's documentary film on Senator McCarthy, *Point of Order*, had horrified me when I saw it in New York two years before: adapting his soundtrack for radio as *The Senator from Wisconsin*, he added a blistering commentary on one of the most unsavoury smear campaigns of all time. Reuben Ship's resounding satire on McCarthyism, *The Investigator*, I had put on the air back in the fifties, but it well deserved a second hearing. The story of a demagogue who begins to investigate Heaven, gets St. Peter dismissed as a political subversive, and is finally thrown out for plotting to indict God, it was one of the most effective satires I had heard on the air. It did a great deal in its time to laugh McCarthy out of business.

Alistair Cooke, whose book on the trial of Alger Hiss is well remembered, covered *The Spy Scare* in his own inimitable way: like the trial itself, he left the question of Hiss's guilt in doubt. John Henry Faulk's account of his own persecution, *Blacklisting on Trial*, provided a fitting close to the reign of fear which McCarthyism had thrived upon. Himself indicting the men who had tried to smear him as a Communist, Faulk finally succeeded in clearing himself completely. Though he never succeeded in collecting them, the three and a half million dollars awarded him in damages proved an adequate deterrent to further attempts at political blackmail.

In *The Folk Song Army* and *Songs of Protest*, Alan Lomax and Guy Caravan traced the evolution of the form from the songs of the thirties through Woody Guthrie, Earl Robinson and Josh White to Pete Seeger, Tom Paxton, Phil Ochs and Bob Dylan—an evolution, of course, to which they had contributed much themselves.

The special significance of *The Beat Generation* was discussed by Kenneth Rexroth, who had watched its coming to birth in San Francisco after the Korean War. His *Subculture of Secession* brought the story of the drop-out up to date, while *Beat Poetry—and After* examined the nature of the work by which the Beats were best remembered, and its influence upon later poetry.*

I had first put my friend Tom Lehrer on Third Programme back in 1957, thus introducing him to the English audience. In *Sick Humour and Satire*, I traced his influence from the prophetic

---

* I had some fun with Allen Ginsberg's immortal line:

America go fuck yourself with your Atom Bomb

which was included in his own recorded reading. As in duty bound, I referred the line to Camacho, who referred it to Marriott, who referred it to Gillard, who referred it to the Board of Management. There I like to think of it being solemnly considered . . .

It was the Director-General himself who sanctioned it for broadcasting. The man who got himself arrested for declaiming it on Brighton Promenade later might well have called him for the defence!

survival hymn *We'll all go together when we go* to the later lucubrations of Mort Sahl, Lennie Bruce and the others. Nat Hentoff reported on *The New Jazz* from New York, and Ralph Gleason on *The Birth of Pop* from San Francisco.

Gleason also gave an account of the demonstrations at Berkeley in *Revolt on the Campus*, a programme which included some stirring words from Joan Baez and a truly inspired outburst by Norman Mailer. Leading up to it, the story of the student participation in the Mississippi campaign was carefully documented by Colin Edwards in *White Integrationism*. A new production of Edward Albee's highly significant *Zoo Story* completed the series, to which Auden's *Age of Anxiety* had formed a fitting prelude.

It was a matter of some satisfaction to me that the most enthusiastic response to *America since the Bomb* came from students at the English universities. For the middle-aged, who normally formed the vast bulk of the Third Programme audience, the series could not have had such an immediate appeal. No doubt many of them were distressed and alarmed by it, for it clearly bore the impress of things that were to come nearer home. But to the younger listeners, this was the story of their own lifetime, and one that pointed the way that many of them were already going. The series was heard on the air in the very midst of the London demonstrations against the war in Vietnam, on which it provided some illuminating American comment. And the names that the series threw up as its heroes were names that made news for a younger generation. Kerouac, Ginsberg, Ferlinghetti and Gary Snyder, Pete Seeger, Judy Collins, Joan Baez and Bob Dylan, Dick Gregory and Godfrey Cambridge, Lennie Bruce and the Fugs—these were names which meant far more to them than ever they could to a generation of dons. With its portrayal of student unrest, social nonconformism, anti-war demonstrations and political militancy, *America since the Bomb* gave a strong foretaste of British unrest in the years that followed it, the later sixties. And I was glad to feel that even as I approached the sixties myself, I could still mount radio exciting to the younger audience. The correspondence that I had from the series, and the steady requests for scripts from the universities, persuaded me that I had done so.

With the completion of *America since the Bomb*, I ended my second year in charge of Arts, Science and Documentaries, and quite long enough the two years seemed. As I pointed out at the time, Oscar Wilde had served no more after giving far greater provocation to the authorities. With a suitable lack of ceremony, I handed over my duties to Lord Archie Gordon—deeply grateful for all he had borne for me already. Without this helpfulness on his part *America since the Bomb* could never have been attempted. My promised return to programme independence was honoured by Frank Gillard and carefully promulgated by Michael Standing. I still had four years left for writing and production before I was due to retire from the BBC—or so I thought . . .

As 1967 was to mark the fiftieth anniversary of the Russian Revolution, I had plenty to think about by way of a possible further series for Third. Permission was granted me—at last—to visit the Soviet Union, to which I was keenly looking forward. As I had not had a holiday for the last twelve months, however, I started the year by taking a month's belated leave at home. I was too tired to bother taking myself abroad, having been working sixty or seventy hours a week for the past three months. The Negro series had meant the mounting of eighteen shows in twelve weeks: *America since the Bomb* had involved the mounting of twenty shows in ten.

My mother, then in her eighties, was failing in health and I went up North to visit her for a few days: no sooner had I returned to London than I learnt of her death. Upset by the sudden news, I set out for Lytham St. Annes once more to arrange her funeral. The arrangements proved sadly depressing, and feeling the need of some exercise, I set myself a race to the stop against a bus I was not in the slightest hurry to catch. Apparently, I was not so fit as I had imagined; no doubt a hundred thousand cigars and as many bottles of burgundy were beginning to creep up on me. I caught the bus, but that was virtually the last thing I man-

aged to do for the rest of the year. I was ordered complete rest
while my arteries adjusted themselves, and settled down to something I had never had time to tackle before. I slowly read my way
through Gibbon's *Decline and Fall* . . .

The following winter, preparatory to getting back to work full
time again, I took Joyce with me on a return visit to Australia.
We were extremely well looked after by her cousins in Sydney
and Melbourne, and I took the opportunity of renewing many
old friendships in and around the ABC. Returning by way of the
Pacific, with short stops at Fiji, Honolulu, San Francisco and New
York, I took the opportunity of flying down to visit Conrad
Aiken in Savannah. Two hours after I left Atlanta on the return
trip, Martin Luther King was murdered there. That night I
watched the near riots in New York, and returned to London two
days later in time to help with the remaking of a programme on
Black Power. It seemed remarkably appropriate.

During my rest cure, the BBC had taken care that I received
what medical attention I needed, additional to that laid on for me
by my own doctor. I had been offered premature retirement on
health grounds, but preferred to see whether there was anything
interesting to do before I accepted it. In the event, I was to come
up with another twenty shows, but by then I had decided that
radio was beginning to look less healthy than I was.

Since I had returned to work, Broadcasting House had been
invaded by a team of management consultants from McKinsey
and Co., Inc., in whom the accents of Oxford and Harvard had
pleasantly cross-fertilised. It seemed that the internal economy of
the BBC was being 'investigated'. Lord Hill of Luton had been
appointed as Chairman of the Board of Governors, and shortly
thereafter, Sir Hugh Greene had resigned. It was rumoured that
'a cool hard look' was to be taken into the future of radio. Gerard
Mansell, with whom I had enjoyed working while he had been
running the Home Service (Radio 4, as it was by then), had retired into the woodwork with various other people to plan the
pattern of broadcasting in the seventies. I had no idea what the

pattern was to be, but remembering every reorganisation to date, I doubted very much whether it would appeal to me. An instinctive sense of timing told me that I should be well advised to arrange for my departure. I had to admit, reluctantly, that I was no longer quite so spry as I had been, and doubted whether the last year of my full time with the BBC would give me all that joy. I applied for premature retirement on the grounds of my arterial trouble, and planned my final shows meanwhile.

Marriage of True Minds, the story of Bertrand Russell's parents, based on the enchanting *Amberley Papers*, had been well received on my fifty-eighth birthday: an adaptation of my favourite impropriety, *A Sentimental Journey*, was followed by a new production of my favourite fairy story, *Pippa Passes*. I paid a nostalgic *Return to Manchester*, in which the start of it all was recalled with those who had made life good there—Joan Littlewood, Ewan MacColl, Francis Dillon, Walter Greenwood, Edgar Lustgarten, Kenneth Adam, Emmanuel Levy and the rest. A final programme on Wyndham Lewis and the Vorticists was arranged; there were farewell repeats of *The March of the '45* on Radio 4 and *The Quest of Gilgamesh* on the Third Programme; and that was about the sum of it.

As I had no need to remind myself, the old Features Department team was rapidly breaking up. Joe Burroughs had died suddenly. Douglas Cleverdon, Christopher Holme, Christopher Sykes and Maurice Brown had all retired. Robert Pocock's contract had lapsed and Rayner Heppenstall—much to his irritation—had found himself retired early. David Woodward was due to retire later that year. All in all, I felt it was time for me also to depart, which I did in May 1969, just over thirty-five years after my first programme had gone out over the air. Over eight hundred broadcasts had had my name upon them since and four hundred had been heard in recorded repeats. It seemed quite enough radio for anyone to have had a hand in. I was happy to resume what was left of a somewhat interrupted career.

POSTSCRIPT

PROSPERO AND ARIEL

As EVENTS WERE to prove, my retirement from the BBC was remarkable for the aptness of its timing. I had become used to getting off the air within seconds of any deadline, no matter how long or complicated the show had been. And my last week in Broadcasting House turned out to be the one when the final nail was driven into the coffin of radio as I liked to remember it. Indeed, the farewell lunch given to me by the new Director-General, Charles Curran, had to be postponed till five weeks after I had left, as it had been set for the very day that the Board of Governors were called upon to hammer the nail home.

Following on that meeting came publication of *Broadcasting in the Seventies*, which had been drawn up in response to the recommendations made by the Mansell Committee. Suffice it to say that it formed the blueprint of radio as we know it today.

There is no need to discuss the nature of the new state of affairs which the seventies brought to radio, for we have come to accept it. Whatever one may have thought about the wisdom of creating the Third Programme in the first place, there can be no doubt at all about the folly of abolishing it in view of its splendid record over twenty-three years. The reversion to mixed speech listening on Radio 4 is meaningless, when offered as an alternative to unmixed pop on Radio 1 and unmixed slop on Radio 2. As for the logic of confining all good music to the narrow groove of Radio 3, it has merely made doubly sure that none but the already converted will ever hear good music again. *Broadcasting in the Seventies* proved to most thinking people that the seventies were for the Yahoos, so far as responsible broadcasting went. The fact emerged clearly enough in the withering editorials and comments which flooded the press for weeks once the threat had been fully understood.

A great deal more effort was made to save the Third Programme in 1970 than had been noticeable in 1957. The letters of protest printed by *The Times*, the *Guardian* and other responsible organs were signed by a reasonable cross-section of independent and informed opinion. All were dismissed by the BBC management as so much special pleading. When the Campaign for Better Broadcasting was belatedly organised, Sir Adrian Boult, Sir Tyrone Guthrie, Henry Moore, Sir Roland Penrose, Professor Max Beloff and Professor G. M. Carstairs were among the signatories of its demand for a public investigation of the new plans before they were put into effect. But despite the able pamphleteering of John Donat and others, no notice was taken of their demand. I celebrated my own retirement by giving them what help I could, though with little hope of their efforts being successful. At least I was glad that my last recorded utterance on the subject of responsible radio should be one more denunciation of the way that BBC management seemed bent upon ploughing good radio programmes into the ground.

Most significant of all, however, was the fact that on this occasion a large number of the programme staff implicated in the changes rose in open revolt against the managerial *diktat*. Petitions were presented to the Director-General, and when these failed to win proper consideration, a letter signed by 134 members of the London radio programme and planning staff appeared in *The Times*, complaining that they had been refused any chance to lay their own point of view before the Board of Governors. Not only was this in open breach of their individual contracts with the BBC: it was the first time in forty-eight years of BBC history that such a step had been deemed necessary in the public interest. The letter was soon followed by others from the BBC Regions in exactly the same terms.

The gist of these protests was contained in a single paragraph from the London letter: "What we object to," it stated, "is the abandonment of creative, mixed planning in favour of a schematic division into categories on all four programmes; and, above all, the refusal to devote a large, well-defined area of broadcasting time to a service of the arts and sciences." What was implicit in all of them was the indignation felt by the signatories that once again the BBC management had taken upon itself to decide a matter of the greatest importance to BBC programmes without the slightest reference to the people whose duty it was to *make* those programmes. If I had still been on the staff of the BBC at the time, my signature would certainly have been among the others. At least it appeared under the manifesto calling for a Royal Commission to review the structure, finance and organisation of broadcasting before the renewal of the BBC Charter and the Television Act in 1976. If such a Commission is set up, let us hope that for once at least the opinion of programme makers will be weighed in the balance against the opinion of programme brokers.

It is natural enough, at the end of a long journey, to look back over the course of it and wonder whether or not the time it has taken has been well spent. Would the time have been better spent in other ways and other courses? Has one arrived, at the end of it all, wherever it was one hoped to be? Is it true that to travel hopefully is sometimes a better thing than to arrive, or is that merely the excuse put upon time wasted by those who refuse to admit the truth?

So far as my time in radio was concerned, there was certainly little tangible to show at the end of it. The money I had earned was enough to make life comfortable, but that could have been done in many ways. I had saved the BBC some tens of thousands of pounds in broadcast fees—for shows that would have had to be paid for if written by somebody else—but that fact was hardly reflected in my salary: I could have earned as much as a producer without having written a line. There had indeed been plenty of empty praise, but no more solid pudding than sitting quietly behind a desk might well have landed on my plate. Few of my scripts had been published, and not many of my shows survived even in recorded form. For the rest, they were blowing in the wind indeed.

The same amount of creative effort in any other medium of communication would have left far more to show for the time taken up. Radio, after all, is the most fugitive medium of any—for even in journalism, back files are there to be read. As it was, I had only my memory of past excitements to remind me of all that was gone for good. Hundreds of millions of people around the world had listened to what I had wanted to say: how many of them remembered a single word of it? If I had ever influenced them, were any of them even conscious of the fact? It seemed highly unlikely.

Even so, the important thing was that I had *said* what I wanted to say. I had said it as persuasively as I could, and millions had been gathered together to hear it. Whether it realised the fact or not, for better or worse the world had mostly gone the way that I—and others like me—had tried to ensure that it would. In greater liberalism, in greater equality and tolerance, the world was a better place than it had been in my earlier years. It might have been far worse, if radio had not been there at work to give it something of a lead.

Only radio itself had failed to retain its power for good in a world where television had largely taken over. But apart from the coming of television—to which radio will always remain a necessary adjunct—far more had been lost to it than ever needed to have been. Radio in the seventies seems likely to make a sorry showing. And for that I can only blame the wrong-thinking of later BBC management, and all the trivialisation that has resulted from it.

But apart from use or misuse of the medium, there is much in radio that I like to remember it for in retrospect. Every successful programme that I have written has left its echoes in my mind, echoes to which mere printed publication could never have given rise. There is something uniquely satisfying to a writer in hearing his work spoken, in choosing his favourite actors to interpret it, and in hearing how his favourite composers can heighten his

POSTSCRIPT: PROSPERO AND ARIEL

dramatic effects. Radio writing and production is a form of shared experience, and without the participation of others, not much creative work can ever be totally enjoyed. As Louis MacNeice remarked of it in his preface to *The Dark Tower*: "The point is that here we have a means by which written lines can emulate the impact of a stage or of a painting and give the writer that excitement of a sensuous experience simultaneously shared with many which is one of the joys of life."

But radio has meant far more to me than the mere pleasure of writing and production. The only end of living, so far as I am concerned, is the enjoyment of life; and there is no doubt at all that the time I spent in radio has helped me to enjoy mine to the full. At every stage of the game, including the most boring one, I have enjoyed my fun and frolic. Radio has taken me to many parts of the world, where I have heard and done far more than falls to the lot of most people. I have seen most of the things that I wanted to see, and shared the pleasure by recreating them for others' enjoyment. I have eaten well and drunk well, made many delightful friendships and had many charming love-affairs. I have spent my life in pleasant ways and among people that I admire and respect. I have been old enough to enjoy the greatest days of radio, and young enough to bow myself out before the worst of them set in. One thing I know for certain: I was right to follow my bent, and given the time over, would avidly follow it again.

As I left Broadcasting House for the last time, I remembered the noble figures which Eric Gill had set up there above the portal —Ariel in his young fervour, Prospero in his quiet and vigilant concern. I was glad to know that my days had been spent in such gracious and friendly company. After all, one could hardly feel much respect for the tutelary deity of Television Centre—a tin man with a prick on a stick. For me, Prospero and Ariel stood for something more meaningful and something rather more inspiring. Ariel had served me well and faithfully, though I had no more been his master than anyone else had been among my colleagues. Prospero, on the other hand, had been the master of us all. He

335

at least had worked for what he knew to be right and just, he had used his art to redress wrongs, and had taken upon himself to shape the lives of others for their own good. There was much of him in all the men I had liked and admired most in radio. There was something of his paternalism in the first bold concept of Lord Reith, and something of him in all the best of Reith's followers and successors. There was something of him in all who had tried to use radio responsibly and from a sense of inner conviction. Much of the devotion to his art had been in the creativity of my friends, the writers and producers that I had been proud to number myself among. There was much of his patience in all those whose craft had been untiring wherever radio was being made. An art such as Prospero's had made radio possible, had given it excitement, integrity and truth.

There was much in serving Prospero that had brought out the best in many people. There was much that had been good for me, much I had been glad to do; and more I should have liked to do, given greater ability. Prospero had been a kind taskmaster —not only to Ariel, but to me and everyone else who had tried to serve him worthily.

INDEX

N.B. BBC productions—features, documentaries, plays, etc.—are listed alphabetically under that heading.

BBC productions—*cont.*

Tower of Hunger, The (Terence Tiller), 200

Transatlantic Call—People to People (CBS–BBC series), 96–9, 101, 115

Trimalchio's Feast (adapted from Petronius' *Satyricon* by Louis MacNeice), 185

Tristram Shandy (adapted from Laurence Sterne by D. G. Bridson), 285

Trouble in Mind (Alice Childress), 306

Tunnel (D. G. Bridson), 71, 184

Under Milk Wood (Dylan Thomas, produced by Douglas Cleverdon), 200, 206

Valiant Years, The (TV documentaries based on Churchill's war memoirs, produced by Robert D. Graff), 257–62

Very Great Man Indeed, A (Henry Reed, produced by Douglas Cleverdon), 200

Vincenzo (Henry Reed, produced by D. Cleverdon), 200

Visual Arts, The (Andrew Forge), 321

Voyage of Magellan, The (Laurie Lee, produced by Rayner Heppenstall), 200

War Report, 51, 116

Waste Land, The (dramatisation of T. S. Eliot's poem by D. G. Bridson), 64–7

We love this land (feature on Invasion of Norway by D. G. Bridson), 83

We speak for ourselves (actuality series by D. G. Bridson), 77, 78

Where do we go from here? (Louis MacNeice; part of *Britain to America* series), 93

Wilfred Pilgrim's Progress (play by D. G. Bridson), 227–8

Window on Europe (feature inaugurated by D. G. Bridson), 123

Women of Trachis (Ezra Pound's translation of Sophocles' play), 196–7

Wound, The (Ted Hughes; produced by D. Cleverdon), 200

Zoo Story (Edward Albee), 327

Zulus, The (D. G. Bridson), 139

Beach, Sylvia, 192

Beadle, Sir Gerald, 262; Director of Television, 243

Beatles, 97*n.*

Beaverbrook, Lord, 73–4, 87

Bechet, Sidney, 168

Beckwith, Reginald, 115

Bedell Smith, General Walter, 118

Bedford, Agnes, 283–4

Beerbohm, Max, 65

Belgrade, 127

Beloff, Professor Max, 334

Bentley, Dick, 144

Bernaškova, Alena, 124

Berryman, John, 278, 279

Betjeman, John, 247*n.*

Bevan, Aneurin, 53

Beveridge, Lord, 159–60

Beveridge Report, 94, 95

Biddle, Anthony Drexel, 89

Bigard, Barney, 168

Birnbryer, Eddie, 185

Blackbirds (Cochran's revue), 109

Blackett, Professor P. M. S., 290

Blesh, Rudi, 168

Bliss, Sir Arthur, 220

Blunden, Edmund, 205

Bonarjee, Stephen, 311

Bontemps, Arna, 305

Boult, Sir Adrian, 334

Bowes, Major, *Amateur Hour*, 97

Boyd, Donald, 28, 116; Talks Producer, 51

Brannigan, Owen, 143

Bridges, John, 123, 315

Bridson, D. G.: life in Manchester, and friendship with Archie Harding, 1*ff.*; resigns job to devote whole time to writing, 33; first

Durrell, Lawrence, 208, 272–5
Dyall, Valentine, 76, 86
Dylan, Bob, 101, 222, 326–7
Dyrenforth, James, 198

ECA (Economic Co-operation Administration), 156–8
Eddison, Robert, 76
Edge, David, 319
Edinburgh, Duke of, 149
Edward VIII, 52
Edwards, Colin, 326
Edwards, Jimmy, 144
Eisenhower, President, 118
Eliot, Henry Ware, 90
Eliot, T. S., 33, 37, 40, 64–7, 165, 191, 233, 276–7, 321
Elizabeth II, Queen, 135
Elizabeth, Queen, the Queen Mother, 51n., 133
Elliott, Bill, 168n.
Emerton, Roy, 86
Englishman looks at Brooklyn, An (D. G. Bridson; NBC production), 108
Englishman looks at Chicago, An (D. G. Bridson; NBC production), 104
Englishman looks at San Francisco, An (D. G. Bridson; NBC production), 106
Entertainment Division, 185
Epoca, 284
Evening Chronicle, Manchester, 45
Evers, Medgar, 307–8

Fallon, Joe, 149
Farmer, James, 305
Farquharson, Robert, 46, 65–6, 183
Faulk, John Henry, 326
Feature programmes: creation of, 30; development during the war, 121–122; a medium for creative writing, 122; variety of styles and material, 122–3; high quality, and decline in creativity, 235
Features Department, 123; effect of 1957 reorganisation of, 234–6, 238; end of, 289, 295–7, 299–304

Features and Drama Department, 73, 75, 80, 82, 121; new and independent status, 123 (*see* Features Department)
Feiner, Ben, 261
Ferguson, Jocelyn, 320
Ferlinghetti, Lawrence, 220–1, 327
Ferris, Paul, 280
Finch, Peter, 146
Fitch, Captain Henry, Director of Administration, North Region, 51
Fitzgibbon, Constantine, 321–2
Florence, 132
Flying bombs, 116
Fogg, Eric, 55
Foot, Sir Robert, Director-General, 95, 113, 143
Forces Programme, 178
Foreign language broadcasting, 80
Forge, Andrew, 321
Forster, E. M., 183
Fortuin, H. B., 199
Fox, Paul, 322
Fraser, Grace Lovat, 32
French, Philip, 320
Frisch, Professor Otto, 292
Frost, Robert, 195, 214–16, 278
Fugs, the, 327

Gamble, Doris, 55
Geer, Will, 115
General Talks and Current Affairs Department, 311, 318–19
George V, King, 53
George VI, King, 62n., 133, 144n.
George Mitchell Choir, 247
Gerhard, Roberto, 198–9, 220, 282–4, 306
Gielgud, Val, 30, 42, 48, 60, 64, 74–5, 156, 159, 182n., 240, 244, 246, 282; Director of Features and Drama Department, 123
Gildard, Gordon, 60
Gill, Eric, 41, 337
Gillard, Frank, 115, 134–5, 299–303, 312–14, 316–17, 328; Director of Sound Broadcasting, 296

Gillespie, Dizzy, 305
Gilliam, Laurence, 36–7, 62–4, 67n.,
    75, 79–80, 82, 92–3, 99, 116, 122,
    126, 134, 161, 168, 186, 199, 240,
    244, 254, 258, 295, 297, 299–304,
    308, 312; in Drama Department,
    62; Head of Features Department,
    123, 237–8; joins Television Ser-
    vice, 152–3; and *This is Europe*
    series, 156–9; death, 309–10
Ginsberg, Allen, 204, 219, 326n., 327
Giovannitti, Len, 261
Giudecca, 132
Gleason, Ralph, 327
Glubb, Sir John, 171
Goacher, Denis, 197n.
Goehr, Alexander, 283
Goehr, Walter, 199
Goldring, Mary, 292
Gollan, John, 268–9
Gordon, Lord Archie, Programme
    Editor, 323, 328
Goring, Marius, 278
Gough, John, 47, 82
Graff, Robert D., 258, 261
Grant, Cy, 254
Graves, Sir Cecil, Director-General
    95–6
Graves, Robert, 118, 219, 258, 269–72,
    278, 286
Greece, 83
Greene, Sir Hugh Carlton, Director-
    General, 154, 288–9, 294, 322, 329
Greenwood, Walter, 28, 146, 330
Gregory, Dick, 327
Grey of Fallodon, Lord, 95
Griffin, John Howard, 309n.
Grigson, Geoffrey, 321
Grisewood, Harman, 187, 193, 208;
    Third Programme Controller, 160,
    185, 189; personal assistant to
    George Barnes, 183; Director of the
    Spoken Word, 198
Guardian (formerly *Manchester Guar-
    dian*, q.v.), 247, 294, 334
Guthrie, Sir Tyrone, 237n., 330
Guthrie, Woody, 115, 222, 326

Haley, Sir William, Director-General,
    96, 113–14, 118, 121, 130, 141, 179–
    180, 182–3; resigns, 197–8
Halifax, Lord, 90
Hall Johnson Choir, 110
Halton, Matthew, 116
Hampton, Lionel, 103
Hanley, James, 82
Harding, Archie, 32–40, 45–8, 50–1,
    54, 160, 184, 283; background and
    characteristics, 28–30; creative atti-
    tude to broadcasting, 30–1; Chief
    Instructor, BBC Staff Training
    School, 60, 63
Harding, Gerald Lankester, 173
Harrison, Rex, 165
Hassard, Peggy, 198
Hayes, Patricia, 199
Heller, Robert, 167
Helveg, Marianne, 152, 168
Hemingway, Ernest, 214
Hentoff, Nat, 305, 327
Heppenstall, Rayner, 123, 200–1, 208,
    235, 303, 309n., 315, 330; *Portrait
    of the Artist as a Professional Man*,
    236, 296
Hill, Lord, Chairman of the Board of
    Governors, 329
Hilton, James, 106, 165
Hilton, John, 53
Hindell, Keith, 319
Hirche, Peter, 237n.
Hiss, Alger, 324, 326
Hitchcock, Alfred, 106, 110
Hitler, Adolf, 86, 124
Hobbs, Carleton, 66
Hogarth, Ann, 50–1
Hogg, Quintin, 53
Holland, Charlotte, 285–6
Holliday, Billie, 103
Hollywood, 106–7, 165–7
Holme, Christopher, 330; Assistant
    Head of Features, 254; Joint Assis-
    tant Head of Drama, 315
Home Service, 177, 224, 226–7, 235,
    237, 286–7, 329; changes in pro-
    gramme emphasis, 233

INDEX

Parks, Rosa, 308
Partnow, Hyde, 107
Pascal, Gabriel, 165
Patmore, Derek, 162
Paxton, Tom, 326
Peacock, Michael, 248
Pearl, Cyril, 149
Pearson, Lily May, 115
Peierls, Professor Rudolf, 292
Pelletier, H. Rooney, Light Programme Controller, 227
Penrose, Sir Roland, 334
Philadelphia, 101
Phillips, Frank, 163-4
Pickles, Wilfred, 53, 70-1, 77-9, 88, 185, 227-8, 247
Pinter, Harold, 182
Pirate radio stations, 316
Playfair, Giles, 32, 51
Pocock, Robert, 315, 321, 330
Poetry (Chicago magazine), 278
Poetry Committee, 208
Point of Order (film), 325
Porter, David, 51
Portman, Eric, 117
Portugal, 158
Potter, Stephen, 75, 122
Pound, Ezra, 33, 39, 41, 164-5, 193-7, 209-14, 249-53, 265-7, 276-7, 283-285
Powley, Bryan, 76
Prague, 124-6
Pre-scripted talks, 52-3
Primus, Pearl, 103
Proud, John, 144
Pudney, John, 64
Purser, Philip, 247
Purslow, Bruce, 50

Radio criticism, 37
Radio Times, 40-1, 226, 229, 294
Radiophonic Workshop, 282-3
Rafferty, Chips, 146, 149
Rapp, Helen, 320
Rawsthorne, Alan, 185
Ray, Nicholas, 102, 165
Read, Sir Herbert, 208

Recorded Programmes Library, 219
Reed, Henry, 51, 235
Regional Programme, 177
Reid, Robert, 115
Reis, Irving, 165
Reith, Sir John (later Lord), 39, 42-3, 45, 53, 73, 179, 227, 288, 317
Religious Broadcasting Department, 246
Rexroth, Kenneth, 219-21, 278-9, 326
Reynolds, Michael, 115
Rhodes, Mick, 319, 321
Richards, I. A., 190, 198
Riding, Laura 206, 286
Rilla, Walter, 82
Roberts, Michael, 205
Robeson, Paul, 110-11, 249
Robey, George, 188-9
Robinson, Earl, 326
Robinson, Robert, 266
Robson, Bill, 165
Rochdale, 115
Rodger, Ian, 255
Rodgers, Richard, 261
Rodgers, W. R., 200, 208-9
Romney, Edana, 76
Roosevelt, President, 89, 102
Rose, Howard, Assistant Director, Features and Drama, 123
Rotblat, Professor J., 290, 292
Roth, Philip, 260
Rotha, Paul, 161-2
Rowe, Joyce (Joyce Bridson), 207n., 258
Russell, Bertrand, 290, 330
Russell, Paddy, 263

Sackville-West, Edward, 122
Sahl, Mort, 327
Salkey, Andrew, 255
Salt, John, 64, 67, 80, 92
Salter, William, 191
Salzburg, 131
Samson, Ivan, 76
San Francisco, 105-6, 168, 221, 326
Schafer, Murray, 283-4
Schary, Dore, 166